TRIALS
AND
ERRORS

D030280

TRIALS AND ERRORS

Experimental UK Test Flying in the 1970s

MIKE BROOKE

First published 2015

The History Press
The Mill, Brimscombe Port
Stroud, Gloucestershire, GL5 2QG
www.thehistorypress.co.uk

© Mike Brooke, 2015

The right of Mike Brooke to be identified as the Author
of this work has been asserted in accordance with the
Copyright, Designs and Patents Act 1988.

All rights reserved. No part of this book may be reprinted
or reproduced or utilised in any form or by any electronic,
mechanical or other means, now known or hereafter invented,
including photocopying and recording, or in any information
storage or retrieval system, without the permission in writing
from the Publishers.

British Library Cataloguing in Publication Data.
A catalogue record for this book is available from the British Library.

ISBN 978 0 7509 6160 8

Typesetting and origination by The History Press
Printed in Great Britain

A DEDICATION

To the memory of
Group Captain John W. Thorpe AFC, FRAeS, RAF

John Thorpe and I pose before my final jet flight as a pilot in an ETPS
Alpha Jet in March 2004. This was also our last flight together. John is
the tall one! (OGL (QinetiQ))

This book is dedicated to my good friend and fellow test pilot John
Thorpe, aka JT. Although we both joined the RAF, as trainee pilots,
straight from grammar schools and learnt to fly at the same Flying
Training School, John was a couple of years behind me on that
particular journey. It was the only time that he was behind me in

anything – from then on he would always be out front. However, I did not meet John until June 1973 when we travelled together from our neighbouring RAF stations in the English Midlands to Boscombe Down in Wiltshire. There we would undergo two days of rigorous examination to see whether we were fit to be selected as student test pilots with the Empire Test Pilots' School (ETPS). He was at that time flying the Harrier and had been on the very first Harrier squadron. We made that journey more in hope than in expectation.

Indeed, after the two days of challenging academic tests, demanding interviews and nervous waiting we departed together with even less hope and no expectation. As we drove up the hill away from Boscombe, John put our thoughts into words:

'Well, I don't know about you but I don't expect to be seeing that place again.'

It was therefore with an element of shock and much surprise that we were both selected to attend the course; in the event, circumstances prevented me from joining the 1974 course, on which John was awarded the prize for Best Pilot; an indication of his outstanding mastery of the art of aviation. I attended the course the following year and John was by then a test pilot on A Squadron testing fighters and trainers. John was one of the two RAF test pilots who carried out the official Preview Assessment of the BAe Hawk trainer.

I next came across him when I joined the ETPS staff in early 1981. John helped me enormously to adjust to this new job and made sure that I was fully comfortable with everything before students were allocated to me. Throughout our time together on ETPS I never experienced anything but kind concern, calm control, good humour and exemplary and consistent professional standards from John.

Our paths crossed again, once more at Boscombe Down, in the late 1980s when he was now the CO of A Squadron and those extraordinary personal qualities came to the fore. He was an excellent leader and always set the highest standard for all in his unit, while maintaining an approachable and friendly demeanour.

John continued to serve at Boscombe Down, as Chief Test Pilot, Director of Flying and, latterly, as a civilian test flying tutor on ETPS. He ended up serving at Boscombe Down for a total of nearly twenty years; which made his remark to me in the summer of 1973 all the more ironic!

John Thorpe died, after fighting cancer, in December 2013 in Calgary, Canada, where he had made his home with his wife Jenny. He was, as they used to say in the Harrier force, a *bona mate*, one of the best I have known. I shall miss him.

I would also like to remember two of my friends and colleagues who lost their lives during flight test activities. The first is Flt Lt Sean Sparks, RAF, with whom I worked at Farnborough and at ETPS. Sean died when the Jaguar in which he was flying crashed into the sea off North Devon after suffering a catastrophic birdstrike. The second is Lt Cdr Keith Crawford, USN, who was a fellow tutor of mine at ETPS. Keith died while testing a McDonnell F-18 Hornet from the US Naval Flight Test Facility at Patuxent River, Maryland. Both these men were good, reliable and true friends who loved their flying.

CONTENTS

Part 3: Researching Radar

Part 4: Back To School

ACKNOWLEDGEMENTS

Once more I have been unstintingly supported throughout this project by my wife, Linda. She has put up with me spending many hours with my nose in my flying logbooks, typing one-fingered, and then she proof-read every page. She has corrected and advised even more thoroughly than she did during the production of my two previous books. I cannot thank her enough. However, if you do spot any errors please don't blame her; the 'book' stops here – with me!

I also want to thank the staff of The History Press for keeping me on their 'books' and doing such a good job of producing this volume. Thanks also go to several people who have helped, provided pictures and advice and helped me to produce something that would not have been as good without their input: John Bradley, Norman Roberson, Allan Wood, Norman Parker, Jenny Thorpe, Natasha King and the folks of the Photographic Division at QinetiQ Boscombe Down. Last, but by no means least, I want to thank Matt Savage of Mach One Manuals (www.mach-one-manuals.net) for providing the cockpit illustrations.

INTRODUCTION: WHAT IS A TEST PILOT?

> To design a flying machine is nothing. To build it is not much.
> But to test it is everything.
> *(Otto Lilienthal, Pioneer aviator, 1848–96)*

From the very early days of flying someone has had to make the first flight of a new flying machine. Usually, in that now far off era of 'stick, string and cloth' flying machines, it was the designer. Crashes were common but not always fatal, so giving those pioneers the chance to change things and try again. Eventually, as men became more expert at aviating, pilots would team up with designers to do the dangerous bit on their behalf, usually for some sort of remuneration. And so the role and profession of the test pilot developed.

As the aviation industry matured and aircraft companies proliferated, bold aviators, often men with a military background, were recruited to fill the posts of company test pilots. Many became famous in their, sometimes short, lifetimes. There were also skilled pilots in the armed forces who were selected to fly experimental aircraft and carry out research and development flights at the Royal Aircraft Establishment (RAE) and the Aeroplane and Armament Experimental Establishment (A&AEE), but the role of the test pilot was not formalised or standardised across the industry or within the services. However, events during the Second World War brought an end to the DIY approach to test flying.

On the day that the war was officially announced by Prime Minister Neville Chamberlain, 3 September 1939, the A&AEE upped sticks from its vulnerable east coast location of Martlesham Heath, near Ipswich, and moved west to the safer, more distant environs of Boscombe Down, on Salisbury Plain in Wiltshire. In 1942 the man in charge of clearing aircraft for service use, known as the Controller Aircraft, Air Marshal Sir Ralph Sorley, made a decision. He wrote to his fellow 1920s test pilot, Air Commodore D'Arcy Greig, then Commandant of A&AEE, ordering him to form a school to train pilots to become effective test pilots. So the world's first such training establishment, the Empire Test Pilots' School (ETPS), was founded, with the first course starting in April 1943. On that course were a mixture of civilian and military pilots.

With the advent of the post-war jet era the image of the test pilot, always known in the trade as the 'tp', became crystallised in the public mind as a dashing character who drove a sports car, flew his jet in a business suit and almost always wore a bow tie. People soon thought that these cool and daring men flew their brand new jets with bravado and a white silk scarf to hand. That image has not really gone away. 'How exciting!' is often the response to the announcement that one is a test pilot.

Well, sometimes it is, but not as often as folk would like to think. The description of 'hours of tedium punctuated by brief periods of terror' could be nearer the truth! These days the military test pilot, which is the remit of this book, never gets to fly the first flight of a brand new aeroplane or helicopter; that is the privilege of the company tp. However, during his career he may well fly many 'first flights' of new systems, weapons and equipment; however, much of the most futuristic research is done in very old and trusted aircraft. Therein lies the definition of another sort of tp – the experimental test pilot.

There are also military test pilots whose work is concerned with the release of an aircraft to the customer – that is the branch of the armed forces that is going to use it. He has to be concerned with its safety and effectiveness for the role for which it was designed. Things have changed in the way that military test pilots work since I was last involved in the business, which is now over 20 years ago. The scale has reduced markedly and collocation, rationalisation and privatisation have all changed the face of military aircraft and systems procurement and assessment.

But the basics of test flying should not have changed. Far from dashing into the air on a solo mission to 'push the envelope' the underlying principle is still a progressive approach, following an in-depth assessment of the potential risks and designing the optimum protocol. That way there should be no surprises; I was once told that the last thing a test pilot should be is surprised! Take it step-by-step and review before moving on. And most of all – BE OBJECTIVE. That means that any problem that turns up, especially in the areas of handling and stability, should be analysed carefully and not blamed on the pilot. That's one of the reasons why service pilots often have disdain for a tp's findings about their own 'wonderjet'.

However, the job of the military test pilot is, or should still be, both challenging and rewarding. I found it so – read on and judge for yourself!

Whereas my story thus far, contained in the books *A Bucket of Sunshine* and *Follow Me Through*, has included some basic technicalities about flying, this tome will, by its very nature, delve a little deeper into the science attached to the art of aviation. So I have included, at Appendix A, some hopefully simple explanations of some of the technical terms this book contains. I know that for many readers, who have followed a similar path into test flying, this appendix could serve at best only as a refresher, if it serves any purpose at all!

But there may be some, indeed I hope that there are many, readers who do not have a deep understanding of aerodynamics and the principles of flight necessary to follow fully all my tales. So to those folk I commend that if you get stuck on a word, phrase or symbol that really obstructs your reading do not hesitate to turn to Appendix A – 'A Brief Lesson in Aerodynamics'.

PROLOGUE

When I was a lad in Yorkshire I was incessantly interested in things that flew. I watched birds. I watched aeroplanes. I went to air shows and often spent hours at the local aerodrome, now Leeds Bradford Airport, just taking in the exciting atmosphere of post-war aviation. There were the diminutive private aircraft as well as the DC-3s of the BKS airline company and a whole collection of flying visitors. An RAF Auxiliary Air Force squadron of Meteor fighters was also based there. To see them making formation take-offs and zooming off into the Yorkshire skies was the height of excitement for a 10-year-old. During those long summer days I used to put up my parachute-panel wigwam in the back garden, get a rug and lay out on the lawn with my dad's best binoculars, an exercise book and a pencil to hand. Then every time anything flew within earshot or eyeshot I would record what it was, at what height I thought it was at and in what direction it was flying. Mostly these identified flying objects were DC-3s!

My favourite Christmas and birthday presents were book tokens. Grasping them in my small sweaty hands I would then catch the bus into Bradford, walk up to a bookshop near the entrance to Kirkgate Market and buy the Observer's Book of Aircraft for that year. When I had got that I would look for any other books about flying that I could afford. Otherwise I would scour the local library for similar literary content. Books about test pilots were particularly favoured; what excitement they contained. I wondered dreamily if one day I too could be a test pilot. Of course, I was naïve and in the full flush of that limitless, youthful expectation of what life could bring. Then every year, on one day in September, I would be glued to the small black and white TV in our living room for the two-hour broadcast of the Farnborough Air Show, with Charles Gardener's wonderful commentaries: '... and over the Black Sheds comes 'Bee' Beamont in the Canberra' or 'from the Laffan's Plain end here comes Neville Duke in the Hawker Hunter. You can't hear him yet, but you will!' And as Roly Faulk flew past in the Avro Vulcan, 'Goodness me! He's going to roll it!' What I would have given to go there and see it all live.

At the age of 11 I discovered the local Air Scouts, then later the Air Training Corps, so it was no surprise to anyone, my parents included, when I joined the RAF in 1962. I became a pilot and I flew the Canberra in Germany in the low-level nuclear strike and tactical interdictor roles. When that was over I became a flying instructor, first on the de Havilland Chipmunk and then on the Canberra again. But, in the mid 1970s, in order to achieve an ambition I had secretly held since my youth, I had applied for, and been accepted into, the ETPS. I also thought that it might break the cycle of flying old aeroplanes!

So, thirteen years after taking the Queen's shilling[1] I was on the threshold of a new career. All that childish reverie of slipping the surly bonds of earth in a shiny, brand-new flying machine to climb aloft and touch the face of God was, perhaps, going to become a reality! Here I was, 30 years old and with 3,200 hours in my logbook, about to become a member of No. 34 Fixed Wing Test Pilots' course at ETPS at Boscombe Down, in Wiltshire. Maybe my dreams could come true?

1   Meaning to sign-on in Her Majesty's Armed Forces.

PART ONE

LEARNING TO TEST

1 GETTING AHEAD OF THE GAME

So here I was on another threshold – the door to the ETPS Ground School. It was a cold January day at the beginning of 1975 and I had walked the mile or so down from my married quarter on the top of the hill on which Boscombe Down airfield is spread, like a concrete and grass tablecloth. I was chilled, not just from the weather but also from apprehension of what was to come. In the summers of 1973 and 1974 I had undergone the rigorous examination of the two-day selection procedure to get here not once, but twice. I had been successfully selected the first time but illness prevented me from attending the 1974 course.[1] But, because the selection procedure was competitive, I had to do it all again in the summer of that year. Thankfully I was reselected, but with one proviso: due to my relatively basic level of mathematics I needed extra tuition before the course started in early February. Because I had joined the RAF at the minimum age of 17½, I had left school after just one year in the sixth form. I had, therefore, only an O Level GCE in maths, although I had subsequently completed one year of instruction in calculus.

My results in the selection board maths paper had reflected my lack of depth in this area. So here I was, ready to receive special attention from the teachers of such mysteries as polynomial equations, differentiation and integration. I was not totally alone as a couple of other guys with a similar background and lack of achievement in sums were here for the same treatment.

We were soon directed to the classroom. I noticed that there was a great view out to the north, over Salisbury Plain, beyond the busy major trunk route to the southwest, the A303. I wondered how often I would

---

1   As described in *Follow Me Through* published by The History Press, 2013.

be looking at that view over the following year. But there was no time for that now. A shortish, balding man in a white coat entered and stood on the slightly raised 'stage' in front of a huge roller-style chalkboard. He had the air of a hospital consultant confronted with a small group of patients who were not going to understand a word of his diagnosis and treatment. He was actually Wing Commander John Rodgers, the Chief Ground Instructor (CGI). He started the morning in the way he meant to go on, taking no prisoners and rolling the blackboard at a frantic rate, while writing all sorts of barely comprehensible symbols and numbers in rapid succession.

Later we would come to know, and sort of love, him as 'Chalky' and become well accustomed to his many catch phrases, such as 'I've done nothing wrong', usually to the accompaniment of erasing something from each side of an equation. There was also his uncanny knack of asking the only person who had not followed what he was doing to explain how he had arrived at some esoteric conclusion. Too often that would turn out to be me.

We did not spend all day and every day in the classroom. That would have been too much for our tiny minds. There were other things to sort out up at the ETPS Fixed Wing Flying HQ, which was situated in offices along the front of one of the hangars. The windows there overlooked the countless acres of the concrete parking area used by the many and varied types of aircraft at Boscombe Down. We had to be issued with flying kit, including bright orange flying suits, anti-G trousers, helmets, lightweight headsets for flying the transport types and an assortment of connectors and other bits and pieces, the purpose of which would eventually become clear. The very affable man in charge of our flying clothing, including anti-G suits, was most appropriately called Tony Gee. His small empire's HQ was located in a wooden hut in front of the second set of hangars. Like all the ground support personnel Tony was a civil servant; however, the majority of the ETPS staff were service personnel.

The Officer Commanding (OC) was a group captain, with a wing commander Chief Test Flying Instructor (CTFI) and four fixed-wing tutors, three RAF squadron leaders and one US Navy lieutenant commander on an exchange appointment. There was also a Qualified Flying Instructor and Instrument Rating Examiner (QFI/IRE), who was there to help with conversions to type for everyone and keep the flying standards up to snuff. The Adjutant was Sgt John Hatschek and the Ops Clerk was LAC Bill Anderson, known ironically as 'Flash'; because the only time he moved faster than a slow trot was when he drove the CO's staff car! The Operations Officer, who helped to ensure that the daily programme ran as planned, was a civil servant called Ted Steer, who could be relied upon to point us in the right direction! There were also three air engineers who helped with the running of the school's Armstrong Whitworth Argosy C1 turboprop transport aircraft and many other ancillary tasks within the school. They were Flt Lts Len Moren, who could often be spotted wearing carpet slippers, Terry Colgan, also the school's entertainment officer, and Terry Jones, who, like us, had just arrived. On the other side of the airfield was the rotary-wing element, manned by RAF and RN (Royal Navy) tutors, plus a Qualified Helicopter Instructor (QHI).

To be ready to fly the diverse fleet of ETPS flying machines we were to be issued with a barrow load of Pilots' Notes and checklists, known as Flight Reference Cards (FRCs). There were also a handful of small, neatly typed cards that gave the essential information on flying each of the half dozen aircraft types. All these documents had to be digested rapidly, but thoroughly, before each conversion flight. Unlike the normal RAF practice of taking several months to be taught how to fly a particular aircraft type, we would only be given a maximum of two flights under instruction before we were going to be allowed off the ground as captains of these aeroplanes. The ETPS fixed-wing fleet of the day was:

- Beagle Basset – two examples; one the standard, twin-prop, piston-engined, 5-seat light communications model and the other a specially modified version to demonstrate in flight the effects of changing parameters of aircraft design and aerodynamics. This one was known as the Variable Stability System or VSS Basset.
- Jet Provost T5 trainer.
- Canberra T4 and B2 twin-jet bomber and trainer.
- Hawker Hunter T7 and F6A fighter and trainer.
- Argosy C1 four turboprop transport and air-drop aircraft.
- Lightning T4 twin-jet, supersonic trainer.

The Ground School was challenging enough, but when I took the assorted volumes of aircraft knowledge home and thought about how much there was to learn in such a short time I began to wonder what I was doing here! However, that anxiety was offset by the frisson of excitement at the thought of being, eventually, let loose on such a wide range of aircraft. And it wasn't long before that started. I was at the hangar offices of the school one morning, my head reeling from the latest mathematical revelations from Chalky. While I was enjoying a restful coffee one of the tutors, Sqn Ldr Duncan Cooke, a South African-born, ex-Harrier pilot, walked in. He had a brisk way about him and, with a friendly smile, he said, 'I think that it's time that you had a break, young fellah me lad. How's about you and me flying the Hunter together this afternoon?' My immediate response was a big grin. 'I'll take that as a "yes" then. Get your flying kit sorted, read what you can of the Pilots' Notes and I'll see you in the Ops Room after lunch.'

It was 16 January, thirteen years to the day since I had joined the RAF and still more than two weeks before the course would start, and here I was getting ahead of the flying game as well as the academic one. This was more than all right by me. The flight in the Hunter was going to be pretty intense, very little of the usual demonstration followed by practice and correction. There wasn't time for all the correct Central Flying School (CFS) instructional procedure that I had come to know so well over the past eight years. This was the start of test pilot training, so finding out for oneself was at the top of the agenda!

I had flown in the two-seat, dual-controlled version of the Hawker Hunter on three previous occasions: twice during a visit to the Royal Navy's Fleet Requirements and Direction Unit at RN Air Station Yeovilton and once when I visited the RAE at Farnborough. I had gone there before I attended the ETPS Selection Boards to find out what the test pilots at Farnborough did to earn their crust. One of them was Flt Lt John Sadler, an old mate who had been on No. 16 Squadron at RAF Laarbruch in Germany with me. When I had flown the Hunter T7 with John we had climbed out over the English Channel so that we could make a dive and go supersonic without annoying people with our sonic boom. That was the first time I had seen a Machmeter exceed one; admittedly by not very much! During those three trips the pilots had let me fly the aircraft for some of the time.

Now I was walking round the very attractive aeroplane that was one of Sir Sydney Camm's aesthetic creations, being shown what to check before getting on board. Once that had been achieved I strapped into the left-hand seat and then looked around. It all seemed somewhat familiar because the seat procedures and the cockpit layout reminded me of the Canberra T4 trainer in which I had spent so many hours in the last three years. The view of the outside world was a little better, but not much, especially when the cockpit canopy had been lowered and locked into position. The Canberra familiarity continued when starting the engine. Essentially it was the same R-R Avon engine that I had used in the Canberra B(I)8 and was started by the identical cartridge system. All the flight and engine instruments were about the same; the only difference was that the aircraft was controlled from a single central stick, and not a yoke, and there was only one throttle.

By the time we had reached the holding point of Boscombe's south-westerly runway, I had got used to using the handgrip brake and rudder to turn the aircraft. After carrying out the pre-take-off checks we lined up for departure. One new principle was that I didn't need to learn the checklist sequences, in fact it was positively discouraged. Because we students would be flying a multitude of very dissimilar types, often three on the same day, then the FRCs were the only way that we could be sure that we had done everything correctly.

Another new approach was that there would be very little demonstration of techniques. Accordingly, I lined up the Hunter on the runway and Duncan just monitored things as I did the take-off. The acceleration was much like a

Canberra: positive but not startling. At the briefed speed I moved the stick back, quite a long way it felt, and I was a little taken aback that nothing happened. Soon, though, the nose wheel started to lift off the ground. I held the slight nose-up attitude and at about 150kt we were airborne. Then I squeezed the brake lever and raised the undercarriage. At this point a gentle side-to-side wing rocking started, which I couldn't seem to stop. In fact my attempts at correction were making it worse so I just held the stick central while the landing gear retracted. Once it was up I raised the flap.

The wing rocking had stopped and it was now very easy to hold the aeroplane still and let it accelerate to the climbing speed of 350kt. The wing rocking after take-off was all down to the relationship between the higher breakout force to initiate movement of the ailerons and the very low friction once the stick was moving. Like all Hunter pilots before me, I would see for myself that pilot compensation was the cure and after a couple of sorties I knew what to expect and how to avoid it instinctively. It was my first lesson that no aeroplane ever built is absolutely perfect in every respect.

The flight itself was an exploration of the Hunter's flight envelope, although we didn't go supersonic. We stalled, with the wheels up and down, the flaps up, part down and fully down. At best the stalling speed was about 110kt. Then a few aerobatics, looping from 400kt, rolling at 350kt and all the while the control forces were very light. Hard turns revealed that the maximum rate of turn at about 360kt was found as the airflow started to separate from the back of the wings, which caused a very clear and perceptible vibration, known as buffet. The resultant increases in G-force inflated the anti-G trousers, squeezing my legs and my lower abdomen: another new sensation for me. It was great to be zooming around considerable amounts of sky in such a responsive and exciting jet.

Probably because I was enjoying myself too much Duncan said, 'OK, let's fly straight and level at 300kt.'

I duly adjusted everything and then Duncan reached out and selected two double-pole switches from the up position to down. The controls stopped working. The control column became a rigid rod sticking up out of the cockpit floor.

'That's what it's like when the hydraulics fail,' explained Duncan. 'Now try a turn.'

I forced the stick to the left and pulled slightly to hold the nose up and stop the jet descending. 'Roll into a turn to the right,' came the next instruction. I had to use both hands to do that. A gentle chuckle with a slight South African accent emanated from the right-hand seat. Eventually we slowed down, dropped the undercarriage and then the flap and manoeuvred some more. After five minutes of this my arms were getting tired, particularly after dealing with the changes of trim with the flaps moving up and down.

'Right, that's enough,' Duncan said. 'Switch the hydraulics back on and we'll go home and do a few circuits. On your next trip you'll do much more of that. I would have thought that a Canberra pilot would have found that flying in manual[2] quite easy.' My wry look at him across the cockpit was sufficient answer.

Soon enough I flew the Hunter T7 again, with lots of manual flying and practice of the forced landing pattern onto the airfield; no landing this machine in fields like I had practised and taught in the Chipmunk! The Practice Forced Landing (PFL) was quite a plunge at the ground starting at about 6,000ft over the upwind end of the runway and ending with a rapid and steep descent at the other end. Once the flaps were fully down it was very easy to unintentionally initiate a wing rocking motion and firm but careful use of the stick and rudder was the only way to stop it.

I was also introduced to something called the One-in-One radar guided approach, used when the engine has failed and the weather precludes the visual PFL overhead the airfield. This involved matching the distance to touchdown given by the controller with the height: 1,000ft for every mile. No great mental strain then, but plenty of physical strain flying it in manual. Nevertheless, I must have done everything to my mentor's satisfaction because, a week later, I walked into the Ops Room and found my name on the programme board to fly Hunter F6A XE 587.

I had already been warned to read up the Pilot's Notes and so I felt ready to take to the air for the very first time in a single-seat jet. As I walked out to the pretty red and grey painted fighter I felt like a kid in a sweet shop. I made sure that nothing was obviously amiss, that it had the right number of wings and wheels and then climbed the short, narrow ladder to get aboard. After the ground crew had helped me strap in I took a minute just to look around the cockpit. Some things were very familiar, some new. There was a switch marked BRIGHT/DIM. I didn't know what it did but I set it to BRIGHT; I didn't want to be dim today. The starting system was different in that it did not use cartridges but AVPIN, a very volatile liquid. I had experience of this system when I had flown the Canberra PR9, which had the more powerful Avon 206 engines. The Hunter 6 also had more thrust than the T7, another thing to look forward to.

After start-up, with the engine idling nicely and all the electrical and hydraulic systems checked I put my oxygen mask on and switched on the microphone. *Oh, no!* I thought. *The wretched thing's not working. I can't hear myself. I hate it when the jet's all ready to go and something breaks!*

---

2   'Manual' was the term used when the hydraulic pressure to the flying controls was
    not available.

Nevertheless, I thought that I'd call for a radio check with the control tower. As soon as I pressed the transmit button on the throttle I could hear myself talking. The controller came back immediately with, 'Tester 70, you are loud and clear.'

Of course! This jet doesn't have intercom. Why should it? Idiot!

After that I just got used to not hearing myself as I ran through the checklist. Soon enough I was lined up at the beginning of runway 24, ready to slip the surly bonds of earth in a really meaningful way. I opened the throttle to about 80 per cent of full power, released the brakes and then put the throttle on the front stop. Two things happened: first an awesome howling noise emanated from just outside the cockpit and then we set off down the runway like a scalded cat. Both effects were due to the bigger Avon engine and the lighter weight of the single-seat model of the Hunter. I was up and off in no time. I climbed out to the west and proceeded to have a wonderful time! I did all the things I had been briefed to do and, after forty-five minutes of unbridled enjoyment, landed. As I turned off the runway and despite the fact that I could not hear myself I shouted, 'What have I been doing for all these years when there were jets like this to fly?'

The following day I flew a second sortie in the F6A. It was just as much fun as the first, although my first attempt at a PFL in manual was hardly text book; but I would have landed safely eventually and probably stopped just before the end of the 10,000ft runway! After a relaxing trip in a T4 Canberra, for which the management had decided that I didn't need a dual check, the time for the official start of our course was getting imminent.

2 AND SO TO SCHOOL

Monday 3 February 1975 was the first day of that year's ETPS graduate courses. There were actually three courses running concurrently. In 1975 they were: No. 34 Fixed Wing (FW) and No. 13 Rotary Wing (RW) for the pilots and No. 2 Flight Test Engineer (FTE) course for a handful of scientific civil servants. All three courses would finish on Friday 12 December. That seemed so far off as to not be worth thinking about. Stamina was going to be a key to survival. We had all been instructed to gather at the Officers' Mess at 8.30 a.m. from whence we were to be transported by coach to the ETPS Ground School building. This would be the only time that we would be afforded such luxury. From the next day onwards it would be bicycles, cars or Shanks' Pony. Some of us, the 'Select Few', had already been together over the past three weeks, getting our brains sharpened through the ministrations of Wg Cdr 'Chalky' Rodgers and his staff. Now we were all together, settling into our desks for the next nine months or so. There was the usual plethora of formalities to be completed and, at 10 a.m. promptly, we were greeted by a series of the great and the good of Boscombe Down.

It is worth explaining how this large and diverse organisation worked in the mid 1970s. At the top of the tree was a senior RAF officer, the Commandant, an experienced test pilot and at that time Air Commodore A.D. Dick, OBE, AFC, MA. He represented all the military services' involvement in the establishment's work in the assessment and development of air vehicles for the three armed forces. He worked alongside a senior scientific civil servant known as the Chief Superintendent, who wasn't a policeman, but oversaw and took responsibility for all the scientific work of the establishment. And that bore the grand title of the Aeroplane and Armament Experimental Establishment (A&AEE or colloquially A²E²), even then a somewhat archaic title, as the establishment dealt with all types of aircraft, not just aeroplanes, and there was not much in the way of experimental flying done there any more. That was more the preserve of the various RAE sites across the UK.

ETPS had its home at Boscombe Down and the Establishment provided all the facilities it needed. In the chain of service command down from the Commandant was the Superintendent of Flying, an RAF group captain, and the three test squadron COs, who were all wing commanders, or other services' equivalents. ETPS was under the supervision of its OC who was, at the time, an RAF group captain. All the customary support services for military personnel at Boscombe Down were provided by the RAF Unit and commanded by an Administration Branch RAF squadron leader.

After listening politely to the CO of ETPS, Gp Capt. Alan Merriman, the CTFI, Wg Cdr Wally Bainbridge and, last but by no means least, the Chief Ground Instructor, the aforementioned Wg Cdr John Rodgers, we started a whole new round of interviews. The first was with Gp Capt. Merriman, who had already grilled me twice before, when I had attended the ETPS Selection Boards in 1973 and 1974! Still, it was nice to chat again in a much more relaxed atmosphere. He was friendly in that special way that senior officers have of making you feel simultaneously at ease but keeping you aware that you are in 'the presence'. When he asked what my ambition for the course was I answered, 'To be at the McKenna Dinner, sir.'[3]

---

3   The McKenna Dinner was the graduating event held at the end of the course and named after Sqn Ldr J.F.X. 'Sam' McKenna. He was an eminent pre-war test pilot with the A&AEE at Martlesham Heath and, in 1944, was appointed as Commandant of ETPS. He was killed in an accident in a P-51 Mustang when an ammunition box left the aircraft and one wing subsequently detached. The aircraft crashed close to Boscombe Down.

That evening we all met up in the Officers' Mess for a 'Meet and Greet' with all the staff. There were guys from many nations among the student body. From the USA was Lt Cdr Tom Morgenfeld, a US Naval Aviator fresh from flying the F8 Crusader. With his black hair and moustache, Tom had a look reminiscent of a Mexican bandito; which was very strange considering that he was from upstate New York and had a German surname! From Denmark was Capt. Svend Hjort, an F-100 Super Sabre driver; a real fair-haired Scandinavian with a fighter pilot's blue eyes and lantern jaw. Then there was a French fighter pilot with an excess of Gallic charm and a total lack of Gallic hair – Commandant Gerard Le Breton, lately from a Mirage F1 squadron of the French Air Force. Gerard would soon become the focus of attention of most of the wives and girlfriends whenever he walked into a room! Later in the course he would turn things around by bringing his excessively beautiful French wife over; then it was the boys' turn to gawp! There were also two guys from Germany, both civilian German Ministry of Defence pilots – Udo Kerkhoff and Eddie Küs. Udo was a very amusing and amiable chap with a mop of blonde hair that was rarely in good Teutonic order. Udo was a transport pilot latterly with the Franco-German Transall. Eddie was a good-looking but follically challenged helicopter pilot. Another pair who shared their nationality were Indian Air Force pilots 'Rusty' Rastogi and P.K. Yadav, both from MiG-21 squadrons. Then there was an Italian, Bruno Bellucci, who had come from the F-104 Starfighter but was actually going to become a helicopter test pilot. I think that all the Fixed Wing students felt very sorry for Bruno; it was going to be hard enough doing the course in another language, but to also have to learn a whole new way of flying at the same time was a very big ask! The final legal alien was our Antipodean, Fg Off (yes, a Flying Officer) Mark Hayler RAAF, ex-DHC Caribou and Mirages; a good background to come here and fly the variety of aeroplanes we were going to use. He was also my next door neighbour on the married patch.

Then there was the RAF contingent. Apart from myself there were two ex-Lightning pilots, Flt Lts Vic Lockwood and George Ellis, and you soon learn that you can tell a Lightning pilot – but you can't tell him much! George was our youngest RAF course member and had only just acquired the minimum number of hours to qualify to be here. However, he was a bit of an academic star, being a Wickhamist and Oxford graduate. George affected his exceedingly English image by the wearing of a deerstalker hat, plus-fours and waistcoats with a pocket watch on an Albert chain. His party trick was to twirl the glittering timepiece around and then catch it in one of the waistcoat pockets. This usually brought loud acclamation from the 'foreigners'. Tom Morgenfeld gave George the sobriquet of 'Mad Dog', taken from the title of Noël Coward's song 'Mad Dogs and Englishmen'!

The other Brits were an ex-Canberra and F-4 Phantom driver, Flt Lt Chris Yeo, and a 'Jump-Jet' Harrier man – Flt Lt Roger Searle. From the V-Force world, a Scottish 'Flying Flat Iron' Vulcan pilot, Flt Lt Duncan Ross, and two helicopter guys, Flt Lt Terry Creed and Sqn Ldr Rob Tierney. Terry was a dead ringer for the missing Lord Lucan and it became de rigueur to proclaim this loudly when we were in public places. Due to his elevated rank Rob was made the Course Leader. As is befitting, I have saved the Senior Service representative to the last among the pilots: a smooth operator called Lt Simon Thornewill RN and yet another Rotarian. Then there were our four civilian FTE aspirants – Neil Sellers, Dave Morgan, Rob Humphries and Jerry Lambert. I had already flown with Jerry in the Canberra, when he occupied the right-hand seat of the T4; he hadn't seemed all that taken with aviating.

But all that flying experience would be put on hold for three weeks of all-day classroom lessons. We were to be put through a rigorous introduction to a wide variety of subjects: from the composition and characteristics of the atmosphere, units of measurement, basic aerodynamics, stability derivatives, the solution of polynomial equations, the fundamentals of aircraft design and many more such esoteric topics. It rapidly became like an intense first year university course crammed into three weeks, and no time off between lectures.

'Chalky' Rodgers didn't operate solo. He had a small but excellently qualified support staff. The first of these was Sqn Ldr Brian Johnson, an education officer who specialised in matters aerodynamic and mathematical, especially the mysteries of non-dimensionality. Vic Lockwood later observed that to measure non-dimensional time we would need non-dimensional watches and the RAF didn't issue us with those. The other ground instructor was a navigator, Flt Lt Harold 'Wedge' Wainman, the Systems Instructor. He had been a navigator on my first squadron, No. 16, in Germany in the mid 1960s. I had known him well there and we had survived a Winter Survival Course together. Wedge taught us all about magic black boxes and how they and their computerised innards worked.

So our amble, at the speed of light, through the fertile fields of scientific academia continued apace. At the end of those first three weeks we felt like there had never been any other existence. I was getting thoroughly bored with the view from the window by now, and it never gave me the inspiration for the questions racing through my head. But there were lighter moments. One morning during a lesson examining the relationship between Imperial and Standard International (SI) Units, French fighter pilot Gerard Le Breton, who sat immediately in front of me, was thumbing frenetically through his *petit dictionnaire*. He did that a lot because the French Air Force kept his posting to England a secret until the last minute, so he had received no English language training! He turned round to me and asked in a whisper, 'Why eez a small animal from ze garden used to measure force?' He had looked up the word 'slug'![4]

Then one afternoon, during one of his by now famous high-speed blackboard rolling sessions, Chalky asked, 'Now how do you think that we could eliminate this variable?'

'Rub it out?' came the reply from Vic Lockwood.

It's funny how time flies when you are having so much fun and so on our third Friday we were subjected to a progress examination; it was actually more like a speed writing test. From now on we would attend Ground School for one or two periods each morning and after that it would be up to the hangar and flying! However, it still being Friday, we all repaired to the Officers' Mess Bar for Happy Hour. I believe that was when we hatched a plot for future Fridays. It was decided that we would instigate Pot Luck Suppers, with our wives each producing a dish of something delicious and representative of their national origins. Fortunately a large majority of our better halves were in favour, so one of us would, each week, volunteer our Officers' Married Quarter (OMQ) as a venue, and the guys would arrive with the booze! Magic!

3 A PLETHORA OF PLANES

Finally we were going to get to grips with some aeroplanes! Resplendent in our bright orange flying suits, small teams of us could be seen crawling over various examples of the School's flying machines. Initially this was for our first written report – the Cockpit Assessment. I, along with a couple of others, had been directed to assess the flight deck of the Armstrong Whitworth Argosy: a transport aircraft and the last aeroplane to be designed and built by Armstrong Whitworth. The Argosy was adopted by the RAF in the early 1960s and had a freight carrying capacity of 13 tonnes; it could also be used by paratroopers. The flight deck crew consisted of two pilots, a navigator and a flight engineer.

We pored over the pilots' bit of the cockpit and assessed its utility. We measured the field of view through the letterbox-like windscreen and side windows. We checked the escape facility, via a long rope, which we deigned to use, as it was about 20ft from the window to the ground! We looked at all the dials, switches and levers and their layout. We assessed the static qualities of the

4   A slug is an imperial unit of force.

flight controls system, looking for such esoteric characteristics as breakout force, centring, running friction and backlash. To do these things we had each been issued, along with our voice recorders and kneepads on which to carry test cards and make notes, various implements that looked like medieval instruments of torture. These tools helped to measure forces and deflections of the control systems. In addition to these we had been able to hone our skill at estimating control forces using an old Hawker Sea Hawk cockpit set up in the ETPS Hangar for just such a purpose; once we had been introduced to this simple but effective apparatus a queue of guys waiting to use it soon formed! After we had finished our Cockpit Assessments we wrote our individual reports and handed them to our tutors for their assessment of our assessments. During the course we would each have three tutors. The course was split into three terms: the first up to the Spring Bank Holiday, with a week's leave to follow, and the second up to the end of July, after which there would be *three* weeks off!

My first term tutor was to be Sqn Ldr Graham Bridges. He had done a tour on the Canberra PR9 with No. 13 Sqn in the Mediterranean and had been a test pilot at Farnborough. Graham took four of us under his accommodating wings and started us on our journey of discovery into the mysterious world of test flying. Alongside me in Graham's syndicate were pilots George Ellis and Gerard Le Breton, and FTE Neil Sellers. Once we had converted to type, Graham would be the one to brief us and demonstrate in flight the required test techniques, as well as use his red pen to constructively criticise our reports; aka 'rip them apart'! Reports had to be handed in no later than ten days after the final test flight of the topic to be examined. Then the reports would progress from the Tutor, to the CTFI and then to the CO for each to make their comments, each with different coloured ink. It really was a school! Graham was a bouncy sort of character and full of boyish enthusiasm. He possessed a good pair of lungs and his laugh and more sarcastic comments could be heard clearly emanating from his office or the Ops Room, all the way down the long corridor to the coffee bar in the crew room. This was Graham's final year on the school, so he was also the Principal Tutor Fixed Wing (PTFW), which meant that he had the unenviable task of organising each day's flying programme. This had to satisfy the needs of the syllabus and match student progress with tutor and aircraft availability; and there was the English weather to be taken into account.

Apart from Graham Bridges and the aforementioned Duncan Cooke, the other two members of the Fixed Wing Tutorial Staff were Sqn Ldr Peter Sedgwick RAF and Lt Cdr Walt Honour USN. Like Duncan, Peter originated from the southern hemisphere – the Falkland Islands – and had joined the RAF and become a transport pilot. He had spent a tour at Farnborough as a test pilot before returning to ETPS to educate and torment folk like me. Walt was the nominal American in the permanent exchange appointment with the

US Navy Test Pilot's School at Patuxent River in Maryland, USA. He had flown the LTV A7 Corsair operationally and tested the Lockheed S3 Viking for the US Navy. A crucial character, who worked alongside the Tutors, was the ETPS QFI, Sqn Ldr Mike Vickers. Mike was one of those people whose experience was written all over his face. He was older than the rest of the staff, indeed he had flown during the Second World War. For a part of that time he had flown Hurricane fighters from naval fleet support ships. This was on what now seems like a crazy, almost kamikaze-like scheme, where the Hurricanes were launched from catapults on ships that had no landing decks. After flying their defensive fighter missions the pilots then had to find their way back to the vicinity of one of the ships and land in the sea! I cannot believe that anyone would have volunteered for that tour of duty. But Mike survived to fly another day and stayed on in the RAF post-war to become a jet fighter pilot and instructor. It would be Mike's dulcet tones and calm instructional manner that would get us through many of the all too short conversion sorties.

Before we started each test flying exercise we had to be checked out on each aircraft type. My first one was the Jet Provost T5; aka 'JP5'. It really was a re-familiarisation for me, as I had flown the T3 and T4 versions during my basic flying training and the T5 when I was at the CFS. The ETPS JP5 XS 230 was an interesting aircraft. It was the second prototype of the mark and had been converted from a T4; its sister ship XR 229, the first prototype, had been lost in an accident during development flying. XS 230 had never been used for flying training, other than at ETPS, and had several slightly non-standard features. We would use it for stalling test exercises this term and spinning next term.

My next conversion was to the propeller-driven Beagle Basset: an odd little dog and an odd little aeroplane. It was similar in size to the Hunter but, as a light communications aircraft, obviously quite different. There were two 310hp Rolls-Royce/Continental engines mounted on the wings and a cabin that could accommodate five people including the pilot. The Basset had first flown in 1961 and then a military version, the CC1, had been developed for the RAF. Twenty examples of this model were built and they were equipped with a new entrance door incorporating steps down from the rear of the cabin; these were known as the Air Stairs. Possibly because they had been designed so that air-rank officers could dismount gracefully while wearing their full regalia including a sword! The Basset CC1 entered service in 1965. ETPS had two Bassets and the one that was not modified to take the Variable Stability machinery was XS 742. It had briefly been on the Royal Flight, when Prince Charles had been taught to fly a multi-engined aeroplane.

With two people on board the Basset's performance on take-off was hardly startling. One wondered whether it would climb after an engine failure near the ground or whether one would just have to steer it to a crash landing somewhere near the airfield. Goodness knows what it was like on a hot summer's day with full fuel tanks and all the seats occupied. But once it was safely away from the ground it slipped along quite well. It also handled nicely, the forces on the manually operated controls being reasonably light and well balanced. The cockpit was not a bad place to work either, with a great view, fairly spacious and well laid out and with a control yoke instead of a stick. The only thing I remember being tricky was the landing. That was because the tailplane and elevator sat in the slipstream from the propellers and there was not quite enough elevator authority at low speeds to keep the nose up. So if I closed the throttles smartly just before touchdown the little beast tended to drop out of the sky, nose first, while I tried desperately to stop it by applying lots of pull on the yoke, usually to little effect. I learnt to take lots of nose-up trim during the final approach and slowly reduced the power as we got close to the runway. It still didn't guarantee a nice, smooth arrival – but it stopped the nose-down lurch and the naval-style arrival! With the Hunter, Jet Provost, Canberra and Basset under my belt I had just two more aircraft types to attack: the Argosy and the Lightning – the ridiculous and the sublime!

Conversion to the Lightning would not come until much later in the term so it was now time to tackle the Argosy. I had a bit of a head start because I had, along with the others in my syndicate, already become very familiar with the flight deck of the big beastie. But that was with it sitting stationary on the ground. Now we each had only two flights, totalling all of three hours, to qualify to act as captain. I had never before flown a four-engined aircraft or operated turboprop engines. The Argosy had four of them, Messrs Rolls and Royce's excellent and pioneering Darts, as installed on the UK's first and enormously successful turboprop airliner, the Vickers Viscount.

The Argosy was known by all and sundry as the 'Whistling Wheelbarrow'; a reference to the high-pitched, ear-piercing whistle of the R-R Darts, the Argosy's twin, handle-like tail-booms and its tendency to land on the nose wheel at the slightest provocation. Some cynics said that the Argosy had been made out of other people's leftovers. It was reputed to have wings of the Avro Shackleton with Meteor rear fuselages used as the tail-booms. It could have been true! Messrs Armstrong and Whitworth manufactured both aircraft types at one time or another! We also learnt that when the Argosy was first tested by the RAF the floor was not strong enough to take the Saracen armoured vehicle, for which it had been procured. Unfortunately, strengthening the floor increased its thickness, which meant that there was now insufficient headroom in the freight bay to get the said piece of Army kit aboard! Moreover the resulting extra weight cut the total load carrying capacity so much that the range with the required maximum weight was now less than the specified requirement! Hence those aforementioned cynics said that the Argosy could carry a maximum volume load of table tennis balls to Cyprus or a maximum weight load from RAF Brize Norton to RAF Lyneham! We were learning how to be very cruel, but not yet very objective.

It was on the Argosy that our air engineers came into their own. They acted as flight engineers and co-pilots for us and often, during passenger flights (more of which later), as loadmasters or rather butch air hostesses! Their mission, it seemed to me, was to make our very brief conversion flights as easy as possible and then make sure that we didn't do anything silly when there were two student test pilots in the driving seats. During the conversion phase the ninety-minute sorties were flown back-to-back throughout the day, there being enough fuel on board to do an all-day, non-stop series of flights. Thus several of us got to do our first 'solos' as captain without ever having started the engines before! This wasn't a real drama, as we tended to arrive at the aircraft, walk around the outside just to marvel at flying something so big and then climb the ladder up to the flight deck in the attic. There, we would find an engineer with absolutely everything ready for us to start the motors. This was done with switches on the overhead panel and all we had to do was put the start selector switch to the correct engine number and push the starter button. The engineer would do the rest. However, we did have one important thing to do and that was to look out of the window to make sure that the propeller started going round. Ex-Lightning pilot Vic Lockwood, who had only ever flown with a maximum of two engines and both of those out of sight behind and beneath him, pressed the engine start button and looked out along the port wing. 'It's not moving, Terry,' he called. A large engineer's hand came down on the top of his head and rotated it 180° to the right.

'The other number three engine,' said Terry Colgan, with not a little exasperation.

'Oh, yes. That one is going round OK,' responded our embarrassed fighter jock!

On board the Argosy there were all sorts of new toys to play with, like a nose wheel steering tiller to manoeuvre the machine on the ground. From where I was sitting, 20ft up, there was a very good view ahead out of the window and ground handling was quite easy, although I had to learn to be aware that the wings stuck out a long way each side. Take-off was a joint effort between the occupants of the pilots' seats. Steering was initially done by the left seat occupant and power applied by the right-hand man, who also restrained the control yoke. At a predetermined point the 'captain' took full control of everything. I had to learn new things to listen to and call, such as the various key speeds on take-off, like 'V1', 'Rotate' and 'V2' – it was all very 'Speedbird' and 'Captain Speaking' stuff! Once up and away we made stately progress above Wiltshire. The manually operated flying controls were, as expected, fairly heavy, but not overly so; but I had a definite feeling that the final connection to the actual control surfaces was made of rubber

– the controls lacked the solidity I was used to. Vic Lockwood came back from his first sortie in the Whistling Wheelbarrow and likened it to driving a London bus from the top deck, but attached to the steering wheel by elasticated bungees.

The most important things we had to experience and learn to do was to briefly explore the stalling characteristics, which were reasonably benign, but with lots of shaking, rattling and a bit of rolling, and flying with three or two engines operating. After my long experience on the Canberra I found that the three-engined flying was pretty much a non-event. However, once two engines on the same side were throttled back, the handling, speeds and control forces were reminiscent of the Canberra. The most challenging item to conquer was a two-engined go-around from about 500ft on an approach to land. It was difficult but my past experience of flying and teaching that sort of thing for several years helped me out. Then there was the landing. I was supposed to call out power settings in pounds of torque to the engineer who would set the requested number using the throttles. However, I did observe that when any of us made a gross error the correct number would mysteriously appear on the gauges. With the landing gear and full flap down the correct call as the aircraft floated over the end of the runway was 'Slow Cut'. Then it was a case of fighting the tendency of the aircraft to want to land on its nose wheel with lots of aft control yoke, but to not overdo it and flop out of the sky from a great height. The poor old Argosy took a lot of punishment in this phase of the course. But it was very satisfying to fly a large aircraft for once – as long as I didn't have to do it for a living!

Although it didn't happen until April, there was just one other conversion to type to complete the 'Full House' of ETPS Fixed Wing aircraft types in my portfolio. And what a way to finish: the English Electric Lightning. Finally the day arrived when my name was on the daily flying programme against Lightning T4 XL 629. Three of us were down to fly it and the plan was that our tutor would stay in the cockpit while the jet was refuelled and we would make the long walk all the way down to the far end of Boscombe Down's huge concrete apron to where the Lightning was parked. I set off as soon as we knew that the aircraft was down and still serviceable from the previous sortie.

By the time I reached it, the refuelling truck was pulling away. While paperwork was being raised and signed I walked around the tall, sleek, red and silver jet. The heat haze was still emanating from the two vertically mounted jet exhaust pipes at the flat rear end, beneath the fin and rudder that towered 20ft above me. I then walked under the wing to marvel at the left undercarriage leg. It was spindly to look at and the wheel and tyre on the end of it looked far too narrow. That was because the landing gear retracted outwards into the 60° swept wing, which was as thin as the structural engineers would allow. The way that the wheel and leg twisted back into the wing was all down to the angle of the bearing on which it was suspended. The normal pressure in the tyre was around 300 psi; I thought that they might just as well have made it out of solid rubber. Our tame Lightning drivers, Vic Lockwood and George Ellis, had regaled us with lots of stories about this potent Cold War fighting machine, one of which was that the explosion from a Lightning tyre bursting on landing, apparently not an infrequent occurrence, could be heard all over the county! The wear on these tyres is so much that they are changed after ten landings; that is if they've lasted that long. Hence we would not be making touch and go practice landings!

Soon I was at the foot of the long ladder on the left-hand side of the nose. The jet was ready to go, but I was beginning to wonder whether I was. As I climbed up to the cockpit I thought, *You're about to overreach yourself now, lad. You won't keep up with this one.* Graham was sitting there beaming at me; I just hoped that he had more confidence in me than I did. I checked the ejection seat, sat down, strapped in and put my helmet on. *No going back now!* After carefully going through the pre-start checks I indicated that I was about to start the No. 1 Engine. At that point I couldn't remember whether the No. 1 was the one on the top or the bottom of the fuselage behind and below me. I then decided that it didn't really matter, as long as I knew which of the shiny levers and switches to use. The engines were 300 Series Rolls-Royce Avons and were started, like the Hunter F6 and the Canberra PR9, with the 'rocket fuel' more correctly known as AVPIN. That meant that when I pushed the engine start button there should be a 'Wheeee' and then a 'Phut'. If it came the other way round we were in trouble!

A few minutes later both the engines were running, the flaps and airbrake operations checked and we were ready to go. Once cleared, we moved off, trying to use as little thrust as possible. In fact, once under way, the machine was like a thoroughbred hacking down the racecourse to the starting gate; it definitely wanted to go flying. Then it was onto the runway, brakes on and run the engines up to 85 per cent power. Cleared to go, brakes off and open the throttles to the stop, check rpms at 100 per cent, Jet Pipe Temperatures (JPTs) in limits and no warnings. We were already accelerating like a Ferrari but now I had to apply the reheat to make this rocket sled go even faster. Rock the throttles outboard, towards the cockpit wall and then push them even further forward. Then something odd happened. It was like we had started to slow down. This was during the short pause while the jet exhaust nozzles at the back end opened, which reduced the thrust, and the extra neat fuel injected into the jet pipe was ignited, which then increased the thrust even more. No sooner had this deceleration feeling registered than it was replaced with a powerful shove in the back. Now we were really motoring. I watched the airspeed indicator and as it reached 135kt I eased the stick back and waited. Soon afterwards the nose came up and we parted company with terra firma. I checked forward slightly with the stick, briefly applied the brakes and reached out for the button that raised the undercarriage.

Now came a crucial bit. The Lightning's hydraulic system couldn't raise all the wheels at once so they were sequenced. The two main legs retracted first and then, when they were up and stowed away, the nose wheel leg went up. However, it retracted forwards into its bay underneath the air intake, right below where we were sitting. If I let the airspeed get above 240kt before it had retracted it would stay down, held there by the air pressure overcoming the hydraulic pressure. The best thing to do in this case was to raise the nose to an almost vertical attitude and let the speed reduce. This wasn't a very pretty sight from the ground and was a very public display that you'd got it wrong. But today, on my first ever take-off in control of a supersonic interceptor, there was a satisfying thump from down below as the speed was passing 230kt. All the undercarriage lights were out and we were on our way. At 430kt, which turned up very quickly, I raised the nose to about 60° above the horizon to hold 450kt, until the Mach meter showed 0.9 (90 per cent of the speed of sound). The machine was climbing at about 20,000ft per minute! It felt like I was lying on my back. I was supposed to level off at 36,000ft and not go supersonic. Graham had given me the hint to start the level off at about 30,000ft and by the time I had pushed the nose down and reduced power we should be at or near the desired altitude. *Phew! And it's less than two minutes since I let the brakes off!* I thought.

After a bit of handling up here we descended to 15,000ft and did some more turns, rolls and a loop, which took up a huge amount of sky. The aircraft was a joy to handle and I found it relatively easy to make it do what I wanted; *maybe it won't be so hard after all?* There was plenty of buffet to warn me when the wing was getting close to its limits and after trying some slow flight with the landing gear and flaps down it was time to go home and try to land the beast. The Lightning has many good features, but neither range nor endurance is on the list. Fuel will only fit in the thin wings or the streamlined bulge underneath, known as the ventral tank. The total amount of fuel was 700 gallons and this even included 33 gallons in the tiny flaps!

Once we got back to the visual circuit at Boscombe Down, my initial anxieties returned. The Lightning had, so far, been a bit like a big Hawker Hunter, but landing it would be quite different. I would only be making one touchdown, there would be no practice landings, as we did in all the other aircraft, so we would just make low overshoots. And we only had enough fuel for three of those! I knew that it was crucial that I didn't do something that had become natural to me over thirteen years of flying; that was to throttle back before the main wheels were on the runway. Otherwise the big jet could drop out of the sky and its tail-end strike the runway. So I set off downwind, with the undercarriage down, reducing speed to about 190kt. At the turn-in point

I opened the airbrakes to increase the drag and dropped the flaps. There was plenty of buffet now and the most important thing to do was to not let the speed fall too low. Once lined up with the runway, at about 300ft, the minimum speed should be 165kt, slowly reducing to 155kt over the touchdown point.

As I flew the three practice approaches I became more and more astonished by how easy things were. The speed and angle of approach could be easily controlled with small movement of the stick and just one of the throttles. But now it was time to land. As I came over the beginning of the runway, known as the threshold, the speed was right and I just held the attitude and then the main wheels touched the runway. I simultaneously lowered the nose and throttled back. Holding the nose wheel firmly on the ground I pulled the handle that steamed the brake parachute. The control tower confirmed that it had deployed and then I started braking, gently at first. We turned off the runway after about 7,000ft of landing run. So I had flown the Lightning – a small step for a fighter pilot, a giant leap for me!

On my second sortie I would have to fly supersonic, then make single-engined approaches, flapless approaches and approaches with the artificial control feel system turned off. We would be doing our test flying exercises in the supersonic regime so I'll describe that later. The other various practice failure cases were, as far as I could tell, almost non-events; this aircraft really was a credit to Teddy Petter who had designed it, test pilot Roly Beamont and the English Electric team who had helped to perfect it. To my mind Petter's genius in designing both the Canberra and the Lightning puts him alongside the greats of aircraft design such as Mitchell, Camm and Handley Page. I was very satisfied that I hadn't, after all, overreached myself; well not yet!

4 SO MUCH TO LEARN

Day by day, as the spring started to dress the trees around our house and along the roadsides of my morning walk down to the Ground School, things academic and practical were getting harder. The staff were conspiring to fill us with such a huge quantity of new knowledge that there was a danger that we would have no little grey cells left to absorb it. However, that did not apply evenly across the course. There were those among us who had university educations in related subjects and brains the size of planets. One even had a Master's degree in aeronautical engineering. These special people were rapidly becoming more and more popular, as those of us who spent an increasing number of classroom hours in a baffled state pumped them for simpler explanations than we were being fed by Chalky et al. What was a

Fourier transform and what was it for? How did a Laplace transform really work? How do you conceptualise non-dimensional time?

On top of all that brain-burning stuff we were ploughing through the test-flying syllabus. The first such exercise for me was stalling in the Jet Provost. There were four sorties in which to explore all the possible stalls that one could do in a trainer. We then had to report, in cogent English and a prescribed sequence, what we had observed, how it matched the specified requirements and our recommendations as to the suitability of the aircraft for service in its stated role. We were also encouraged to report on all unsatisfactory items that we found, and argue sensibly as to why they might need corrective action.

The JP did not have any automatic recording equipment so everything would have to be quantified using the normal flight instruments, a stopwatch, a hand-held force measuring gauge and a tape measure. Neil Sellers was my Flight Test Observer (FTO) and he grappled with the tape measure to measure how much the stick was moving. It worked well until we were doing the stalls while turning hard and then the tape kept bending under the increased force of gravity or G. Eventually Neil brought a lump of Blu-Tack and stuck it to the instrument panel to stick the end of the tape to. Talk about the cutting edge of white-hot technology! The big surprise at the end of the exercise was that the JP failed to meet the requirement for the margin of stall warning laid down in the regulations. Yet it had spent almost twenty years successfully training pilots.

By the time we had finished those flights and started writing the report I was flying the next test exercise, something called PECs. The acronym stands for Pressure Error Corrections. Air-sensing instruments, the altimeter and airspeed indicator, rely on accurate measurement of the atmospheric pressure the aircraft is flying through. This is done with a sensor or sensors positioned somewhere on the aircraft. However, wherever the sensors are positioned they never give perfect results because the aeroplane itself can induce errors by its very presence. These errors usually vary with speed and configuration, whether or not the flaps and undercarriage are up or down. The way that we had to quantify these errors turned out to be rather good fun and took the form of a legal, low flying competition. Our syndicate was allocated the Basset. What we had to do was fly down the runway at different speeds and in different configurations and measure our height very accurately with a special altimeter fed from the static pressure sensor on the aircraft; the same one as fed the instruments.

On the top of the main HQ building, which overlooked the airfield, was a small observation post from which the FTE would take photographs of each flypast and note down each run number as per our previously agreed test plan. He also had a similar special altimeter. Later the readings and photographs were compared with the aircraft's sensitive altimeter readings and the errors then calculated. Some guys had the Hunter, lucky devils, and others the Jet Provost. The low flying element was restricted by one factor: something called 'Ground Effect'. This was not, as one wag had it, what caused the wheels to go round on landing. It was the influence of the slightly higher pressure caused by the air getting squashed between the aeroplane and the ground if it was flown too low; this would then cause a pressure error of its own. As a rule of thumb if you flew higher than half the wingspan the effect would be negligible. However, I did spot a couple of guys determined to ignore that!

In the classroom we were starting to master the concept of stability derivatives. They were represented by a whole collection of Greek letters mixed up with normal characters that were shorthand for certain features of an aircraft's stability and control characteristics. At the time we used the British system of axis, moment and derivative designators and we soon picked up this new lingo. No longer would we spend Happy Hours just shooting down our wristwatches with our hands when describing the week's flying events. Now we would start talking about Nv and Lv and $T\sin\theta$; but not for long. After a couple of beers, it would soon get back to shooting down wristwatches again!

The next challenge to our test flying abilities was to be a longitudinal static stability exercise, which our syndicate was to fly in the mighty Argosy. There would be three trips: that was one each for George Ellis, Gerard Le Breton and me. Each would be with the aircraft's centre of gravity (CG) in a different position: forward, mid and aft. The two extremes were achieved by lots of bags of lead ballast being strategically positioned in the cargo bay. George won first prize, having to fly the big beast with the CG at the forward limit, I got the aft CG trip and Gerard the mid. The Argosy had a full test instrumentation pack, so there would be lots of automatic measurements of things like airspeed, elevator angles and trim positions. Of course we had to prepare our test plans, the many test cards for each condition and then go off and fly. We pilots acted as co-pilots for each other, Neil Sellers was along as the observer and one of the engineers was there to make sure that we didn't do anything too naughty to his precious 'Whistling Wheelbarrow'.

The only memory I now have of this exercise was when I was flying co-pilot for our French fighter pilot, Gerard. We were getting progressively late for our planned return in order for the next crew to take over. I was trying hard to persuade Gerard to forget his Gallic pride and set off home, even if he hadn't got all his planned test-points completed. Eventually he relented and we set off back to base.

''Ow fast can eet fly?' he asked the engineer and me. We told him what the maximum allowed airspeed was.

'OK, give me ze power for zat,' came the captain's command.

As we got closer to the airfield I told the control tower that we would join the landing pattern directly onto the downwind leg; he cleared us to do so.

But when we arrived opposite the upwind end of the runway Gerard the Mirage driver was still going too fast to put the landing gear down. I apprised him of this fact.

'No problem, *mon petit copain*,' he said. 'Zero thrust *s'il vous plaît*, engineer.'

As the airspeed dropped below the limit speeds for undercarriage and the various stages of flap I selected them. Gerard had his head down now and turned onto the final approach as if he was still in his Mirage. I called 'Finals to land, gear down and locked' on the radio. The controller cleared us to land, but with a little uncertainty in his voice. He was obviously watching our high-speed arrival carefully. Gerard just pointed the big machine at the threshold and waited for the speed to drop. The power setting had not been touched since zero thrust had been set! As we crossed the big white stripes at the beginning of the runway the speed was just right. How did he do that? The landing was immaculate. It all went to prove that not all bad approaches end in a bad arrival!

The test flying exercises during the first term were all related to longitudinal stability and control. In addition to those I have already described I flew two sorties in my dear old pal the Canberra T4. The aim of the exercise was to measure the elevator angles as the aircraft neared its maximum Mach number of around 0.84 at high altitude. Assessment of the aircraft's handling and reporting on any limitations was also expected. There were no surprises for me; the Canberra did its usual thing of having a short period of longitudinal instability as it exceeded about 80 per cent of the speed of sound followed by a return of very strong stability with a nose up lurch at the maximum attainable speed.

A memory of this period is one of a red-faced, ginger-haired George Ellis storming into the crew room after his first sortie in the Canberra, looking directly at me and saying, 'That aircraft should have been put down at birth!' He really was a Mad Dog that morning! The truth was that George was desperately disappointed because he'd always, from afar, admired the look of the Canberra and had long harboured a desire to fly it. However, the uncomfortable, un-ergonomic cockpit and poor view, plus the struggles with flying it on one engine had totally disabused him of his previous admiration. No amount of me extolling the later marks, like the B(I)8 and PR9, would change his mind! Unfortunately his perspective was upheld by unprintable comments from our US Naval aviator, Tom Morgenfeld, after his first trip. He was somewhat mollified when I told him that he had joined the ranks of a very special group of elite pilots – those that had flown the English Electric Canberra and survived!

But the best was to be last. This time another longitudinal stability exercise, much like that we had done on the Canberra, but going through the 'sound barrier' in the Lightning. To do this we had to fly out to the southwest at around 36,000ft and get ourselves positioned at the south-west end of something called the 'English Channel Supersonic Corridor'. A London Military Radar controller would watch us closely to make sure that we didn't stray out of the corridor or fly out of the north-eastern end of it while still going supersonic. The usual eye-watering climb after take-off was followed by a cruise at 0.9 Mach until we were in position to turn into the corridor. Then it was full afterburner and hold the aircraft level to accelerate up to 1.3 Mach. That was a slightly harder task than I expected because as the speed increased, but with no change to the aircraft's attitude, the altimeter steadily unwound until at 99 per cent of the speed of sound it had dropped by 1,500ft. Intuitively I knew that we were at the same height. This phenomenon was a huge, transient static pressure error caused by a shockwave passing down the long probe on the nose of the jet and over the little holes that measured the local static air pressure.

In fact the most obvious sign that we had gone supersonic was the altimeter bouncing back up to the correct height. Then it was a case of carrying on to 1.3 Mach and letting the onboard test instrumentation do all the measuring. There was very little in the feel of the aircraft to tell me that we had passed the speed of sound. This really was a beautiful aircraft; but with one very important limitation. By now we were getting low on fuel, and we'd only been airborne fifteen minutes! In fact, as we had accelerated I could see the needles of the two fuel gauges slowly swinging towards zero! But we weren't there yet. Now we just had to get back to Boscombe; about 60 miles away. The nice man at London Military Radar helped a lot and co-ordinated our hand-off back to Boscombe's Approach radar controller, whom I informed that we would get to the runway using the Instrument Landing System (ILS).

The ILS sent out radio signals from the ground and the receiver in the aircraft converted them into the displacement of a horizontal and a vertical bar on the Lightning's large Artificial Horizon display, right in front of the pilot. This could be used to find the runway in bad weather with no need for any voice radio transmissions. But an even better scheme was to use the Lightning's autopilot and autothrottle to help take all the effort out of the task. So, for practice, that's what I did. I had used a very similar system in the Canberra PR9 before, so its operation was not new to me. What was new was the final approach speed of 165kt! It worked perfectly and at 200ft I disconnected both the autopilot and the autothrottle and landed the aircraft. The fuel gauges showed the minimum allowed fuel quantity for the day of 1,200lb and we had been airborne for all of thirty-five minutes!

It was a great way to end my first three months at ETPS. We now had a week's leave coming, so my wife and I hired a caravan on the south Dorset coast and set off on the Saturday morning for a well-deserved break. She was working for me as well: she typed all my reports. This was long before the days of PCs, tablets and laptops! The weather broke, in a good way, that weekend and it remained hot and sunny for the rest of the week. But it wasn't all play and no work. I sat in the sun for several hours and analysed the in-flight recordings from my Lightning sortie, plotted strange-looking curves on graph paper and wrote my report about the results of that final exciting trip! The ten days from 'flight-to-write' was included in the week's leave – a hard school with hard rules!

5 OUT OF CONTROL

It was now blazing June. We returned to school, like so many students had done for centuries, refreshed from our late spring break and ready to tackle the new mental and physical hurdles to be put in our way. This second term meant a change of syndicate, thus a change of tutor and fellow syndicate members. Our tutor was to be Sqn Ldr Duncan Cooke during this short but very busy nine weeks in which the main event would be that most exciting and potentially unpredictable mode of flight – spinning.

A spin is sometimes called autorotation, and it is the aerodynamic result of flight beyond the point where the aircraft no longer responds normally to control inputs. In other words, the aeroplane is no longer flying where normal control is possible and exceptional steps must be taken to regain control. What does a spin look like? Well, the clue is in the name. A spin happens when the aircraft rotates around all three axes simultaneously and describes a spiral downward path, usually at a very high rate of descent.

In the early days of flight, when there was a dearth of experience and understanding of stability, loss-of-control accidents were very common events. However, not all were fatal because, thankfully for some of those early aviators, their wood, wire and fabric contraptions flew at very low speeds, so the collision with terra firma was often a low energy impact. Many an early pilot, with his goggles, white silk scarf and flat cap on backwards climbed out of the ragged wreckage, dusted himself off and strolled away to find, or build, himself another flying machine. Hopefully a more stable one.

By 1912, when aeroplanes were starting to become much more common, the spin had become notorious. The dynamics of the spin were still not fully understood and it was simply something that was to be avoided like the plague. However, in that year a Royal Naval Air Service officer called Parkes was the first pilot to be recorded as recovering successfully from the usually fatal 'spiral dive', as the spin was then known.

He was flying an Avro trainer and while turning towards the landing field he mishandled the controls so badly as to cause his aircraft to depart from controlled flight. It is said that he felt a strong side wind so applied full rudder to oppose it. At the same time he did something else that was totally non-intuitive: despite the ground coming up at him he moved the control stick forward. The Avro recovered and cleared the ground by not very much. Shaken and probably more than a bit stirred, Parkes climbed his aircraft away from the ground and then made a successful approach and landing. After a change of underwear Parkes analysed what he had done and it wasn't long before the application of rudder to oppose the yaw and movement of the stick forward became known as the 'Parkes Technique' for recovering safely from a spin. However, it wasn't until the advent of the First World War, with the consequent increase in the numbers of military aircraft and concomitant flying training, that intentional spinning became part of the syllabus. In 1917 a senior scientist at the Royal Aircraft Factory at Farnborough, Professor Frederick Lindemann, who, ironically, was a naturalised German, undertook a study of the physics and mathematics of the motion of the spin. He even flew some of the test sorties to prove his theories. A rare animal – a test pilot boffin!

By the end of the 1920s the aerodynamics and the inertial forces on an aircraft in a spin were much better defined and understood, and designers were taking these factors into account, particularly in the design of fighters and trainers. All flying training now included intentional spinning so as to teach the correct method of recovery, as well as to dispel some of the fear of the spin's rather disorientating, rotational aircraft motion. However, spins, especially those accidentally entered during combat or training, were still killing people and losing aircraft.

One story from the test-flying world that I came across involved the US Air Force's acquisition of the McDonnell F-4 Phantom. This formidable, supersonic, two-seat fighter had first flown in May 1958 and was initially acquired solely for the US Navy. It performed so well that, in the mid 1960s, the USAF decided that it too could usefully employ the Phantom. During the initial test programme, at Edwards AFB in California, the occupants of the appropriate ivory towers decreed that the F-4 should undergo a full spin test programme. These sorts of tests are always high-risk and the coalface guys at Edwards pointed out that the USN had already completed very comprehensive spin testing; why not use their results? This very sensible input was overruled and the general then in charge of the USAF aircraft procurement system was reported as having said, 'If this spin programme saves just one USAF F-4 it will have been worthwhile.' This wisdom was then translated into a banner, which was prominently displayed in the Ops Room of the F-4 test squadron at Edwards AFB.

Some way into the programme the test aircraft was, once more, put into a spin and the required control inputs for that particular test point were applied. The spin very rapidly became much flatter, that is the nose rose from about 50° below the horizontal to only 15°. The rate of rotation increased and the Phantom was now in a classic flat spin; usually a very difficult spin mode to recover from. High definition cameras in the desert below were filming all this. It was a recording of this spin that we were shown at ETPS as part of the briefing before we started our spinning exercise. It was fascinating to watch. After more high-speed rotations the anti-spin chute, always fitted for these trials, was deployed. It simply fluttered like a large pocket-handkerchief above the Phantom's spinning fuselage and so had no effect on the recovery. Then the brake parachute, normally used to help shorten the landing run, popped out and just as quickly fell away. The next event was the departure of the two crew using their ejection seats; back-seater first. The camera then continued to follow the stricken fighter all the way down to the desert floor and the inevitable impact and cloud of dust. This brought appreciative whoops from the audience in the ETPS classroom! I later learnt that the punchline came when the uninjured crew had been picked up and returned to their Ops Room. The first thing the pilot did was to walk over to the banner, get out his grease pencil, cross out 'ONE' and replace it with 'TWO'.

By 1975 there were still many military fighters, like the F-4 Phantom, that could be manoeuvred to a point beyond which a spin might be generated. As the twentieth century progressed into its latter quarter, computers were increasingly being used in the flight control systems of all classes of aircraft. The phrase 'fly-by-wire' was, even in the mid 1970s, becoming part of the language of flight control system design. As these specialised magic boxes became smaller and yet more powerful they could be programmed to protect pilots against losing control of their increasingly skittish steeds. A new phrase then appeared: 'carefree handling'.

However, that was, for us, somewhere in the future. The aim now was to get us to intentionally spin suitable aircraft, observe their characteristics while spinning, recover them safely, report on what we had seen and make recommendations. Sounds easy when you say it quickly! Apart from carrying out a couple of brief spins during our conversions to the Jet Provost earlier in the year, none of us had intentionally spun an aeroplane for many years. So we needed, literally, to be wound up before we tried to apply ourselves to the demands of this exercise.

So it was back into the dear old JP. However, this was ETPS; it was to be for only one sortie, with my tutor in charge, which would function as both a re-familiarisation on operating and handling the JP and a demonstration of the required test techniques. One hour was all I would get before I went off and did a whole series of spins on my own. That trip happened about one week later, during which I had to perform about a dozen spins and gather all sorts of information, without the benefit of automatic data recording equipment. I would have a voice recorder and a kneepad holding a handful of neatly drawn up test cards. However, the voice recorders that we used were notoriously unreliable and it was very easy to lose track of the test cards while doing all the things necessary to fly safely around England's busy southern skies!

The day of 12 June 1975 was a fine one for flying, so I had no excuses for not getting airborne. Once I had climbed Jet Provost XS 230 to 20,000ft, which took about ten minutes, I set up for the first spin. I looked all around, particularly below, made sure that my straps were tight and that there were no loose bits in the cockpit with me. All was well so I told the radar controller, who was keeping a friendly eye on me, that I was about to enter the first spin. I closed the throttle and held level flight until the speed had dropped to about 100kt. Then I simultaneously pulled the stick fully back and pushed the rudder bar as far as it would go with my left leg. This meant that the little JP's wings stalled but the yaw to the left caused by the application of full rudder started the autorotation that was essential for a spin to develop. All the time that this was happening I had to make sure that the stick was held fully back and central, so that I would not be applying any roll control input. The aircraft pitched up and then performed a tight barrel roll to the left as the nose dropped quickly below the horizon.

To imitate a real spin test programme, but much abbreviated into one flight, the first two spins were very short because my test schedule was first to check that the recommended immediate recovery action of simply centralising all three controls would stop the spin. If this was done before the end of the first full rotation then the aircraft should recover. In fact this was an essential requirement for a training aircraft, which the JP was. I had to check this result for a spin in both directions, left and right. Sure enough it worked. But it wasn't enough to come back with one's white silk scarf flying in the breeze and say, 'It's fine chaps, don't change a thing!'

No, the designer and engineer chappies need to know all sorts of esoteric information, like the rates of pitch, roll and yaw; angles of attack; time from application of the recovery controls to the time that the aeroplane stops gyrating; how much height was lost until normal, safe flight was re-established. And lots more! Once those so-called incipient spin recoveries had been done, all the while with me chatting away to myself and, hopefully, the tape recorder, I had to move on to the fully developed spins. These also had to be completed in both directions and the same sort of data recorded in my increasingly illegible handwriting. Recovery from the fully developed spins would be taken after at least three full rotations had passed. The entry method was exactly the same: throttle closed, full rudder and stick fully and centrally to the backstop. Once settled into the spin the JP was rotating through 360°

in about four seconds and losing about 2,000ft while it did so. The recovery action was to check that the throttle was closed, then look at the turn indicator on the instrument panel to confirm in which direction the aircraft was yawing.[5] After that the rudder bar had to be pushed fully in the opposite direction to the yaw. This was followed by a short pause before the stick was moved progressively and centrally forward, only stopping once the spin had stopped. There were other tests required, such as applying the recovery actions in the wrong order, to see whether the aircraft would still recover (again a mandatory requirement for a trainer). Then there were different entry conditions to check, such as during turns in each direction.

After an hour I had done a dozen spins and was very ready to go home. I had used the few minutes between each spin, while climbing back to a safe height, to make notes and talk to my voice recorder. How I would make sense of it all was a challenge that I would face later. But that would be in our spare bedroom, in the quiet of the long evenings that I was used to spending there. The JP spinning exercise was just the beginning of a period in which rotation in a variety of forms would fill my summer days. The next step was the Hunter spinning assignment.

The Hawker Hunter was a product of the immediate post-Second World War era. In 1946, recognising that the future lay with jet engines and swept wings, the Air Ministry had issued Requirement Number E38/46 for just such a fighter. One of the industry responses was from the Hawker Aircraft Company of Kingston upon Thames. Their chief designer, the brilliant Sydney Camm, who had designed the wartime Hurricane, started work on a series of prototype fighters powered by a single jet engine. In March 1948 the Air Ministry issued a new Requirement – F3/48, which called for a high-speed, high-altitude, gun-armed fighter with a rapid rate of climb. Camm took on the challenge and came up with a swept-wing aircraft powered by a Rolls-Royce Avon engine that the company identified as P1067. The first version had an air intake in the nose, much like the North American Sabre, and T-tail. But during manufacture of the first prototype the intake was moved to the wing roots and the tailplane lowered to a position about halfway up the fin. It had a wingspan of just over 33ft and was about 45ft long.

So, looking much more like the Hunter that it would become in RAF service, the P1067 took to the air for the first time on 20 July 1951 in the hands of Hawker's Chief Test Pilot (CTP), Neville Duke. That flight was from the very place that I had flown my first flight in a Hunter, only five months earlier: Boscombe Down. There was just a twenty-four-year time gap between the two events!

5   Yaw is rotation around the aeroplane's vertical axis; much like a flat turn in a boat.

Eventually nearly 2,000 Hunters of many variants would be built and they would serve with no less than twenty-two air forces around the world. The RAF would use Hunters in the operational fighter/fighter-bomber and fighter-reconnaissance roles from 1954 until 1971. But the Hunter would continue in RAF service as a trainer until the eventual demise of the Blackburn Buccaneer in the early 1990s. And it was the two-seat T7 trainer version, which first flew in 1955, that I would spin first.

As I walked out with Duncan Cooke towards the always eye-pleasing and elegant-looking Hunter I reflected on the several briefings that I had received about what we were going to do in the next hour or so. It had been made abundantly clear to us all that no other flying establishment in the world carried out intentional spinning in a swept-wing aircraft. The reason for this was that the shape and thus the distribution of mass in such a design meant that the dynamic forces acting on the aircraft in the spin were different to the rather 'squarer' straight-winged trainers, like the Jet Provost. This could lead, and had done so in operational and training service, to pilots being unable to recover from spins. However, once the relationship between the aerodynamic and inertial forces had been fully understood and special instrumentation fitted then safe recoveries were almost guaranteed. But just to be on the safe side every spin would be monitored from the ground by another pilot.

To do that a radio system, called telemetry, in the aircraft's nose would transmit data on a range of parameters that could then be displayed on a panel to show the 'ground pilot', sitting in a building on the margins of the airfield, exactly what was happening 8 miles above and usually many more miles away. Before each spin was entered the 'test' pilot had to tell the ground pilot the details of the type of spin, entry and recovery that was intended. The ground pilot would then monitor everything carefully and call the airborne pilot if anything looked amiss. The ground pilot could, and should, also aid the airborne pilot in calling out recovery actions if they did not appear to be working.

The complementary instrumentation in the aircraft was on a small panel, right in front of the pilot's eyes (where the gunsight would usually be); for obvious reasons this was called the Spin Panel. It had instruments to show the position of the ailerons and rudder, a turn indicator (to show the direction of yaw), two small lights to indicate the direction of roll, an angle of attack (AOA) indicator and a special altimeter with a single needle and a scale marked in tens of thousands of feet from 0 to 4. There was also a big red light that would illuminate at 10,000ft. That was there to show that the aircraft had reached the height at which, if the spin had not stopped, the pilots should eject. It might seem high but the rate of descent in the fully developed spin in the Hunter was getting on for 20,000ft per minute; so 10,000ft was only 30 seconds from impact!

Despite all the added safety measures the exercise was still classified as 'high-risk' and the frisson of excitement was mounting as I strapped into the left-hand seat, next to my South African skipper. But once I was winging my way through the start-up checks and getting the machine to come to life the butterflies subsided again. While taxiing out to the runway we had to check the special radio frequency that we would use to talk simultaneously to our ground pilot and the nice folks at London Military Radar, while we were up and away on our exercise. All was well and with the checks of our telemetered data and the aircraft completed we rolled onto Boscombe's long runway and I wound up the engine for take-off.

About a quarter of an hour later we were up at 40,000ft ready to do our first spin. I went through the radio procedures, looked out around and, as best as I could, below and put the aircraft in level flight, closed the throttle and waited for the speed to drop. At about 140kt I did just what I'd done in the JP: pulled the stick fully back and pushed the rudder bar as far as it would go. The stick in the Hunter is actually cranked slightly to the right. This was done to give the pilot a better view of the lower instrument panel, but it also made it easy for the stick to be pulled to the right as well as back. This is where that funny little gauge marked 'Aileron' on the Spin Panel came into its own. It was important to make sure that no aileron was applied during the spin. The reason for this would become abundantly clear to me during the next half hour or so.

The result of this coarse and rather rude handling of the controls was a big surprise. No rapid roll or pitch up – in fact nothing rapid at all. There was lots of buffet, a slow roll until the jet was inverted and then it all stopped. The nose was well below the horizon and after around eight seconds we still had not done a whole turn. As in the JP exercise the first recovery was going to be by putting all the controls to their neutral positions. As soon as I did so the rotation stopped and we were wallowing earthwards at an ever-increasing airspeed. I pulled out of the dive and recovered to level flight at about 250kt. At least I didn't have to scribble things down on a notepad; the on-board instrumentation was recording it all and I would be provided with the output on the following day.

We had lost about 5,000ft so I put the willing old lady back into a climb to regain 40,000ft. The next two were fully developed three-turn spins. During them the aircraft showed me a stubborn reluctance to want to do this rather ungainly and unseemly exercise. There was nothing smooth, consistent or really predictable about each turn. There were times when the spin rate would suddenly increase and then decrease again, and the aircraft's nose was going up and down with associated flicks of the AOA needle in front of my eyes. It was like a fairground roller coaster ride. But the standard recovery action, modelled on the old Parkes' Technique, worked every time; the aircraft stopped spinning after not much more than another turn. These fully developed spins brought us down to around 25,000ft each time, so the climb back up to 40,000ft took much longer.

But we had to explore more things. One of these being the effect of having aileron applied during the spin and the recovery. So once the aeroplane was spinning properly then, under Duncan's direction, I applied full aileron smoothly in one direction. When that was in the same direction as the spin then the whole thing became much more oscillatory; the roller coaster changed to a bucking bronco! When the aileron was applied in the opposite direction to the spin then it speeded up but became much smoother and the nose was visibly closer to the rotating horizon. But what about recovery? Well, with aileron applied, especially out of the spin, the aircraft just kept on spinning even after the rudder had been applied and the stick was moving forward. Using the neat little aileron gauge in front of my face I could incrementally reduce the deflection of the stick from central and wait a few seconds to see what happened. The aircraft did not recover until the ailerons were within about 10° of neutral. No wonder so many Hunters had been lost in spins. There was no aileron gauge in normal service, although there was a large white spot painted on the instrument panel which, when the top of the stick was lined up on it, meant that the ailerons should be central. So any Hunter pilot who suddenly found himself in a spin would have to concentrate very hard to make sure that there was no aileron still applied during his attempt at a recovery.

By now we had used about half the fuel load, which guaranteed that the two 100-gallon wing tanks were now empty. This was significant because until they were empty Duncan could not show me the final and most challenging feature of today's lesson: the inverted spin.[6] Now the butterflies came back to life. I, like most pilots at my stage of life, had never experienced an inverted spin and lived! In fact, inverted flying of any sort did not occupy much of the time I had spent aviating. However, I had to steel myself for a new experience. Duncan was going to demonstrate one and then I was going to have a go myself. Then we would have to go home before the fuel ran out.

So the first step was to get the jet to do this unusual manoeuvre. Duncan took control, asked me to follow him through lightly on the controls, so that I could sense what he was doing. We levelled at 40,000ft, told the ground pilot what we were going to do, got a clearance to do so, and then accelerated to 180kt. Once there Duncan closed the throttle, applied full left aileron and held the stick just forward of neutral to make sure that the nose stayed above the horizon. After about 270°, as we were about to come upright again, he firmly

6   Tests had determined that the stresses and inertial forces with indeterminate amounts of fuel in the ungauged wing tanks could have a detrimental effect on the recovery from inverted spins.

applied full right rudder. There was a bit of a pause while the jet seemed to work out that the only way it could roll left and yaw right was upside down.

Then it all happened. I could feel the yaw rate increase and at the same time the strong sensation of negative G came on; that very definite 'upside down' feeling. The loose ends of our seat straps flew up in front of our faces and a quick glance at the accelerometer showed that we were under the influence of about −2G. Duncan pointed out on the Spin Panel that the roll and yaw were indeed opposite to each other. He then told me to look at the JPT gauge. I tried to find it, but for the life of me I could not locate it! That was the effect of the extreme disorientation on my tiny brain during the brief time that we had spent in my first inverted spin.

The reason Duncan had asked me to look at the JPT gauge was because it was showing that the temperature inside the Hunter's exhaust pipe was heading rapidly towards the red line that showed the maximum permitted in-flight value. I would later discover that this was because the airflow entering the air intakes was being disrupted because we were dropping earthwards upside down; Sydney Camm had designed the air intakes to work best when the aircraft was the right way up. As the JPT was now at the limit Duncan carried out the recovery actions, which oddly were exactly the same as for the upright spin. The Hunter responded with alacrity, almost as if it had had enough of this bizarre mode of flight.

Once I had recovered my composure and Duncan had put the aircraft back in straight and level flight he gave me control and asked me to climb back up to 40,000ft again and repeat the exercise myself. Within ten minutes we were in our final inverted spin. I had successfully got the aircraft into the spin using the same technique as Duncan and now I had to observe what was going on. The spin was much smoother than the upright one, with nothing like the wild variations in pitch and roll and, although there was that strong upside down sensation, the Hunter's nose did not appear, from where I sat, to be in a classic inverted position. After three or so turns, which took about four seconds each, I checked the direction of yaw, applied full opposite rudder and eased the stick forward. Once more the recovery to a straight dive was fairly rapid and all I had to do was recover from that and take us home.

I thought that I might have been feeling a little queasy by now, but I was not. I had never suffered, like some poor souls did, from airsickness and I was pleased that my stomach had not been too badly affected by the gyrations of the past hour. After coffee and a good debrief I was sent away to think about what I had seen and prepare myself for another similar sortie. Then I would be going off in a single-seat F6A Hunter to carry out a full spinning assessment of my own.

The second sortie in the T7, again with Duncan, had a positive, reinforcing effect on my knowledge, powers of observation and my equilibrium. We repeated much of what we had done on the first trip but there was something new to experience. This was related to the spin recovery with aileron applied, which I would have to do during the solo exercise. During these tests it was important to apply the aileron before starting the recovery, so the stick had to be moved smoothly and fully in the chosen direction while the aircraft was still spinning. However, if this was done during one of the periodic hesitations, when the jet was just sitting there, buffeting but not rolling or yawing, then it could cause the aircraft to flip into an inverted spin. As we students were not permitted to carry out intentional inverted spins during our solo test exercises we had to be shown how best to avoid this unwelcome outcome. So, towards the end of our second spinning sortie together Duncan talked me through the whole procedure.

First, I applied full left aileron while spinning to the right just after the second time that the Hunter's natural reluctance to spin had caused a short hiatus in the proceedings. Sure enough the spin continued, sped up and flattened out a bit, and I recovered as I had done previously, gradually reducing the stick deflection until the spin stopped.

But that was not to be the end of the day's rotational excitement. The next and final event was the application of aileron at the hesitation – just to prove to me what would happen.

'It's not guaranteed, lad,' said Duncan. 'But the odds are in favour of an inverted outcome.'

I duly put the Hunter into yet another spin and waited until things slowed down for a second or two. While the aircraft was wallowing in uncertainty as to what to do next I whacked on full aileron. There was a barely perceptible pause and then with breathtaking rapidity the dear old Hunter flipped into the upside down mode. The negative-G sensation seemed even stronger than before and the rate of rotation whipped us around with eye-watering speed.

'OK, Mike, recover,' came the words from Mr Cool on my right.

I complied and so did the jet. By the time I had got us back to normal flight I had recovered my composure; I hoped that Duncan had not noticed that I had lost it. Time for home and tea.

During the last ten days of June I flew my four spinning assessment sorties; three in the F6A and one in the T7. Much of what I had seen on my two introductory sorties was repeated, but this time I had my voice recorder, test cards and the output from the on-board data recording system. Being in the single-seat Hunter did make a difference, especially in being able to see out better and climb back to height a little quicker. Most of my test plan went as it should have. There was just one occasion when I was exploring the application of out-spin aileron that I felt that sudden onset of negative G! I recovered promptly. The ground pilot, watching the instruments from so far away, just chuckled.

Without doubt this ETPS exercise was the most demanding physically, if not intellectually. We had to record and present a lot of data, facts and give an opinion in the form of a recommendation as to whether intentional spinning should be authorised in the Hunter. I thought that it could but only if a spin panel was fitted. However, the preferred solution was 'No'! Although most of us would never be called upon to participate in a full spin programme it did teach us how to conduct high-risk tests properly, how to learn to overcome disorienting and disturbing motions and how to record and report in a high stress environment. All skills we were going to need in our future test flying roles, wherever they took us.

Of course, spinning was not the only test exercises we did during those two glorious summer months of June and July 1975. That would have been much too easy. No, the school had to keep loading us up with ten-day deadlines for reports; it was part of the ethos. I also flew the Lightning again, trying to establish its rates of roll under a variety of conditions. This test exercise was a constant competition between the number of test points I could complete against the amount of fuel left in the inadequate tanks. Then there were more sorties, similar to those we had flown in the first term, in the Variable Stability Basset, supposedly solving more aerodynamic mysteries. Then I did yet more flying in Hunters, this time exploring the speed, turning and climbing capability of this ageing fighter in an exercise called Manoeuvre Boundaries. This was a way of turning lots of fuel into barely comprehensible lines of recorded data. Much time was spent, late into the evenings yet again, deciphering, reducing, calculating, assessing, reporting and recommending; all without the use of computers! For the course I had spent what was then an enormous amount of money to replace the slide rule that my dear old dad had given me with the latest Hewlett Packard pocket calculator; and your pocket would have to have been quite copious!

The term finished with a series of flights in the little dog – the Beagle Basset. This was under the auspices of an exercise called TOL, the acronym for Take-Off and Landing. This was predominately a handling exercise, although, as usual, a great deal of numerical (known in the business as quantitative) data had to be recorded and used to back up the pilot's observations (known in the business as qualitative data). The final event of the term for me was yet more rotational flight: a trip in a helicopter, which I was allowed to fly for some of the time. This was in the Westland Scout, possibly called that because it could lift, in addition to the crew, just one boy scout. That is a bit unkind, but I was mightily impressed how quickly it came down once the engine was no longer powering the whirly bits above my head. I suddenly came to see why helicopters have windows just above your feet. It's so you can see where you are going to land when the engine has quit! It was good to reach the end of a frantic nine weeks and look forward to three weeks holidays. No reports to write. No data to analyse. Just novels to read. A lot of sleep to catch up on. Chance to spend a lot of quality time with my wife, Mo, and the two little ones, Sonia and Peter.

6 THE LIGHTER SIDE

The day-to-day workload on the course, especially for the more academically challenged like me, was hard and unrelenting. Most of us worked at home well into the evenings. But the secret was not to burn the candle too far into the night, otherwise the consequent fatigue would drag down the next day's performance and soon become a vicious, detrimental circle. I used to work until, at the latest, 11 p.m. every evening from Monday to Thursday inclusive. Saturday mornings were designated family time, usually for shopping. Sundays were also promised to the family. However, if I was 'getting behind the drag curve' with writing reports or preparing for the next exercise then I might eat into Saturday afternoons and Sunday evenings. My wife, Mo, was very understanding and supportive and she typed all my reports for me. I might not have made it through without her encouragement and effort.

You might note, dear reader, that Friday night has not yet featured in my weekly schedule. That was because, virtually to a man, we had come collectively to the decision, as mentioned earlier, that Fridays would start with attendance at 'Happy Hour' in the Officers' Mess Bar. This was usually followed, in the absence of any other pre-arranged Mess function, by a gathering with our ladies at a pre-nominated married quarter for the international food festival known as the 'Pot Luck Supper'. That underpinned our social life for the ten months of the course. Another regular feature, introduced by tutors Duncan Cooke and Pete Sedgwick, was the 'Sunday Tutorial'. This was a get together in either a nominated local hostelry or at the domiciles of these two colonials for drinks and eats. Then there were the parties and Mess functions. Some Saturday evenings were spent on- and off-base, at shindigs thrown by course members. These were many and varied, from more formal dinner parties to really relaxed informal social events. The Summer Ball of 1975 was scheduled for Saturday 4 July. It being some sort of special anniversary for them, the American contingent at Boscombe decided that they would hold a pre-ball drinks party. This band of Yankee brothers comprised the exchange USAF test pilot with A Squadron, John Blaha and his wife, Walt and Lorraine Honour and Tom and Norma Morgenfeld. The latter two couples occupied the specially adapted[7] pair of semi-detached (or duplex in American) quarters at the end of Bawdsey Road. To make enough space for us all to attend and, in typical rebel fashion, they removed the fence between their two gardens. Then, as if to prove that God was on their side, the weather complied with yet another warm and sunny evening. This wonderful celebration of their independence from the tyranny of Crown rule was so good that there was a very real risk that no one would leave to attend the Summer Ball! Of course we did eventually and a great time was had by all. The usual wide variety of food and drink was available in the main public rooms, which were decorated to the normal high standard. There was both live and disco music and dancing in two locations; much frequented by us all. Very late in the proceedings Vic Lockwood and Svend Hjort were to be found examining a plate of leftover whole smoked trout. They each picked one up and pretended they were cigars. 'Svend, I can't get this one to light,' says our ex-Lightning pilot.

'Of course you can't,' replied the Dane. 'It's already been smoked.' To kick off things for our third term, Svend and his lovely wife, Jette, threw a memorable and predictably wild Viking party in their married quarter. We all dressed up as Scandinavian warriors and their 'vimmin'. Lots of horned helmets appeared from goodness knows where. Tom Morgenfeld was more inventive and turned up with what looked like an inverted colander filled with spaghetti on his head and a really scary sink plunger instead of an axe! His wife Norma, not to be outdone, had plaited her spaghetti and was carrying a brush in a very threatening manner; she was quickly christened 'Broom-hilda'.

There were lots more parties like that – too many to recall clearly! But it all went to prove that, although it was difficult to believe at times, there was a 'normal' life running in parallel to our academic cloistering. There were a couple of skittles nights in one of the many local pubs equipped with the old-style alleys. Some folks even had babies; the wives of Simon Thornewill, Rob Tierney and Bruno Bellucci going well beyond the call of duty for this very busy year by producing bouncing offspring. All three new dads were on the rotary element of our course so rather risqué jokes about 'choppers' became prevalent.

And one thing that the staff could not repress was our collective and individual sense of humour. Even when the going got tough there were memorable amusing happenings and witty repartee. Many of these were recorded in the course 'Diary and Line Book' composed, written and illustrated by yours truly. One such bon mot was the response of one of our Indian brethren, 'Rusty' Rastogi, to a notice concerning the conduct of one of the many written examinations. This announced that extra time would be

---

7   These two houses had special transformers to allow the Yanks to use their 110-volt domestic appliances.

given to those students whose first language was not English. Having looked at the list of names and found that his and PK's were not on it he declared, 'Damn racial prejudice, that's what it is!' Obviously 'Chalky' Rodgers thought that all Indians spoke perfect English!

In similar vein on our return from our first period of leave during which the sun had shone unremittingly on us all, someone was heard to remark, 'Even Rusty's got a suntan.'

We were surprised by an announcement in late June that the Course Photograph would be taken on Tuesday 1 July. As that was not far beyond the halfway point of the course many students were heard muttering things like:

'Does that mean that those on the photo are guaranteed to pass?'

'Oh no,' said Vic Lockwood, 'each section is perforated!' In the event the taking of the course photo was delayed by two days. Graham Bridges declared, with some glee, that this was to give the staff a chance to 'chop'[8] a few of us!

Not long before this milestone on our long journey towards the McKenna Dinner, ETPS had taken delivery of another Lightning. This was a two-seat T5 version and was destined to replace the older, faithful T4 – XL 629. Management decided that the staff and students of 1975 would therefore range themselves in a pretty and eye-catching manner in front of not one, but two, supersonic interceptor trainers. Thus ensuring a unique background in the history of graduating course photographs. However, the T5 still had its red and white 56 Squadron markings prominently displayed each side of the RAF roundel on the nose. The CTFI and CO decided that this was not appropriate and decreed that they should be covered. This was done with very large sheets of brown paper, sprayed with silver-grey paint. So, on the morning of 3 July 1975, both aircraft were towed into position and we gathered for the big event, all in our little-used best uniforms and ready to be arranged in neat rows. At this point the CTFI, Wg Cdr Wally Bainbridge, was seen smoothing down the silvered paper on the nose of the T5 and making sure that it was satisfactorily stuck in place. Some wag called out, 'That's no good, sir, it'll come off at about 500 knots.'

It was later in July that a bunch of bright-eyed, bushy-tailed British serving officers turned up at the Officers' Mess to go into battle with the staff and compete for places on next year's courses. As the Brits on our course had all done this at least once before, we now became the doomsayers: 'Go home now while you still have your sanity!' We found out later that the answer that won the ETPS equivalent of the wooden spoon was: 'Why did they shorten the Victor Mk 2's wings even though it was heavier than the Mk 1?'

---

8   Common RAF parlance for failing the course.

Answer: 'So they could get more of them in the hangar, sir.'

But, according to Walt Honour, the commonest answer of the week was: 'I'm sorry I don't understand the question.'

Each year at ETPS the end of the second term is marked by a staff versus students cricket match. Like all ETPS events this was preceded by a briefing for those not familiar with the rules of the game. Which went as follows:

> You have two sides, one out in the field and one in. Each man that's in the side that's in goes out, and when he's out he comes in and the next man goes in until he's out. When they are all out, the side that's out comes in and the side that's been in goes out and tries to get those coming in, out. Sometimes you get men still in and not out.
>
> When a man goes out to go in, the men who are out try to get him out, and when he is out he goes in and the next man in goes out and goes in. There are two men called umpires who stay out all the time and they decide when the men who are in are out.
>
> When both sides have been in and all the men have been out, and both sides have been out twice after all the men have been in, including those who are not out, that is the end of the game!

Our Indian cricketing experts, Rusty and PK, were left to answer the questions from the Americans and other non-cricketing aliens. Despite the excellence of the briefings the execution was not up to snuff and we students lost. The recompense was that, after a pitch-side barbecue and the consumption of copious quantities of ale, we went off on our three weeks of summer holidays.

Soon after that blissful break came another event that was the only part of the flying syllabus that was voluntary: the parachute jump! On the morning of 4 September we found our way across the airfield to the HQ of the resident parachutists. Their day job was to carry out and supervise personnel parachute trials, many for the Special Forces. But today a couple of them had charge of a bunch of chattering, giggling aircrew, all a little high on nervous energy driven by the prospect of actually doing something aviators usually want to avoid at all costs: falling out of a serviceable aeroplane!

We spent a couple of hours learning how to attach our parachutes' rip-cords to the aircraft's static line, then shuffling forward towards the exit, then (having unhitched the rip-cords) learning the correct way to exit. We were not going to have to practise the landing, as we would be jumping into water; so no broken legs or ankles in prospect – just drowning. In fact that too was most unlikely as the Drop Zone was Studland Bay, just off the Dorset coast and the Royal Marines from nearby Poole would be out in the Rigid Raider boats to pick us up. Even more encouragingly we were told that they have a competition at this annual event, with a prize for the marines who collect their parachutists the quickest; they apparently aim not to let us get wet!

When the gallant Parachute Instructors (PIs) had told us everything that they thought we ought to know, we were sent to the flight lines where B Squadron's Argosy, XN 817, was waiting to take us on a one way trip to the seaside. There we stood in line, collected and then donned our main parachutes. Once that was done to the satisfaction of the professionals we were given our reserve parachutes, but told not to put them on until we were seated on board. The reserve parachutes had two handles, one for carriage and one for opening the 'chute. Perhaps it was predictable that at least one person would pick theirs up by the wrong one. Sure enough there was a sudden apparition of what seemed like acres of white silk from among the assembly followed by an expletive from the guilty party – an A Squadron back-seater! 'If you think that's goin' to get you out of the jump, sir,' intoned one of the PIs with heavy and resigned sarcasm, 'you can think again. Here's another one – and when you get back report to the parachute section to learn how to re-pack your first one!'

We climbed aboard the Whistling Wheelbarrow via the rear ramp and took our places in the canvas seats ranged down the side of the aircraft's hold. By now I had spent many happy, if sometimes stressful, hours up in the cockpit so this was going to be my first experience 'down the back'. This was not even 'economy class'; it was the aviation equivalent of 'steerage'. Soon we were airborne and winging our way south. The chatter and merriment level was quite high. But that all stopped abruptly when the jumpmaster opened the door. It now really sank in that we were not going to be here when the Argosy landed back at Boscombe Down.

Soon we were on our feet, queuing up to do this ridiculous thing, all predicated by the school philosophy that test pilots should experience ALL forms of flying. Static lines were attached. Buddy-buddy checks were done on each other's connections and straps. Then, in groups of three, we moved towards the open door, where a definite draught was now blowing in. Then one of the parachute section staff suddenly disappeared out into space; he was gone in a microsecond. The aircraft was flying at 1,200ft and about 120kt. It would take us about a minute to reach the water.

Then it started. The green light came on and three ETPS staff members followed each other out of the door. Then we moved forward as the Argosy was turned around for the next run. I watched about four other sticks of three go before I was standing in the doorway. As the aircraft banked to turn downwind for its next run, the one on which I would be taking my leave of this warm cargo bay, I stepped back slightly. Illogically I was afraid of falling out. A large PI's hand was placed on my back as he encouraged me to stand in the right place – right on the sill.

The aircraft turned again onto the final run heading towards the Drop Zone.

'Red ON … Green ON. GO! GO! Goooooooo!'

I stepped forward into nothing, encouraged by a friendly but firm shove, and felt myself falling.

Oh my goodness, I've just fallen out of an aeroplane!!! I thought. Then there was a jolt, I looked up and the blue sky was now partially obscured by the canopy of a parachute – my parachute. The lines between it and me were twisted, a result of my poor exit technique, I learnt later. However, a bit of kicking resulted in me being given a rotating panorama of this bit of Dorset before I settled into a much more pleasant straight descent. I had already reached up and grabbed the parachute webbing straps above my shoulders – more for comfort than for doing anything useful!

Now, for the first time since stepping out of the door, I looked down. I was probably at about 500ft. There was a blue-green sea being cut to ribbons by the marine's boats as they collected my fellow jumpers from the water. My next job was to bring both hands down and inflate my lifejacket and then put them on the circular box that locked all the parachute straps together. I rotated it through 90° to the 'UNLOCK' position, placed my thumbs at the back of it and my fingers on the front face. If I now squeezed the box it would release all the straps. However, I was still too high for that final plunge. I had to wait until I was at less than 20ft. But that was exceedingly difficult to judge over water. So I now looked ahead and watched the horizon close in on me, I watched one of the boats until it looked as if it was about 30ft below my eyeline. I squeezed the box and raised my arms so that I would fall clear of the parachute. I hit the water quicker than expected, went down a bit, popped up like a cork and found that two pairs of strong hands were hauling me out of the water. I would say that I had been wet for all of five seconds. Let's hear it for the Royal Marines!

We had all sent clean, dry clothes and a large plastic bag down on the coach that was going to collect us from the RM base in Poole. Multiple retellings of the experience of falling out of an aeroplane and surviving punctuated the journey back to Boscombe; as did a stop at the High Post Hotel for refreshments – well it was a bit too early for the bar to be open! Oddly enough I was back in the same Argosy the very next day, but this time on the flight deck with P.K. Yadav, refamiliarising ourselves before we started another high-risk test exercise – asymmetric flight.

So much for the lighter side of life as an ETPS student!

7 TRAVELLING LIGHT

Just as the parachute jump was a part of the ETPS syllabus that took us away from the real flying, as well as providing an escape from Ground School, report writing and data analysing, so was the curriculum of visits to places of aeronautical and educational interest. In many ways these diversions were a relief from the daily grind, but they also increased the pressure on our workload, and that of the staff, to fit all the required sorties into the only 'test programme' at Boscombe Down that had a fixed end date – in our case 12 December 1975. As I would soon learn in my test-flying career, all other test programmes invariably slip to the right!

The first visit we made was one we would repeat about four times during the year. It was an evening out in London; but one that was to be not quite as attractive as it might sound. These visits to 'The Smoke' were made so that we could attend lectures given by various elder statesmen of the flight test community at the Royal Aeronautical Society (RAeS) HQ at 4 Hamilton Place, near Hyde Park Corner. The morning before the first visit a rather stern Chalky briefed us on his 'rules of engagement' for the event. We were to dress smartly, not miss the bus either going or returning (at this juncture times of departure were written on his rolling blackboard) and he told us everything that we needed to know about the internal layout of 4 Hamilton Place. Because more than adequate time had been allowed for the journey we disembarked outside the RAeS far too early, only to find that the doors were closed and we were not yet entirely welcome. However, a scouting party soon discovered that just around the corner in Old Park Lane there was a fine hostelry called the Rose and Crown. Also not far away was a Hard Rock Cafe so choices were made and we split up, with Chalky's shrill counsel for us to ensure that we would be back in good time to take our seats in the auditorium.

I, with Lockwood, Ross, Morgenfeld and other regular imbibers of fine ales, went to the pub. Snacks were consumed along with at least a couple of pints of the landlord's best bitter. Unlike the passage of time during the tedious coach journey the hour now flew by. 'It must be my non-dimensional watch,' quipped Vic Lockwood. We were in danger of missing the deadline! So we quaffed our drinks and set off at a quick trot back to Hamilton Place. Finding the doors open, we surged in to find our way to the lecture hall and took seats not too near the front.

Rolls-Royce test pilot Harry Pollitt, from Bristol Filton, was giving the lecture that night. The topic of his talk was the test programme of the Olympus engine, carried in the belly of an Avro Vulcan, for the Anglo-French supersonic airliner Concorde. It turned out to be fascinating stuff and I soon became an attentive student once again. However, that did not last much more than thirty minutes. The aforementioned imbibing was making itself felt!

During our briefing we had been apprised of the fact that the gents' toilet was in the basement. Moreover, we had been asked that 'in the unlikely event of needing the facility during the lecture' we should leave the amphitheatre by the double doors at the back, then enter the door immediately on our left, go down the stairs behind it and travel along an underground passage until we reached the gents. I whispered to Tom Morgenfeld that I needed to get past him in order to creep out and relieve the increasing pressure on my innards. He whispered back that he would join me.

We sneaked out as quietly as we could, hoping that Chalky Rodgers would not spot us. We left the lecture hall and found a pair of double doors ahead of us. They looked like fire doors but, following this morning's instruction, we pushed them open and stepped through. The doors slammed shut behind us. Then a big red London bus went from right to left in front of us. We were outside! There was no way back; the doors had no external handles. Tom and I then made one of those rapid decisions that only jet pilots can make: we would return to the Rose and Crown. That was for two reasons – first, there would be a gents' toilet there and, second, we could have another beer while we waited for the others to come out of the lecture. It was then that Tom shared one of his many adages. 'My trouble is that I have three-pint kidneys but only a two-ounce bladder.' I admitted to the same configuration. Dear old Chalky did have a kind streak after all, because he had allowed us all an hour's freedom before we would hit the road westward again.

We later learnt that the glazed double doors at the back of the lecture hall, to which the briefing had referred, were actually open so we did not spot them. Hence we ended up like two lost boys standing in Park Lane with our mouths agape and a fearsome need to visit the loo! We went up to the RAeS three more times during the year. I cannot recall the specific lectures, but Tom and I discovered the aeronautical gents' toilet on our next visit.

The first of a series of educational field trips to British aerospace establishments and companies happened on Wednesday 9 April and did not take us far. It was to the RAE and the Institute of Aviation Medicine (IAM) at Farnborough. Once we got there, we were shown round various RAF departments, introduced to a variety of experimental airborne systems and the mysterious world of the structural engineers. The latter's Structures Building, containing a heavily restrained Concorde, was probably the highlight. After lunch we visited the IAM where RAF doctors and other civilian specialists spend their time researching and refining anything medical that interfaces with flying. There we were shown a multitude of ways of putting the human body through the sorts of things that would, in any other world, be regarded as degrading and inhuman. The Centrifuge, Climatic Chamber, Decelerator Track and Vestibular Laboratory being just some of the areas that the doctors delighted in and their subjects no doubt dreaded. Little did I know that, within a year, I would be letting the same medical madmen loose on my small but perfectly formed body!

The next item on the field trip agenda was to be on Thursday 24 April and even closer to home: A&AEE Boscombe Down. After an introductory talk by the Superintendent of Engineering we were divided into four parties and each bunch of students was bussed to one of four on-base research and development facilities. The first of these that our party visited was an impressive piece of machinery called the Blower Tunnel. All the wind tunnels I had seen photographs of and films about were enclosed in huge buildings and had big fans. This one was totally different. First it was outdoors and there was no sign of a tunnel. It looked like a Victorian engineering construction of which Isambard Kingdom Brunel in his stovepipe hat would have been very proud. There were wires and pulleys in a framework of vertical and horizontal girders, all producing a dark presence of mysterious purpose. At one end was a huge tapering nozzle, not unlike the back end of a massive jet engine. This is where the eponymous 'blow' emanated. To achieve the enormous airflows required the big fan inside the duct was driven by not just one but no less than four Rolls-Royce Merlin engines, no doubt left over from the huge production run that powered many of the RAF's air assets during the Second World War. If, thirty years after that conflict was over, this seemed a risky strategy, we were also shown a substantial pile of wooden crates, each containing a brand-new Merlin. It seemed that spares would not be a problem for some time to come! After a guided tour around this wondrous artefact we were then treated to the sight and sound of the Blower Tunnel in action. It did indeed emit a noise like a runaway Lancaster bomber or a flight of four Spitfires! And the amount of 'blow' was very impressive. We were told that all sorts of things were put just downstream of the nozzle including whole aircraft, cockpit sections (for hood jettison and ejection seat tests) and missiles. Using liquid nitrogen the monstrous thing could even be made to produce calibrated ice particles for testing anti-icing systems. It was fascinating and showed our foreign pals just how inventive and cost-conscious we Brits really can be. As we departed the boffins gave us each a brochure about the Blower Tunnel, in which we could read that it would cost £250 per day to hire it!

Declining this offer, we then moved on to a shabby-looking hangar on the south side of the airfield and we were invited to step inside. It was the Environmental Test Centre. In the roof were radiant panels that could heat the place up to Saharan temperatures and around the walls were ducts for blowing freezing cold air in to mimic arctic conditions. Being a hangar a whole medium-sized aircraft could be wheeled in and either heated up or cooled down so that the onboard systems could be run-up and tested for complicity with the requirements for the range of operational temperature. When we had been shown around, the folk who managed the test facility turned the heaters on. It was amazing how quickly it warmed up in there. Having only recently come out of the end of a Wiltshire winter I was glad that they did not demonstrate the cooling.

Having chilled off a little outside we were then told we were going to visit someone called Reg. In fact Reg was not a person but a location. While flying I had noticed a large sunken area alongside the main taxiway. It had concrete parking areas and all sorts of wires on poles and nets of thick cable suspended 20 or so feet off the ground. There were also pointy radar transmitters around the place. Every now and then an aeroplane or helicopter would be parked there. This was the Radio Environmental Generator: hence REG. A boffin showed us round and soon lost all of us that did not have electrical engineering degrees as to what they did and how it worked. The best bit was when he told us that they had recently put a Jaguar fighter-bomber in there and when they had fired their electrical death rays at it all the bombs had fallen off!

The final visit was to the 'new' computer building. This was where all the flight-test instrumentation, processing and analysing was to be centred. Only some of this had been done by the time of our visit but we were still expected to get excitedly interested in looking at a series of large cupboards with flashing lights and whirling magnetic tape on them. All this was now beginning to saturate our minds, so glazed looks, similar to those seen at the end of three hours in Ground School, started to appear. Thankfully that was the end of the visit and we retreated to ETPS and what had become normal life.

The introduction to the next Visit Instruction, under Operation Order ETPS 2/75, read:

> Object of the Visit. The object of this visit is to enable students to gain some knowledge of: the current research programmes of the Royal Aircraft Establishment Bedford; the design and manufacture of aircraft engines by Rolls Royce Bristol Engine Division; and Concorde's flight test programmed by the British Aircraft Corporation, Fairford. In addition the visit will enable students to meet design staffs, test pilots and other personalities with whom they may work in the future.

The visit was to be two whole days out of school, on 30 April and 1 May. So it would be our first trip with an overnight stop, at the Royal Hotel in Bristol.

For all these visits we had to wear our best uniforms during the day and suits in the evenings.

The venerable Argosy was wheeled out again, with the senior staff at the helm, ably assisted by at least two of our air engineers. We all boarded in time to be airborne by 8.30 a.m. We were in gleeful mood, like so many boys going on a school trip; hardly surprising because that was very close to the truth. Our first destination was to be the large airfield at Thurleigh, near Bedford, with its 10,000ft long runway. It appeared over the horizon about half an hour later; hardly time to get into the good book I had brought. We were soon whisked away, in separate parties, around the place looking at and even 'flying' various research simulators. We were told of the current experimental flight tests being undertaken on aircraft such as the BAC-111 and HS 748 airliners, a highly modified single-seat Folland Gnat and a Wessex helicopter. The trials varied from Civil Aviation Authority sponsored work on landing safely in zero visibility, steep approaches and esoteric research into air turbulence. As well as talking to and being talked at by the scientists, most of the resident RAF and RN test pilots were there to chat to us and give us a foretaste of what the next few years might bring.

By the end of the morning, lunch was beckoning, but we had to travel to Bristol to get it. After another hour or so in the innards of the Argosy our own, by now empty, insides were replenished with a magnificent spread laid on by the marketing department of Messrs Rolls and Royce; it really was a Rolls-Royce of a buffet! The company's itinerary then very sensibly avoided the post-prandial trap of putting us into a warm, quiet and darkly-lit room for lectures, where most of us would have had no difficulty in dropping gently into the arms of Morpheus. Instead we were taken on a tour of the engine assembly areas and test facilities. As might be expected there were lots of cylindrical constructions of varying sizes all wrapped in tortuous pipework, which we all recognised as jet engines. The best bit was watching an RB 199 Multi-Role Combat Aircraft (MRCA) engine being run up to full reheat in one of the test facilities.

Having got us through the post-lunch soporific danger hour we were then taken into the aforesaid warm, quiet and darkly-lit lecture room where we met the R-R test pilots: Graham Andrews, John Lewis, Ken Robertson and our recent acquaintance from the RAeS, Harry Pollitt. They talked to us about various test programmes on their current range of engines, including the RB 211, Olympus, Adour and Gem. Then came a talk that many of the UK contingent speculated might be a late April Fools' joke. Apparently the company had proposed an airborne simulator for asymmetric flight. As I knew all too well, from my many hours as a Canberra pilot and instructor, teaching pilots to handle correctly and safely a multi-engined aircraft following the failure of one or more engines was a hazardous business. Certainly on the

Canberra force, more aircraft and aircrew had been lost practising these procedures than had been lost under actual engine failure cases. Thus R-R had come up with an idea for a Jet Provost trainer to be modified in an imaginative and unique way to give student pilots a fairly realistic opportunity to learn how to fly an aircraft under asymmetric power.

Their idea was to put a vane inside the end of the jet exhaust pipe. On selection of the 'engine failure' system by the instructor this vane would then be deflected to give the student experience at correcting the yaw and the engine thrust would be reduced. On the face of it this would cause the same effects as losing an engine in a twin-engined aeroplane and had the potential to be a safe and cost-effective way of introducing pilots to the principles and handling techniques of asymmetric flight. During the tea break that followed a few notable remarks arose following the presentation of this cunning scheme. The most memorable were:

Duncan Ross: 'Only the British could build the Jet Provost and then reduce its thrust and give it an asymmetric problem!'

Chris Yeo: 'It's a great idea ... the ultimate stall turn device!'

The evening was spent playing skittles at the White Lion hostelry in Thornbury. But this time there was a trophy to be won. It was a large bone, mounted on a wooden stand. This strange prize was known as the Bone of Contention and was played for annually between teams from Filton and ETPS. We had been told that we should not try too hard to win as the CTFI, who had to keep the Bone in his office, was not partial to the suppurating and smelly object! However, the opposition was even worse than we were and, anyway, telling a bunch of pilots not to be competitive was a bit of a waste of time. The skittles match was followed by another sumptuous meal, several nightcaps and return to our hotel.

During the afternoon we had been asked to provide ten student volunteers to go flying the next morning, the only drawback being that we would have to rise at sparrow-break and forego breakfast; I volunteered. The bus duly turned up to collect us at 6.30 a.m. and, within the hour, we had boarded a strange-looking aeroplane called a VFW 614, which was a 40-seat, short-haul airliner of German origin. It was at Filton for tests on its M45 engines, which were uniquely mounted on pylons above the wings. The logic of the bizarre configuration was driven by a desire for the aircraft to sit low to the ground for ease of access and maintenance. R-R test pilot John Lewis was at the pointed end and kindly invited us each in turn to go up to the cockpit and 'have a go'. I actually don't remember much about that, other than there was nothing out of the ordinary there. The aircraft handled much as one might expect for a fairly simple machine of its size and weight. What was odd from a passenger appeal view was that the rearmost rows of seats, two each side of the aisle, had no sight of the ground but an excellent view of the engines, which, in any turbulence, tended to wobble sideways on their pylons. The VFW 614 did not turn out to be a success story; however, we were all very grateful for the opportunity to fly in it and experience handling it.

After we returned to Filton we transferred to the Argosy for the final stage of our visit and we were flown the short hop to Fairford, in Gloucestershire, the home of the British Concorde test team. There we met two of Concorde's celebrity test pilots Brian Trubshaw and John Cochrane, who talked to us about that beautiful flying machine's flight test programme. There were lots of questions followed by a look around the impressively graceful aircraft itself. 'Awesome, astounding, amazing' were just some of the words emanating from the gobsmacked student body – except the Frenchman, who was telling everybody that Concorde was really a Gallic invention! After that we were treated to our final buffet lunch and then boarded our faithful old freighter to return to Boscombe Down; from the sublime to the ridiculous!

If we thought that was a good outing, we had something even better to come. On Friday 6 June we were due to visit the Paris Air Show. Passports were retrieved from almost forgotten places, alarms set for an early start and best suits donned. The Argosy was airborne by 7.45 a.m. and an hour or so later we arrived at one of the French Air Force's Flight Test Centres, a place called Brétigny, about 60km south of Paris. From there we were bussed (yet again) north, past Orly Airport and then via La Périphérique around Paris, to Le Bourget and the Paris Air Show; or as the French call it: Le Salon International de l'Aeronautique et de l'Espace. No wonder the French talk so much, they have to get in so many more words!

We arrived at coffee time and melted into the considerable crowds. Looking round the static aircraft display there was a lot to see: the latest American F-14, F-15 and F-16 fighters, French Dassault Mirages of all sorts and, most impressively, an Aeroflot Tupolev Tu-144 supersonic 'Concordski' airliner. We were allowed to walk under it and I couldn't help noticing boiler-plate strengthening with huge round-headed rivets under the aircraft's centre-section. Engineering more reminiscent of shipbuilding than aviation!

Each of us had been given the name of a UK aerospace company to remember; those that did so and managed to locate the appropriate chalet were rewarded with lunch and drinks. As I sat there in the sunshine, with a prawn cocktail and a glass of wine, watching the latest products of the worldwide aircraft industry being put through their paces I could hardly believe my fortune. It made all the long hours of report writing, Ground School, test card preparation and demanding flying worthwhile. I could have stayed there for the whole week. But that was not to be. At about 5 p.m. it all came to an end and we took another hour-long coach journey through the jams around Paris back to CEV Brétigny, where we wearily climbed back aboard the Argosy and set off to return to good old Blighty. However, it was

far too late on a Friday night for Boscombe Down to be open so we landed at
RAF Lyneham. Then, yes you've guessed it; there was another coach journey.
By the time we reached Boscombe the Officers' Mess Bar was closed! Back
to reality!

We had only one day back at school before we were off again. The man
trying to keep the flying programme running to schedule, Graham Bridges,
was now pulling his hair out – all these beautiful summer days going by with
no productive syllabus flying being completed! This next trip was to the
seaside, landing at Shoreham aerodrome on the English South Coast for a
visit to the Singer Link Miles factory in nearby Lancing. Transport this time
was courtesy of the RAF Handling Squadron and their Andover military
transport aircraft. The purpose of this visit was to see the civil and military
flight simulators that the company produced for customers around the world.
The lunch at the Chatsworth Hotel in Worthing was definitely real and not
simulated, nor were the wines. The gourmets among us were starting to draw
up a league table of the quality of field trip lunches. To date Rolls-Royce had
a narrow lead over Singer Link Miles. Who would be next?

Well, the answer came soon enough. This time we would be 'on the road'
for a whole three days on what became known as the Midlands Tour. On to
the Argosy (by now the sobriquet 'All-soggy' was being used in a variety of
foreign accents) and our first destination was to be the airfield of Hawker
Siddeley Aviation (HSA) at Dunsfold in Surrey. As usual, the high-priced help
was up in the cockpit while the rest of us sat in the cheap seats downstairs.
We had not been airborne long when our Fleet Air Arm (FAA) rep, Simon
Thornewill, started complaining that he couldn't see out of his 'porthole'
too well.

'There's pink, gooey stuff all over the window,' he moaned. As I was sitting
close by I had a look. It was hydraulic fluid! An engineer was requested. Terry
Jones arrived, confirmed the diagnosis, fell about laughing and then rushed up
top to inform management. As we were now nearer Dunsfold than Boscombe,
the whole flight being not much more than half an hour's duration, we pressed
on eastwards. Not much later the flow of raspberry juice reduced. We were full
of admiration for our flight deck engineer, Lenny Moran, whom we assumed
had taken the correct remedial action. After landing we found out that our
confidence was misplaced; the flow had slowed because the tank had emptied!
As we walked away from the sad-looking aeroplane there was an easily
seen cherry red stripe down the side of the fuselage. US Naval Aviator Tom
Morgenfeld said, 'If that was a Crusader (his operational steed) we'd just go
ahead and launch it.' Vic Lockwood said that if he walked out to a Lightning
(his operational steed) and it wasn't leaking hydraulic fuel he wouldn't take
it because it was empty! We left the engineers to try to fix our sole means of

onward transport and spent the day learning about Harriers and Hawks, the latter then still being in development as the RAF's next advanced trainer.

By teatime the Argosy had been repaired and the fixed-wing students re-embarked for our onward journey north to visit Rolls-Royce's Derby Engine Division. This time our arrival destination was East Midlands Airport. The 'rotor heads' returned to Boscombe Down in an aged and clattering Pembroke communications aircraft. No second Rolls-Royce entertainment for them!

After arrival at East Midlands Airport we were taken to our overnight accommodation at the Pennine Hotel in central Derby, where we had an hour to spruce ourselves up before being treated to dinner. Most of us used only ten minutes of that allowance for its stated purpose and spent the rest of the time in the bar! The evening passed very pleasantly with Messrs R-R living up to the standard set by their West Country brethren in Bristol: a splendid multi-course dinner, ample wine and excellent company. This all took place at the Palm Court Restaurant at Allestree in north Derby. Some of our number thought that our venerable CGI, Chalky Rodgers, was disappointed not to find a matronly string quartet playing under the eponymous palms. After a very pleasant evening the coach returned us to our hotel before we all turned into pumpkins.

Our hosts were very kind to us the next morning. After arriving at their factory in Moor Lane we were deposited in a softly lit lecture room and regaled with all sorts of mostly useful and interesting information on the company and its two major engine projects of the time: the military Adour for use in the Jaguar and Hawk; and the giant RB 211 for commercial airliners. Crippling costs of the development of this advanced powerplant had led to the whole of Rolls-Royce, in business since 1914, being nationalised by the Conservative government in 1971. The world-renowned car division of the business had been separated from the parent company in 1973 as Rolls-Royce Motors.

After a talk about their future aero-engine projects, a visit to the research labs and lunch, we were taken on tours of the production facilities and test rig. The most fascinating part was watching a 2ft-long RB 211 fan blade that was under test waving like a reed in a gale force wind. We were also intrigued by the precision casting of tiny compressor and turbine blades through an interesting moulding technique called 'The Lost Wax Procedure'; this gave rise to some very dubious humour! With that highly educational gem in our heads we were conveyed back to East Midlands Airport where our transport of delight was waiting to take us on our way for the third leg of our voyage around England. This time to an airfield even us Brits had never heard of: Holme-on-Spalding-Moor, not far from Beverley and Hull in the East Riding of Yorkshire. We would soon learn that it was invariably referred to as

'HOSM'. The forty-minute flight passed uneventfully, with no reappearance of pink liquid. However, a few seconds after landing there was a very audible *thump-thwack* from underneath the aircraft. This was because we had passed over a rigged arrestor cable on the runway that was there for the emergency use of the resident Buccaneers and Phantoms. This event brought on much chatter from the assembly of amateur Argosy pilots in the belly of the said flying machine. That was because we all knew that the Argosy's Release to Service only allowed it to go over ('trample' in the trade) a rigged cable at walking speed! We reckoned that as the aircraft was being flown by two very senior test pilots they should write a report, to be handed to the appropriate authorities (within ten days of course!), to extend that clearance. However, it might be worth inspecting the underside of our dear old Argosy before they did so!

Back in my native Yorkshire I, for one, was hoping that this would be a fitting climax to this time away from school. I was not to be disappointed. After a group photograph was taken a coach took us to HSA's aircraft factory at Brough Aerodrome, on the north bank of the wide, grey River Humber, within sight of the splendid Humber Suspension Bridge. There had been an airfield at Brough since the days of the First World War, when Robert Blackburn set up a factory there for the manufacture and testing of his aircraft. In the 1930s Blackburn built a side-by-side, two-seat, biplane trainer called the B2 and this allowed the company to gain a training contract with the RAF. Many soon to be RAF aces, such as Ginger Lacy, were trained at Brough. The airfield had a splendid Art Deco building on its western boundary, which was the Brough Flying Club HQ. It was in this building that we were to be accommodated and fed.

After the by now usual rapid sprucing most course members were to be found in the bar imbibing their first aperitif of the evening. The TV was on and showing *Top of the Pops*. When the troop of gorgeous girls called Pan's People appeared and started their musical gyrations Vic Lockwood was heard to call across the room to one of our air engineers, sipping his port and lemon, 'Hey, Lennie, turn up your pacemaker and come and watch this lot!'

Things got a bit more staid and serious when we sat down to a formal dinner hosted by the Executive Director, Mr Essex-Crosby, and many of the company's senior staff, including CTP Don Headley and his deputy Tom Gilmore. The evening included a splendid slide show of the company's wide range of aircraft from the 1910 monoplane to the modern Buccaneer, still being made on-site. At the end of dinner the sensible ones went to bed and the rest hit downtown Hull; I'd been there before and didn't reckon it was worth the considerable taxi fare on a Thursday evening!

The next day dawned fair and, by way of a change we walked to our first appointed rendezvous. This was to be a long perambulation through the factory, looking at large billets of metal being fashioned by huge precision milling machines into bits of aeroplane for the Buccaneer. There were other areas where more conventional manufacturing processes were fabricating sections of Hawk, Harrier and Trident airliner. Brough was the only place in the UK where one could still see huge blocks of metal going in one end of a factory and aeroplanes coming out of the other end. Within a few years it was to be the last.

After coffee we were taken out onto the edge of the airfield to find that a shiny little biplane had been wheeled out for us to look at. This was the aforementioned Blackburn B2 trainer of the 1930s that the company had preserved and kept in flying condition. It was a bit like a chubby Tiger Moth but much prettier. After we had all had a good look at it our gallant leader, Gp Capt. Alan Merriman, was invited by Don Headley to climb aboard and try it for size. They went off and flew around over the airfield while we all watched jealously from below. After a couple of gentle aerobatic manoeuvres the machine puttered back to just outside the hangar where Pete Sedgwick was waiting for his turn. We students, however, walked back to the Aero Club to retrieve our suitcases and get ready for our departure. That was after a wonderful lunch, in keeping with Yorkshire tradition on a Friday – fish and chips, with mushy peas, accompanied by strong tea in decent sized cups! The fish was as fresh as it should have been so near to the North Sea.

It was now time to head back to HOSM, look over and into Buccaneers and Phantoms, and inspect some of the very modern test equipment and instrumentation, which were incongruously housed in 40-year-old single-storey wartime buildings. After final chats with the flight test folk we climbed aboard the Argosy for the last time, at least this week, and were flown back to Boscombe Down. Thank goodness it was Friday. We could have two days to recover before we tackled the next set of test exercises!

Apart from a one-day visit to Westland Helicopters Ltd at Yeovil in Somerset we had almost the whole month of July to allay the Principal Tutor's worries and catch up with the syllabus. Then, almost at the end of the second term we were off again! On 30 July we were taken, again by Andover, to Rochester in Kent to spend the day discovering the electronic gismos and thingamajigs that the company of Marconi-Elliott put into modern aeroplanes and helicopters. Head-Up Displays (HUDs), navigation and attack systems, automatic flight controls systems and the company's thoughts on the future of digital technology in aircraft were all on the agenda. So was another sumptuous lunch at which the steaks that were served were definitely not Marconi sub-miniatures!

On Tuesday 23 September, a rather special visit was laid on; but only for three of our number, plus a responsible adult in the form of Fixed Wing Tutor, Pete Sedgwick. Ted Steer drew the names out of a hat and the three lucky

winners were: Edward Küs, Svend Hjort and yours truly (well done, Ted!).
The visit was to be a few hours aboard the RN aircraft carrier HMS *Ark
Royal*, which was working up in the reserved sea-space off Dorset. We flew to
the ship in the ETPS Puma and arrived in time to be taken below for coffee.
That was followed by a tour of the ship's main operations centres finishing on
the bridge. Flying was taking place and landings were about to commence so
we were escorted onto the balcony overlooking the flight deck, known to all
in the trade as 'Goofers'. From there we watched Phantoms and Buccaneers
arriving, some making hook-up practice landings and go-arounds, others
being arrested by one of the four wires strung across the deck.

A Buccaneer arrived and missed the wires altogether. This led to him taking
off again, only just achieving sufficient lift before the deck ran out. This is
known in the trade as a 'bolter'. I later learnt that this was a Boscombe Down
test pilot; his name will be withheld to save embarrassment. Then a Phantom
arrived and seemed to be a bit lower on its approach than all its predecessors.
Just as the aircraft arrived over the back end of the ship a wave lifted the stern
and there was an almighty impact with what is known as the 'round-down'.
Bits could be seen coming away from the Phantom's undercarriage. The pilot,
no doubt a bit shaken, made a low, slow flypast with the landing gear down.
The powers that be decided that he would have to return to land ashore. By
now all the brave aviators were back on deck and it was time for us to depart.

The final of our educational expeditions around the UK was to be
christened 'The Great Northern Gourmet Tour'. This excursion would go
first to the British Aircraft Corporation's (BAC) airfield and production
facility at Warton, near Blackpool in Lancashire, then onwards, even further
north, to Scotland, the 'Home of the Brave', to visit Ferranti Ltd in Edinburgh
and Scottish Aviation at Prestwick in Ayrshire. As had become the norm that
year the 'Whistling Wheelbarrow' was to be our preferred conveyance and we
departed Boscombe Down at an early hour to arrive at Warton in time for
coffee. But about twenty minutes after lift-off, when most of the company
had dozed off, there was an almighty BANG, accompanied by a lurch and a
flash. Most folk blamed Duncan Ross, but there was no accompanying bad
odour. In fact the aircraft had been struck by lightning. Svend Hjort pondered
that it might be Thor's revenge for the irreverent and rowdy Viking party he
had held the previous Saturday night. The captain, Wg Cdr Wally Bainbridge,
decided to carry on to our destination where the airframe would be examined
for damage while his passengers got on with the business of the visit to BAC.
In fact, the engineers found a hole burnt into the port elevator horn, which
they patched up in the tradition of their trade with linen and dope (for our
younger readers – dope is a liquid that shrinks and strengthens the linen, not
a drug!). What no one spotted was that the lightning had also struck the end

of the long pole sticking out forward from the top of the cockpit. This carried the moveable vanes to measure angles of attack and sideslip. It wasn't until later, during the first asymmetric handling exercise, that some very strange results were found. Expected sideslip angles were much lower than indicated. This was because the vane had been welded into its neutral position by the lightning bolt! Goodness only knows what sideslip angles had really been generated by Duncan Ross and his tutor Walt Honour!

The visit to Warton went off much as expected. There were the usual presentations on products followed by a look at some of them: Jaguars, the MRCA prototypes and the new Combat Simulator, housed in a dome kept in shape by positive air pressure. Most of us were allowed a short attempt at shooting down an adversary in the simulator; some did well, funnily enough mostly the bomber pilots! The MRCA and its testing were probably of most interest as it had first flown only a year earlier and was still heavily involved in its development programme. Its two test pilots, Paul Millet and Dave Eagles, were very open about how the programme was progressing and what they had found to date.

After the completion of the visit we were taken to the Fernlea Hotel in St Annes for the usual routine of changing and preening. At the appointed hour we were taken from there into Blackpool and the evening's watering hole, the Savoy Hotel. En-route our overseas guests were able to marvel at 't' lluminations' and the famous Blackpool Tower. However, our Frenchman, Gerard Le Breton, appeared underwhelmed by the latter, which he found to be an inferior copy of Monsieur Eiffel's original. BAC had reserved a room at the Savoy for our dinner. However, just after our arrival some souls ventured a look around inside other parts of the rather grand edifice. It transpired that the annual conference of the Labour Party was being held in Blackpool that week and on that evening many highly recognisable political faces could be spotted in the hotel. One of our number was later seen dragging the Home Secretary, Roy Jenkins, by the arm in our direction. However, the Right Honourable Gentleman was heard protesting that our company was far too young for him to join! It was probably all a bit right wing for him as well.

After a very enjoyable dinner with our hosts, several of our number had been told by our hosts that the place to seek for further amusement was called Jack Pye's Club: an establishment where ladies publicly divested themselves of their garments. During their search, a local Bobby (police constable for foreign readers) was accosted with a demand for directions to the said establishment.

'We closed it down two weeks ago,' came the reply.

Someone piped up with another similar place of entertainment that he had heard about, 'What about Jack London's?'

'Not open on Wednesdays,' replied the officer of the law.

'Is there anywhere like those places open?'

'Not really. You could always try the disco,' came the reply.

The scouting party decided to go where the BAC hosts and our less adventurous companions had said they were going: a nightclub called 'The Lemon Tree'. Like most such establishments the beer was sold in half-pints for the price of a pint, any other drinks needed a small mortgage and the women there were only slightly more attractive than the men!

The following morning started with an amusing conversation between Gerard Le Breton and the spotty youth serving us breakfast. When asked what he would like to eat Gerard replied, 'I weel 'ave ze scrambled eggs, *s'il vous plaît*.'

'I'm sorry, sir, but we don't do scrambled eggs,' came the reply.

'But you 'ave eggs. My friend 'ere is 'aving poached eggs, *n'est ce pas?*'

'Oh yes, sir, you can have your eggs poached or fried – which do you want?'

'I want ze chef to take ze eggs and break zem into a bowl and stir zem up to make scrambled eggs,' was the insistent answer. 'Or per'aps an omelette?'

'Poached or fried, sir,' was the next bargaining position in this escalating war of culinary words.

Gerard knew when he was beaten (unlike his desired eggs). '*Sacré bleu!* Just toast!' came the exasperated denouement.

Those who had stayed out late, sampling the dubious delights of a midweek night out in Blackpool, had ample time to catch up on their beauty sleep as we droned even further north from Warton to Edinburgh Turnhouse Airport. As we did so Duncan Ross became definitely perkier, and the braw twang in his speech definitely became more noticeable. However, the welcome he had no doubt hoped that our company would receive on his native turf was less than full of warm Scottish hospitality. We spilled off the Argosy to await a coach that, after ten minutes, still had not appeared; and it was perishing cold out on the tarmac. 'I speak the lingo, so I'll go and find out what's happening,' declared our son of Scotia. The rest of us retreated out of the cutting wind back on board the Argosy. Duncan was obviously successful as, eventually, a coach arrived and took us to Ferranti's Crewe Toll factory on the outskirts of Scotland's capital city. Those that had still not caught up sufficiently on their shut-eye were able to continue the quest in the warm darkness of the lecture room into which we were led. Those that stayed awake were given the opportunity to learn about such esoteric airborne electronic equipment as Inertial Navigation and Attack Systems (INAS), Military Lasers, Airborne Radar and Ferranti's wish list for the future. Lunch was taken on site and after a tour of the factory we were whisked away to our final overnight accommodation, which was the modern and upmarket King James Hotel in downtown Edinburgh. The evening was rounded off by an excellent dinner, much like a service dining-in night, back at Crewe Toll. There was an open forum of after-dinner jokes, hosted by ex-RAF tp Bill Morrison (Gp Capt. retired), Ferranti's military liaison man. Those gags offered by Vic Lockwood were definitely the worst!

The Great Northern Tour, our last such visit of the year, ended the following day with a short flight from Edinburgh to Prestwick, on the west coast, to look over Scotland's only aircraft manufacturer – Scottish Aviation Limited. This followed the usual pattern of warm welcome, coffee, several lectures, lunch and a tour of the factory where the workforce was turning out shiny new piston-engined Bulldog trainers and twin-turboprop Jetstream aircraft. The former was an indigenous design but the latter had been taken over from the Handley-Page aircraft company of Radlett, Hertfordshire, which had gone into liquidation in 1970. By the time that we made our visit the Jetstream was in service in both the RAF and the RN, as well as in its civilian guise around the world, notably in the USA.

After lunch, as we winged our way homewards, we realised that we had been greatly privileged to have had the opportunity to see at first hand the full gamut of British aerospace expertise and capability. Despite some of the light-hearted attitudes we had taken, a lot of new and useful knowledge had actually sunk in. A fact not lost upon the folk who had hosted us. It was now early October. In two months' time we would have just about finished our time at ETPS. The final exercise would be upon us – the McKenna Dinner. However, before that there were still test cards to prepare, data to analyse and reports to write. On, on!

8 ROCKING AND ROLLING

By the time we arrived at our third term of penance we had achieved a reasonable understanding of how aeroplanes flew and why, occasionally, some odd things happened. We had learnt how to seek out answers to questions that previously we had never even thought to ask. But just as things were becoming a little clearer we were introduced to lateral and directional (L&D) stability. In the first term our collective knowledge and use of mathematics and aerodynamics had been tested and extended through the ministrations of the Ground School staff's teaching of longitudinal stability. We had learnt about such factors as the position of the aircraft's CG, the size of the tailplane and its relationship to the airflow from the wing, the way that the elevator worked and how important all these things were to the stability and safety of flight. But that was only in one plane (if you'll forgive the pun!) – the horizontal – that is in the sense of the aircraft's nose moving up or down as viewed by the pilot. The relevant equations were complicated enough, as was the manipulation of the stability derivatives, but in the case of L&D stability the two were inextricably interlinked.

So we were now dealing with a cat's cradle of dimensions and inter-connectivity. So, after much study and chalkboard rolling, we were subjected to another examination to ensure that we had at least a moderate grasp of the theory. Then we were dispatched to prove that we knew what we were doing by completing the flight test exercises laid down in the syllabus. First we had to fly the VSS Basset so that we could learn the correct test techniques and explore the effects of some of the variables. The Basset's clever analogue computer, which controlled the aircraft when it was flown from where we students sat, in the right-hand seat, provided most of the fun. The occupant of the other pilot's seat was a tutor who fiddled knowledgeably with one or two of the computer controls on a panel between us. When he did so some factor in the aeroplane's aerodynamic make-up, called a stability derivative, would be changed and the resulting variation in the handling of the Basset would quickly manifest itself. After each such selection a task would be flown and we had to see how difficult it had become. That meant that we had to come out with an opinion using the excellent Cooper–Harper rating scale, leading to a number. We were also encouraged to opine as to what the problem might be and how it might be fixed. The VSS Basset was an excellent tool for this but it did have one drawback. In order to protect the aeroplane from damage the automatic cut-out system, which warbled at you when the right-hand set of controls was automatically disconnected, was set a bit too far on the safe side. That meant that some of the more extreme modes were available for only a few seconds. Nevertheless we got the gist of it all.

The three main test techniques that we applied in order to discover the aircraft's L&D stability were steady heading sideslips, rolls on one control and something called Dutch rolls. I thought the latter the most interesting. The Dutch roll was ostensibly named after the rolling motion exhibited by the speed skaters of that flat land beyond the North Sea. In flight the motion was initiated by pushing the rudder bar in one direction until the nose had yawed off heading; a roll, normally in the same direction, accompanied that. As the motion got to its limit then the rudder bar was moved smoothly in the opposite sense and the nose and roll would reverse direction. After a couple of cycles the frequency of the aircraft's natural response could be sensed and measured. However, an eye had to be kept on the sideslip gauge. If the limit was exceeded then structural damage could be caused, especially to the fin. A lot could be learned from this relatively simple test. Looking out towards the wingtips, the circular or ovoid path that showed the ratio between the yaw and the roll generated by the sideslip induced by the rudder deflections could be observed. If the wingtips were not in view then a mark on the canopy or side window would do the same job. Watching the heading change on the gyro-stabilised compass on the instrument panel meant that the yaw angle could be quantified. Of course with a fully instrumented prototype or development aeroplane then all of this stuff would be automatically recorded for post-flight analysis by the boffins. But for us it was very useful for those times when we would not have those luxuries on board.

The two L&D exercises that I did were Asymmetric Flight in the Argosy and the L&D Assessment in the Lightning: chalk and cheese! I now had two new compatriots in our syndicate: Flt Lt Roger Searle and one of the Indian students, Flt Lt P.K. Yadav. As usual with the Argosy we were each given a different CG to fly, forward, mid and aft, and we would each fly as co-pilot and captain at least twice. From my seven years flying the twinjet Canberra I had plenty of experience of flying with thrust coming from only one side of the aeroplane, whereas Roger and PK, being single-jet pilots, had very little. On the quiet I was made aware that I would have to keep a bit of a supervisory eye on the other two; but I didn't really have any fears about their ability. In the end everything went off safely and no undue excursions were made beyond the sideslip limits of the dear old Argosy.[9]

As to the Lightning exercise we were allowed just two sorties, one subsonic and one supersonic. As usual, due to the Lightning's enormous thirst for kerosene and its tiny fuel tanks, neither sortie lasted long enough; especially the second one. It was the Lightning's highly swept wings that made it interesting, especially at the speeds around Mach 1. In fact, several Lightnings had been lost through pilots manoeuvring in the transonic regime. That was because the aircraft's directional stability, reduced by the transonic shockwaves, then the application of large amounts of aileron, had generated much more sideslip than roll, so the aircraft had entered a spin. Which was something that was not easy to recover from in this particular fighter.

Swept wings, along with wings that rise from the root, where they are joined to the fuselage, to their tips – known as dihedral – normally generate quite a lot of roll when sideslip occurs. Unsurprisingly this outcome is known as 'dihedral effect' and has its own stability derivative. It can be very important

9　The dangers were there. During the following year's course an Italian student lost control during a two-engined asymmetric go-around and XR 105 crashed on the edge of the airfield. Both the student and the Air Engineer, Terry Colgan, lost their lives and the ETPS QFI, Mike Vickers, was very badly injured but survived, having been thrown from the cockpit as the Argosy crashed. The aircraft was totally destroyed.

in some regimes of flight. For instance when landing an aeroplane with large dihedral effect in a crosswind. Because it is not good for the tyres it is highly desirable that the aeroplane's wheels are in line with the runway when it lands. So when there is a wind blowing from the side of the runway, instead of the much-preferred direction of straight ahead, then something must be done to get the machine down in that direction – straight down the runway. One option is to allow the nose to point into the wind during the final approach; this will set up an angle known as drift and manifests itself as a crab-like approach. Then, just as the wheels are about to touch down, a judiciously judged boot-full of rudder is applied to bring the nose round to point at the other end of the runway. As in much of life, timing is crucial. Too early and the aircraft will start to drift sideways across the runway and perhaps be in danger of missing it altogether. Too late and the tyres will squeal in protest at being forced sideways onto the ground. Your popularity with any passengers, the ground crew and the logistics folk will also suffer.

However, in an aeroplane with lots of dihedral effect, even if your timing is perfect, the amount of roll generated by the sideslip that the aforementioned boot-full of rudder produces may be too much to correct with the ailerons, especially at the low speeds that landing brings. In aircraft with low-mounted wings or underwing stores then, there may be a danger of those things hitting the ground. So another method had to be found. In the early days of swept-wing fighters, especially in the USA, pilots found that they could fly the aircraft straight down the runway centreline by using rudder and aileron in the opposite directions. This technique became known as the 'wing down' method and became widely adopted. Although a little more difficult to fly than the 'crab' technique, all the pilot has to do at touchdown is to put the crossed controls back to neutral. However, neither of these methods was safely successful for one large aeroplane – the USAF Boeing B-52 bomber. So an ingenious solution was engineered. The B-52's main wheels are all housed in the fuselage and the clever folk at Boeing made it possible for them to be moved by the aircraft's navigation system and set them to the correct drift angle. So all that a B-52 pilot had to do was fly a 'crabbed' approach all the way to touchdown in the knowledge that the wheels would stay in line with the runway. I've often wished that my flying machine had that facility on a dark and stormy night with the wind howling at some ridiculous angle across the runway!

As a footnote to this chapter I cannot move on without a tribute to the man who was my tutor during that last term, although he was away for most of it. Walt Honour, the US Naval exchange tutor, was a man who possessed a wry sense of humour, a plethora of knowledge and great integrity. He was a hard but fair task master and I used to make fun of his American zpelling, in which he inzizted on uzing the final letter of the alphabet as the first, rather than the second, alternative; it was, in my opinion, all the fault of Webster's dictionary and the US education system. A couple of weeks into that third term Walt was diagnosed with lymphatic cancer. He had first noticed a lump in his armpit while playing the unfamiliar game of cricket at the beginning of August and by mid September he was to be sent back stateside for treatment at the National Naval Medical Center [sic] in Bethesda, Maryland. In typical Walt fashion he threw a champagne party the evening before he and his wife, Lorraine, left us. We drank to his return, to both health and ETPS, hoping that would be before the McKenna Dinner. In the event it was not to be. However, Walt did go into remission and was able to return to Boscombe Down the following year. But tragedy was to strike again. Just after take-off the engine of the Hunter that he was flying exploded and he and his companion had to eject. They both landed safely with their parachutes, but perhaps the stress brought the cancer back into action. Walt died later that year. I believe that he still lives on in the minds of all of us fixed-wing student test pilots of 1975.

9 BEAVERING ABOUT

By the middle of October autumnal tints were appearing on the trees outside our house and lining the long walk that I was still making down the hill to the Ground School building. Those warm colours were the first harbinger of winter, which we hoped would see us graduate from ETPS and move on. But before that we had the final hurdle to successfully put behind us: 'the Preview'. This was the ultimate and most extensive test flying exercise of the course. We would each be put into a team of two or three and then undertake a comprehensive assessment of a current in-service aircraft against a set of requirements. The worst bit was we then had to report our findings in the by now familiar manner. This exercise would draw together all the test techniques that we had learnt and practised throughout the previous nine months, and it would be done using an aircraft type on which we had no previous flying experience.

However, this sort of 'testing to learn' was not going to be completely new to us. In mid September we had each to complete a lesser version of the Preview, when we flew an unfamiliar but simpler type of aeroplane in order to assess its suitability for its role; this mini-Preview was called the Pilot's Assessment. Again it was done in teams of two or three. Svend Hjort and I were allocated the de Havilland DHC2 Beaver. The exercise took place at the 'Beavers' Lodge' – The British Army Air Corps (AAC) airfield and HQ at Middle Wallop, Hampshire, not more than a thirty-minute drive from Boscombe Down. We had each been given a copy of the Pilot's Notes a few days beforehand, along with a role description and some basic requirements. That gave us time to work out what tests we should prioritise, as we would be allowed no more than an hour and a quarter to complete them. Although we were in teams the reports were to be written individually.

The Beaver was a late 1940s product of the Canadian arm of de Havilland Aviation and was designed to be a rugged, all-metal aeroplane with a Short Take-off and Landing (STOL) capability. It had a high wing, fixed landing gear with a tailwheel and was powered by a single 450hp (340kw) Pratt & Whitney Wasp radial engine. Like the animal it was named after it was a relatively rare sight in the circles in which I had moved. The DHC AL Mk 1 Beaver was adopted by the AAC in the 1950s for the light transport and observation roles. So I thought that its prime characteristics should be good longitudinal stability and control, a decent field of view from the cockpit and vice-free low-speed handling, with clear, unambiguous warning of an impending stall. It should also possess high-quality manoeuvrability for the observation role and for positioning during approaches to short and possibly semi-concealed landing strips.

I wrote up the test cards to take into account the normal sequence of a general handling flight. So field of view and ground manoeuvrability would be assessed before take-off. Then engine handling, take-off handling and performance, trimmability in the climb and the rate of climb would be the first airborne tests. The aircraft's control characteristics, longitudinal stability, both static and dynamic, and stalling would be next. After that turns up to the normal G-limit, roll-rates and L&D control and stability would be on the menu. I was aware that if I was not careful to fly the tests quickly and accurately I could reach the time limit while I was still miles away from Middle Wallop. However if I did manage the time for each test properly I should still be able to look at the glide performance for the engine failure case, before having time to do at least a couple of landings on the grass runway back at Middle Wallop.

When the day dawned Svend and I were sitting in the ETPS crew room waiting for our supervising tutor, Pete Sedgwick, to take us up the road for our day with the Army. 'Transport for all going to Centre Thump,' he announced cheerily as he appeared in the doorway. Svend gave me a questioning look. 'Centre Thump?' he intoned.

'Yes. It's Sedgwick's attempt at wordplay – Middle Wallop – Centre Thump. See?'

'Not really,' replied my exasperated Danish friend.

An hour later we had arrived, found our way to the appropriate hangar and were guided to the Ops Room. After introductions were made I met the poor soul who was going to sit next to me and suffer my pitiable imitation of a test pilot! He was a mature, grey-haired chap called Mr Mackenzie; most, if not all, of the instructors on the Beaver Flight at Middle Wallop seemed to be civilians of an older persuasion. After I had briefed Mr Mac about what I wanted to do he told me what I would be allowed to do. Fortunately the two were not irrevocably different. He then sent me to the Officers' Mess for lunch and asked me to be back in time to walk out to our steed by 1.30 p.m. Steed was a good description because, having observed the way that things had been done during the latter part of the morning, it seemed that the Beavers were treated a bit like horses in the cavalry. They were stabled overnight, groomed and fed with fuel in the morning and then just topped up between flights. I supposed that at the end of the day someone was going to give them an encouraging pat and a sugar lump.

We walked around the green and matt-black beast together while my mentor was checking that all the required bits were still attached. The next task was to mount. It was a bit of a climb up the side and in through the car-style entrance door. Once inside there was a definite retro ambience, but the seat was comfortable and most of the required knobs and levers fell readily to hand. As with radial-engined aeroplanes starting the motor was a bit of a lottery and required a fairly high level of ambidextrousness. After priming it with extra fuel, the starter flywheel was spun up electrically until the noise it made reached around treble C, then the switch was moved to the engage position, ignition switches selected 'on' and the throttle opened slightly. The propeller spun up, encouraging pops and bangs emanated from the exhaust pipe, along with a good deal of oily smoke, and then the engine started to run more smoothly. Such machines are much more fun to get going than jets!

Despite being a 'taildragger'[10] the view ahead was not too restricted by the big round motor just in front of us and I found that the Beaver could be manoeuvred and steered in the desired direction without too much effort. After the typical engine run-up and pre-take-off checks we lined up on the grass and I opened the throttle progressively while keeping straight with deft jabs on the rudder pedals. After raising the tail, which happened readily, the Beaver rose in the air in a very stately manner; there was obviously plenty of lift being generated by that long, high wing. To be honest I cannot remember much detail of the next seventy-five minutes in the Beaver and my report has been lost in the many house moves since! But I do remember that there was one unhealthy characteristic that I uncovered. Astonishingly there was no discernable warning of the stall in the landing configuration. The transition

---

10 A taildragger is an aeroplane with its central, third wheel at the back end, as opposed to the more frequently found location – under the nose.

from a normal descent at the correct speed to a stalled condition at too low a speed was marked only by the rate of descent, indicated on the appropriate dial, suddenly increasing to an alarming quantity. No buffet, no nose-drop, and no feeling that the aircraft was about to fall out of the sky; although that was what it was doing. Against the stated requirements and plain common sense this outcome was highly undesirable and should have been fixed. However, the Beaver had been doing its job for ages without crashing too many times. Moreover, the Beaver was nicely manoeuvrable and steep turns with a very small radius could be flown as long as the speed was held at a safe value. But in doing that the view into the turn was limited by the leading edge of the wing above my head. Back at Middle Wallop I managed to fly some circuits and landings without disgracing myself too much.

Overall this Pilot's Assessment exercise was a great experience. I had flown an aeroplane that I would be very unlikely to have got my sticky hands on otherwise. I had seen at first hand how another flying service operates and I had learnt to manage a test flight that covered all the main stability, handling, performance and qualitative assessment aspects of the past nine months' syllabus. I now felt better prepared for the 'big one' – the Preview – whatever flying machine might come my way.

10 A-BUCCANEERING WE WILL GO, ME LADS!

The final walk to the Ground School came on Monday 13 October; our Indian colleagues thought this date was very inauspicious. I told them that it was fine – it wasn't a Friday. However, it was actually very special because it was the day when we sat the last ever, final and ultimate examination of our academic knowledge. That meant that we were getting close to the end of the course and now, ever more hopefully, to graduation as test pilots and FTEs. We had handed in our penultimate reports and our next test assignment would be our last. But it was also going to be the biggest. By the concluding week of this year's course, in early December, we would have, in teams of two or three, written what amounted to a good-sized, illustrated book on our evaluations of a current operational aircraft that we had never flown before. On top of that would be a nerve-wracking thirty-minute presentation to the great and the good from the school, test flying establishments and representatives of the operational worlds we had dared to enter. We pilots would be allowed a maximum of five hours flight time each to achieve this not inconsiderable aim. But the question now doing the rounds was, 'Which aircraft will it be?'

The day soon arrived when we would find out. We all assembled for the briefing on the Preview exercise and listened to all that was said, but all the time we wondered where and to what we would be headed in a few days time. Wherever it was we would be allowed a maximum of three weeks from start to finish, before we had to start burning the midnight oil to produce our reports, as ever, within ten days.

At the end of the briefing the new CO of ETPS, Gp Capt. Mike Adams, announced the allocation of teams to aircraft and the locations where the exercises would take place. They were:

Flt Lts Vic Lockwood and 'Rusty' Rastogi were to assess the McDonnell F-4 Phantom as an interceptor/fighter, at RAF Coningsby in Lincolnshire.

Flt Lts Duncan Ross and P.K. Yadav were to assess the DH 125 Dominie as a light transport and training aircraft, at RAF Finningley in South Yorkshire.

Flt Lt George Ellis and Lt Cdr Tom Morgenfeld were to assess the BAe Harrier in the ground-attack Short Take-Off and Vertical Landing (STOVL) role, at RAF Wittering in Lincolnshire.

Flt Lt Chris Yeo and Maj. Svend Hjordt were to travel all the way to RAF Lossiemouth in northern Scotland to assess the BAC/SEPECAT Jaguar in the fighter-bomber role.

Flt Lt Roger Searle, Capt. Gerard Le Breton and Herr Udo Kerkhoff were to assess the Folland Gnat as an advanced trainer at RAF Valley, on the Isle of Anglesey in North Wales.

A big team of no less than four were allocated to assess the Westland Sea King at Royal Naval Air Service (RNAS) Culdrose in Cornwall. They were: Sqn Ldr Rob Tierney, Flt Lt Terry Creed, Capt. Bruno Bellucci and Mr Rob Humphries.

As befitted a small helicopter only two guys were sent to RAF Ternhill, Shropshire, to assess that particular 'whirlybird'. They were Lt Simon Thornewill and Herr Eduard Küs.

Finally, yours truly was teamed up with Flt Lt Mark Hayler and Mr Neil Sellers to go to RAF Honington in Suffolk to assess the HS Buccaneer in the low-level strike/attack role.

Our departure date was to be Monday 27 October, so the ten days following the Preview Briefing was taken up with reading into the Buccaneer's Aircrew Manual, Operational Data Manual and Flight Reference Cards (FRCs or more colloquially 'Checklist'). I also tracked down a book that gave the history of the Blackburn NA 39/Buccaneer project. Mark, Neil and I had several get-togethers in which we decided what tests we would do, in which order and who would do what. Then it was time to prepare our individual test cards, which was a bit of a lottery as we had no idea how much of our tests we would be allowed to do. Our ETPS staff 'overseer' for the exercise was to be Graham Bridges. I found that pleasing in the sense that I had started the course under his wide and capable wings and I would finish it in the same manner.

There was one thing that was different for us, compared to the other teams. There were no dual-controlled Buccaneers. It was for this reason that previous attempts by ETPS to use the RAF's Buccaneer as a Preview aircraft had come to nought.[11] However, before we went to Honington, Mark and I flew a Boscombe Down Hunter T7A, which had the Buccaneer's flight instrument panel fitted, and we each gained an Instrument Rating using that panel. That meant that we would be allowed to fly the Buccaneer, with a No. 237 Operational Conversion Unit (OCU) staff member in the back seat.

On the evening of Sunday 26 October the Preview adventure started with us driving the long diagonal across the country from Wiltshire to Suffolk. We settled into our rooms in the Officers' Mess and then met up in the bar to toast what we hoped would be a rewarding and successful stay. We were not late to bed as 'tomorrow was another day' and likely to be a very demanding one; like many of the tomorrows to come over the next three weeks.

As with any flying training situation our first destination was the Ground School where we would be introduced to the Buccaneer's many and varied internal organs: its electrical, hydraulic, fuel, flying control and electronic systems. These lessons would normally be given to student pilots converting to the aeroplane over a period of weeks; we had just a few days. So it came at us fast and furious in condensed packages always signed off with '... and you can read more in the appropriate section of the Aircrew Manual.'

Then it was into the simulator. Within a week of arriving at Honington I had been crammed with knowledge about this rather odd naval fixed-wing bomber. I had started to become accustomed to the often-haphazard layout of the cockpit and the naval aviators' apparent obsession with black and white magnetically operated indicators, rather than the lights and illuminated captions that I was more used to. I had also flown two further sorties in the specially instrumented Hunters with the poor soul who had been allocated to look after me; his name was Lt Alan Crabb, an FAA pilot who, thankfully, had lots of Buccaneer time in his logbook and plenty of experience of sitting in the back with no method of control over his students' actions other than shouting!

11 In fact there had been one Buccaneer Preview by ETPS. However, that was by using a Boscombe Down-based aircraft operating under MoD Procurement Executive rules and not RAF Regulations.

It was on the afternoon of Bonfire Night, Wednesday 5 November, that we met in the flying clothing section to gird our loins in a fit manner to commit aviation in the erstwhile Mr Blackburn's high-speed, low-level, nuclear-capable bomber. Perhaps this is the right time to introduce this piratical attacker? The Buccaneer was conceived by the then Blackburn Aircraft Company, based at Brough in East Yorkshire, in response to Naval Staff Requirement NA 39 issued in June 1952. By July 1955 the tendering process was completed with Barry Laight's design from Brough winning the development contract. Initially the aircraft was not named and was simply known to the public as the Blackburn NA 39. Secretly it was referred to as the Blackburn Advanced Naval Aircraft – BANA – and that soon became the 'Banana Jet'. A soubriquet somewhat enhanced by the curvy look of the fuselage.

The NA 39 possessed several innovative features, most notably the use of air piped from the engine compressors and ducted to blow over the wings at low speeds to delay the onset of the stall. Using this natty system, with the flaps down and the ailerons drooped, the Buccaneer could 'come aboard' its aircraft carrier about 30kt slower than it would have done without it. This ingenious system was correctly called Boundary Layer Control or BLC, but soon became known as 'blow'. After a fatal accident during development flying the blow system was extended to include the tailplane and its extendable flap that preserved longitudinal trim when the wing flaps and aileron droop were fully deployed. The original Buccaneers were powered by two de Havilland Gyron Junior engines, which each produced just over 7,000lb of thrust. However, as the aircraft became operational in the early 1960s, the weight it had to carry had increased markedly and it soon became apparent that the Gyron Junior was just that – not man enough for the job.

After a couple of in-service losses the FAA Buccaneer fleet was grounded. But the company had an answer and by late 1966 a new version was introduced that had a pair of bigger, more powerful engines: Rolls-Royce RB 168/Mk.101 Speys. They shoved out a total of nearly 25,000lb of thrust; about 40 per cent more than their predecessors. These splendid motors gave the Buccaneer a new lease of life with more range, increased payload capability and safer operation, especially during take-off and the approach and landing phases of flight. There were also changes to the airframe and operational equipment, the most noticeable of which were the enlarged intakes each side of the cockpit to suck in all the extra air demanded by the bigger engines. To make it work correctly the blow system required a minimum air pressure to go through the narrow slots in the wing leading edges and ahead of the ailerons and flaps. That, in turn, meant that the pilot had to select more throttle (thus thrust) than was needed to make the descending final approach path at the correct speed. So another unique element of the Buccaneer's shape arose.

It had a huge airbrake at the back end which, when it was fully opened on the approach, added drag to offset the surplus thrust. This design feature was achieved by a large tail cone that was split vertically and opened and closed by a hydraulic ram operated by a switch on the right-hand throttle.

Another feature of the Buccaneer's operation and layout that was new to all landlubbers like me were the folding wings. The hinge-line was a metre or so outboard of the main landing gear. The wing-fold was operated by hydraulic power and selected by a big guarded handle on the right-hand console in the cockpit. Of course, being a naval design, the aircraft also had a hydraulically operated hook at the back end, underneath and just ahead of the tail cone/airbrake. A hook-shaped switch in the cockpit, near the undercarriage buttons, selected this. With all this hydraulically operated stuff the company had decided to use the higher than usual operating pressure of 4,000 psi. An added bonus of this was that the wheels came up very quickly after selection; this was another highly desirable outcome for aircraft carrier operations. Once you had been unceremoniously slung off the deck by the steam catapult what you really did not want was unnecessary drag slowing you down.

But the Buccaneer had now become a land-based, strike/attack aircraft operating with the RAF. How did that come about? In 1965 the Labour government scrapped the BAC's TSR2, and then in early 1968 the order for its replacement, the American General Dynamics F-111K, was also cancelled. Thus the RAF was forced to cast about for a replacement that was available and affordable. They reluctantly selected the Buccaneer; the only realistic choice left to the Air Staff. The Buccaneer was seen simply as an interim solution, but delays in the Panavia Tornado programme would ensure that the 'interim' period would stretch out, and the Buccaneer would remain in RAF service for over two decades, long after the FAA had retired the type. With the phased withdrawal of the Royal Navy's carrier fleet during the 1970s, FAA Buccaneers were transferred to the RAF, which had taken over the maritime strike role. From 1970, the RAF Buccaneer force re-equipped with WE 177 nuclear weapons. At peak strength Buccaneers equipped six RAF squadrons assigned to NATO for overland strike duties in support of forces opposing the Warsaw Pact, plus one squadron (No. 12) for maritime strike duties.

After a week of technical briefings and five hours in the Buccaneer flight simulator we felt ready to start flying; we just hoped that our hosts felt the same. So I found myself climbing up the narrow ladder that led to the front cockpit of Buccaneer XV 348. Actually getting dressed to fly had been a long and arduous task. Although I had infrequently worn one before, the donning of an immersion suit over a green fluffy 'onesie' and anti-G trousers had proved a bit of a trial. Then there were the flying boots, lifejacket, leg restraint garters and the harness that would connect me to the ejection seat to go on over it all. The encumbrance of all this flying kit made climbing the ladder, strapping in and the pre-flight checking process much more difficult than it had been in the simulator, when I had just worn a normal flying suit, lifejacket and harness. Once I was correctly strapped in I raised the seat and found that, just for once, despite my short back-length, I could see out very well. The only snag was that I could no longer apply full rudder, even with the pedals selected all the way back towards me! Actually, my feet barely reached the cockpit floor. It was a shame, but I would have to lose a bit of that great view over the nose to be able to apply full rudder. I adjusted the seat height accordingly.

However, given time, and a lot of patience from Mr Crabb in the back, I eventually got the checks all done and the engines going. Unlike all the aircraft I had flown before, the Buccaneer did not have a self-contained engine starting system. A large, low profile trolley was rolled up and a flexible hose was plugged in to the side of our flying machine. This apparatus was known as a Palouste, named after the little French jet engine inside the trolley.

When all the switches and levers had been arranged correctly a wind-up signal was given to the ground crew and they opened the throttle at their end. The wee turbine wound itself up, the slack hose went rigid with the air pressure and one of the mighty Speys started to turn. All I had to do was give it some fuel and off it would go. When the engine was pushing out more air than the Palouste the latter gave up the battle until I selected the second engine. Then it bravely did the whole thing again. Once that and the electrical ground power unit had been disconnected we only had to complete a long list of functional checks of all the moving bits before we were allowed to go. So with the wings now where they should be, sticking out on each side, and the flaps and 'droop' set for take-off, we set off towards Honington's 9,000ft-long east–west runway.

On the ground the Buccaneer was easy to manoeuvre and the view from the cockpit was good. The nose wheel was steered by pushing a button on the right throttle and pushing the rudder pedals in the natural sense. As befitting a large flying machine that needed to be manoeuvred quite precisely on a busy flight deck it was quite sensitive. But for going long distances on an airfield it was a bit of a pain to have to hold the button in all the time. It became quite an inconvenience when Air Traffic Control (ATC) started asking complicated questions about our desired departure plans! Each time an answer was required the same thumb had to be used to press the transmit button on the same throttle, so leaving the nose wheel to its own devices. Nevertheless, we reached the beginning of the runway without incident and I ran the engines up, checked that all the needles were pointing at the right numbers and that there were no red lights anywhere. Brakes released and off we went.

The Buccaneer's large tailplane made lift-off a very easy affair and I selected the undercarriage up as soon as I sensed we were safely off the ground. The green 'down and locked' lights turned to red and then went out faster than I could say it. I held a shallow climb and the aircraft accelerated well. Not like a Lightning, but adequately enough. Before we reached the limiting speeds for the flap, aileron droop and tailplane flap setting I had used, I selected them up using the curious split selector on the left-hand side of the instrument panel. By checking three small gauges I could tell that we were now 'clean' and ready to climb. The man-in-the-back was talking well!

The sortie proceeded along the lines of the traditional first trip, with me doing a little ad hoc test flying when I could. We went as fast and as slow as the Buccaneer was allowed to go. Put all the things that we could down and back up again. Put out the enormous airbrake at high speed: that really worked well – it felt like my teeth had migrated into my oxygen mask! We had rolled, turned at maximum rates and generally thrown the machine about a bit. Another new thing for me to master was that the engines each had two rpm gauges, something I'd not come across before. That was because Mr Rolls and Mr Royce's excellent Spey engine is what is called a low-bypass turbofan; the military version of which was specially tailored for the Buccaneer and its low-level role. Inside the engine there are two concentric rotating bits. The inner is a small conventional turbojet engine with a compressor, combustion chambers and a turbine that drives it all around. Surrounding that is a larger, low-pressure (LP) compressor and turbine, this is the 'fan' bit and it produces the majority of the thrust. The design of the Spey gives it much better fuel consumption than a pure turbojet of the same total thrust – great for a low-level bomber that needs to go a good distance. I soon learnt that it was important to balance the rpms of the LP fan in preference to the inner high-pressure (HP) compressor. If the LP rpms were not balanced then the thrust from each engine wasn't balanced either and the jet tended to fly a bit sideways.

Being especially interested in gathering L&D stability and control data I built those things in where I could, chattering into my voice recorder like a mad thing and making estimated measurements when I could. The notes on my test cards were a bit sparse – but that was nothing new! However, I had already noticed that the Buccaneer was not over-endowed with directional stability. It was easy to generate sideslip and at high speeds the machine continued to fly askew with the alacrity of a hovercraft. Judicious use of the rudder trim could correct this, but any significant input of aileron to roll the aeroplane at those high speeds generated an inordinate amount of sideslip; later I would find the same characteristic at low speeds when the BLC was active. At the higher speeds this could lead to weapon delivery inaccuracies as well as potential structural overstress of the fin and rudder. While doing these tests I remembered that I had read that the NA 39's original design had a fin that was a foot or more higher. Unfortunately that height was such that the aeroplane wouldn't fit in the aircraft carrier hangars below decks; so, like a

Springer Spaniel's tail, it had to be docked.

By the time that we started to head back to Honington I had obtained a favourable overall impression of Mr Blackburn's naval bomber. It was a bit like a slick Canberra with powered controls. In fact the mechanical characteristics of the control column were exemplary. The stick was mounted in an unusual way for a fast jet. The handgrip, with its usual trim switch and weapons selector buttons, was fixed vertically to a steel tube that passed horizontally into the lower part of the instrument panel. Its movements were so smooth and with so little friction I thought that it must be mounted on glass bearings. In fact I learnt later that the tube moved over ceramic wheels.

Now all I had to do was to land this machine. The recommended method had been handed down from the Navy and I had one of its best practitioners in the back. It was going to be a bit like landing the Lightning: fly the approach until you meet the ground. No attempt at raising the nose or taking power off to smooth it out. The unbelievably sturdy undercarriage legs would absorb the impact (it says here). So we joined the circuit with enough time left to do a couple of touchdowns.

It was while getting the aircraft set up for landing that things got busy and that the rather haphazard layout of the cockpit made itself felt. The flap/aileron droop/tailplane flap settings had to be progressively selected and closely monitored. A warning in the Aircrew Manual had stated that any significant split could lead to a loss of control. The flaps and droops were selected, usually together, in stages and these were identified by the degrees of deflection of each surface. There were three normal settings: 15/10/10, 30/20/20 and 45/25/25 and as each moved the little yellow arcs on the indicators had to be watched. Perhaps unsurprisingly these indicators were known as 'cheeses'. Another action required was to change hands on the stick so that the right hand could be used to pull up a lever on the right lower panel. This was the aileron gear change and it allowed the ailerons to move further at lower speeds, so retaining plenty of roll authority during the approach and landing stages of flight. It was important that this lever was down for higher speed flight as the use of the full 'low-speed' aileron might lead to structural overstress. In fact, at very high speeds pilots were instructed to make sure that they only deflected the stick laterally over half its travel, again to retain structural integrity. I thought that was a very big ask during high-speed, low-level terrain-following or enemy aircraft avoidance manoeuvres. Whilst I was holding the stick with my left hand to do the aileron gear change (it must be an automatic box as I didn't have to use the clutch!) I then had to move my right hand up to a small panel below the right windscreen to change the settings on the auto-stabilisers from 'high-speed' to 'low-speed'.

Once beyond the first flap and droop setting, that is 15/10/10, the wings needed to be blown, so I had to make sure that the pressures in the BLC system were satisfactory. There were two large gauges on the top of the instrument panel for the wings. However, the tailplane BLC gauge, being a later addition, had been put on the left-hand cockpit wall. That meant that I had to lift my left elbow, while retaining my grip of the throttles, and peer down into the gloom inside the cockpit under my left armpit. By now the speed was below the limit for selecting the next flap and droop setting of 30/20/20, watching those 'cheeses' again, and then dropping the wheels. Three green lights appeared rapidly and by now we were approaching the end of the downwind leg. The turn onto the final approach began with the final selection of flap and droop (45/25/25), pulling on the sliding switch on the left throttle to extend the huge airbrake on the stern-end, adjusting the throttles to give sufficient power to keep the BLC pressure up as well as putting the aeroplane on the correct approach angle of 3°. Gosh this was a busy business!

Although the man-in-the-back had calculated a minimum safe approach and landing speed for the weight of the aircraft, the approach was flown using a small gauge right in my field of view when looking ahead. The gauge represented the AOA, that is the angle between the airflow and a datum line on the aircraft, usually a line that bisects the wing from front to back. As well as driving the needle on the gauge the sensor on the side of the Buccaneer's nose fed its signals to an electronic noise generator, which gave an audio signal on the intercom, so that both crew could hear it. The noise generator system was set so that at the correct AOA, which was 20 units, a steady note was heard. If the angle was too small, that is the speed too high, a higher pitched, interrupted 'beeping' happened; if the AOA was too large, thus speed too low, a low-pitch beep came out. This latter sound got louder and lower pitched the larger the angle became. In this case, which was dangerous, there was a real need to get the pilot's attention because it was possible that a large rate of descent would build up and a crash ensue. As one of the instructors, the irrepressible Flt Lt Bruce Chappel put it so succinctly, 'Ignore that noise at your peril or you could very quickly end up with Suffolk around your armpits!'

Once lined up with the runway, using the red and white lights at the side of the runway touchdown area to show the correct glidepath angle, it was simply a case of holding the AOA at 20, the noise in my headset steady, and doing nothing else until the wheels hit the runway. I imagined that it was going to be a bit similar to a parachute landing – whatever you do, don't flinch! There has long been an argument, especially among flying instructors, as to which control does exactly what when flying an approach. Does the throttle control the speed, as it does in normal level flight, while the stick points the aircraft to where it is going to land and so controls the angle of approach? Or does the stick control the AOA and thus the speed, while the throttles control, through the thrust of the engines, the rate at which the aircraft is descending and so the flightpath? Well, the answer, like in many things in aviation, is – it all depends.

In the case of the approach to landing in the Buccaneer, flying well behind what is known as the drag curve, it was easy to discern that the stick directly and rapidly affected the AOA and, thus, speed while the throttles had a slightly slower, but no less discernible, effect on the approach angle. However, it soon became apparent that things would be a whole lot easier if I could reduce both the frequency and amplitude of my left- and right-hand inputs on the controls. Unfortunately there was a strong westerly wind and quite a lot of turbulence so 'smooth' was not an option. One thing that I noticed straight away was that when I pushed the throttles forward the nose of the jet went down, so I had to pull back a little on the stick. When I reduced the power then I had to lower the nose. This bizarre behaviour led me to imagine that there was a fixed length cord from my left hand to my right hand, passing around my neck, so that movement of one begat the equal and opposite movement of the other.

By now, of course, the ground was rushing up towards my sturdy steed and me. We were doing about 130kt and Honington's 9,000ft-long runway was stretched invitingly ahead. I just held everything steady and waited. The steady middle C noise continued and then there was a thump as the wheels impacted terra firma. I whacked the throttles shut and used the stick to hold the nose up; this would help us slow down before using the brakes. At about 100kt I lowered the nose and started to apply the brakes with the foot pedals on the rudder bar. As we slowed down further I pressed the nose wheel steering button to keep straight and in readiness for turning off the runway. Once I had done so we stopped while we carried out all the after landing checks, which included another new experience: folding the wings. I taxied back with mixed feelings. I had successfully flown an in-service, relatively modern operational jet and would do so again, but I also had a pile of data to sift, prioritise and discuss with my team.

We met up that evening to analyse what we had got so far from our first flights. The cockpit assessment was essentially complete, including a 'night lighting' assessment done one evening in a darkened area; we were not going to be allowed to fly the beast at night. Neil had already collected a lot of information for his engineering systems evaluation. I had some, if not all, of the L&D data, as well as a few performance numbers, and Mark had gathered a good amount of his longitudinal stability and control data. We had started but still had a long way to go. I was due to fly again on the following morning and Mark was scheduled for his second sortie in the afternoon. So, after a very quick drink, it was off to our rooms to prepare our test cards.

My trip the next day was with another naval aviator, but this time not a pilot but an observer, FAA-speak for navigator; however, the accepted naval nomenclature was 'looker'. The brave Lt Beddoes and I boarded our Buccaneer, XV 388, and he waited patiently while I ploughed through the checks, got the engines going and taxied out to runway 09. This time I had been able to dictate more of the flight profile to suit my tests, so we set off, via the appropriate departure procedure, to start at around 30,000ft over the North Sea and about 30 miles off the East Anglian coast. But we hadn't been airborne for long before I noticed that one of the many fuel tanks that lay along the top of the fuselage, above the bomb bay, was not decreasing. Because of the arrangement of those fuel tanks it was important that they fed evenly, otherwise the CG could possibly go outside the limits and that might endanger our safety. We declared a minor emergency and set off home, while carrying out what remedial action was possible. Forty minutes after taking off we were back on the ground with very few lines of my test cards completed. I hoped that Mark would have better luck in the afternoon.

Indeed he did. But he was not airborne until somewhat later than planned. The effect was that he might not achieve the full time allowed, as he had to be back on the ground before the official start of night flying, at 'Civil Twilight', usually taken to be thirty minutes after sunset. We had agreed that one of the assessments we should make would be an arrested landing, using the arrestor cables[12] installed about 400m from each end of the runway. These were there for use by hook-equipped aircraft with certain types of emergency. The request had met with the approval of management so Mark had volunteered to do it and I decided that I would go to the control tower to watch the event.

I duly arrived to discover that Mark was on his way back and I settled into a spare chair in the glass box on the third floor of the tower, universally known as 'Local'. The aforementioned Bruce Chappel was there, acting as the OCU's Duty Instructor. We chatted about mutual memories and mates from our Canberra days while we waited for Mark's callsign to come out of the ether. We didn't have long to wait. But no sooner had Mark's aircraft appeared overhead than the Approach Controller, in his darkened room downstairs, called up to say that he had an OCU aircraft with a hydraulic emergency coming back to make an arrested landing using the cable. I had told Bruce that Mark was also hoping to end his trip with a cable engagement, but it now looked like he had been beaten to it. Mark was asked to hold in the overhead; in fact he declined this kind offer and went off to do another radar-directed approach.

12 The cables installed on airfields work on the same principle as those on aircraft carrier decks. However, because there is a lot more space the run-out length can be longer so the stress on the aircraft is less. The cable is supported by discs of dense rubber, so that the hook will go under it and successfully engage. The cable is restrained and retracted afterwards by hydraulic motors. That is why the installations are called Rotary Hydraulic Arrestor Gear or RHAG.

Meanwhile the pilot with the hydraulic system fault was making his own approach. Bruce had briefly disappeared downstairs to cross-check that the rookie crew had done all the right corrective action in the right order and had four green lights in the cockpit – three for the landing gear and one for the hook – 'down and locked'. By the time he had scooted back up the stairs the object of his attention was appearing out of the steadily lowering light of a November dusk. I watched with interest because I had never before seen an arrested landing on an airfield. The landing looked normal with the exception of a trail of sparks emanating from below the stern of the Buccaneer, where the hook was in contact with the concrete. Then there was a marked deceleration as the hook picked up the wire. But it was nowhere near that of the 'trapped' landings I had seen on HMS *Ark Royal* a couple of months earlier. In fact I was really surprised just how far the cable allowed the jet to go. Bruce, who had seen and probably done many more of these events than I, suddenly leaned over the local controller's shoulder, took the microphone and said, 'It's OK, sir, we've got you. You can throttle back now.' The tension of the emergency on one of the student crew's early trips together had led the pilot, who was actually quite senior in rank, to having been so relieved as to have picked up the arrestor wire that he had forgotten to close the throttles!

On the following day I flew once more and Mark flew his third and final sortie. At last we were making progress. My sortie, which I flew with RAF navigator Flt Lt Vaughan Morriss, was memorable for only one reason. When we returned to Honington the wind had swung round to the north and was blowing so hard that it was nearing the Buccaneer's crosswind limit. From messages passed to us I gathered that the high-priced help were worrying about this relatively unknown and inexperienced person in charge of one of their precious aeroplanes. Even worse, it was someone who had not really received all the normal gamut of training. Of course, when you realise others are worrying about you it does beg the question, 'Should I be worried?' I looked at the situation philosophically. Over the thirteen years that I had been flying I had done a lot of crosswind landings (something that naval aviators don't often get to do!) and if I couldn't get this machine down safely then I would go to an airfield that had a runway more aligned with the wind.

We arrived in the circuit and I flew the pattern as well as I could. It was a right-hand turn onto the final approach on Runway 09, so the wind was making life even more difficult by pushing me into the turn towards the final approach line. By now I had got accustomed to the synchronisation of left and right hands to achieve a satisfactory approach angle and hold the AOA correct. Apart from a bit of turbulence and an adjustment to avoid the wind blowing us through the final approach line it all went much as usual. I set up a drift angle and watched the runway through the left-hand quarter panel of the windscreen. As we came over the runway I prepared myself to prod the rudder to straighten up just before the wheels impacted the runway. *About … NOW!* I thought and, as the aircraft very obediently responded, to my surprise the nose came up a little: I just held the attitude and power. The wheels just kissed the runway. It was like one of my better Canberra landings. I closed the throttles and immediately lowered the nose wheel onto the ground so that I could keep straight more easily in this sideways gale. I was quietly congratulating myself when there was a gruff censure with a Scottish accent from the back seat: 'That's no way tae land a Buccaneerrrrr, laddie!' He obviously preferred the teeth-jarring naval arrival!

Team conferences in the Officers' Mess bar and my room followed and we now found ourselves in a position to do some mopping up of some of the data points and qualitative assessments that we were still a bit short on. My final sortie was not programmed until the following Tuesday, so we decided that we go home for the weekend and travel back on the Monday.

The weather in East Anglia during November can be dire. Low cloud, cold easterly winds, fog off the North Sea and poor visibility are all typical. When we returned to Honington that is exactly what we found. As the local management would not recognise my instrument rating I was getting nowhere fast with completing that final trip. After four days, and with not a glimmer of hope for decent weather over the horizon, I contacted Graham Bridges at Boscombe Down and asked his permission to return to base and perhaps fly the final sortie in one of A Squadron's machines. After a suitable time lapse for negotiations he came back with a response: 'Pack yer bags, lads and come home.'

Monday 17 November dawned bright but breezy, in fact downright windy. It was the day scheduled for my final Preview Exercise sortie. The aircraft was to be Buccaneer S2 XV 337, allocated to A Squadron. The short straw for back-seat occupant had been drawn by Flt Lt John Kershaw; an ex-FAA pilot who had transferred to navigational duties with the RAF. I was in safe hands – I just hoped that he felt the same! We planned a trip of about one hour to cover some of the outstanding items of our overall flight test programme. This included some single-engine handling and a brief spell of low flying in Wales to assess low-level flying, handling and gust response. The day was near perfect for the latter, but with northerly winds of 25–35 knots.

The trip went off much as planned. At low level the Buccaneer handled very well and was easy to fly at 250ft over the undulating territory of the principality. It was bumpy but I reflected that I could not have sustained such flight in my old Canberra B(I)8. The response to the turbulence of the highly wing-loaded Buccaneer made operating in such conditions totally safe and effective. I reckoned that we were probably the only fast-jet barrelling down the Welsh valleys and over the mountain ridges that day. Here the Buccaneer was at home; doing 450kt at 250ft. Now it was fun and felt perfectly safe and effective.

When we got back to Boscombe the wind was now so strong that only the shorter, north–south runway was available to us. I did one practice approach and then set up for the final landing. The gusty wind and turbulence made it more challenging than my previous arrivals; there was to be no smooth 'kissing' the runway this time – Flt Lt Morriss would have approved! And that was how my initial encounter with Mr Blackburn's naval bomber ended – with a good carrier arrival: a positive impact.

So the flying was over and the writing continued. By the end of our allotted time our report ran to over 150 pages. Against the requirements given to us we had found that, overall, the Buccaneer was unacceptable for service in its strike/attack role. Of course that could be construed as a surprising outcome, given that the aircraft was still in service and would go on to operate with the RAF for almost another twenty years. However, the grounds on which we found the aircraft unacceptable, as it was presented to us, were two-fold. First, there was a high probability of the loss of the aircraft if a significant split occurred between the elements of the flap and droop system. We felt that the reliance on aircrew monitoring the three indicators (the aforementioned 'cheeses') was an unreasonable expectation; especially in a high stress environment, such as during an emergency. Neil had done an engineering analysis of this system and had worked out a solution that would automatically halt the movement of the flap and droop elements, as well as signal an alarm warning in the cockpit, if a split occurred. This solution involved quite simple and cheap electronics. If it was to be incorporated then the system would become acceptable for service use. The second item that we felt was not acceptable in the mid 1970s and beyond was the overall utility of the pilot's cockpit; to be a bit less than objective we had heard it called an 'ergonomic slum' – and that by some of the Buccaneer's aircrew. No individual item was bad enough to cause the unacceptable assessment (with the possible exception of the tailplane blow gauge under the pilot's left armpit!) but there were too many such poor locations and there were multiple possibilities of mis-selection and omission for adequate overall safety.

The final act was to give a presentation in the large A&AEE HQ Building Lecture Theatre to an audience of our fellow students, ETPS staff, Boscombe Down aircrew and scientists and, most dauntingly, a few folk from the Buccaneer force. Our presentation went quite well but there were audible mutterings when we came up with the final answer. We could not recommend that the HAS Buccaneer Mk S2A be procured for the RAF in the low-level strike/attack role without significant and essential modifications to the flap/droop system and the cockpit layout. We also thought it highly desirable that a more effective yaw auto-stabiliser be fitted, a physical restriction on aileron deflection above 530kt be installed and warnings be issued about the poor longitudinal stability at speeds between 270 and 360kt. Of course this was an academic exercise looking in detail at a 15-year-old aeroplane against contemporary requirements and standards.

Once we had answered all the questions from our audience, some of which were quite penetrating and even hostile, we repaired to the nearby ETPS crew room where Udo Kerkhoff had stashed several bottles of German schnapps to refortify each team's post-presentation coffee. After a short while the knowledge that we had nothing else to do started to sink in. It was a very strange feeling. The next event of note was the McKenna Dinner and our graduation. Hurrah!

11 GRADUATION AT LAST

Those last days at ETPS were a paradoxical active limbo. By now we RAF guys had received our postings; the overseas course members were going to return to their own flight test centres and become involved in their national aerospace projects. As for the Brits most did not even have to move house because they were staying at Boscombe Down to join one of the test squadrons: Chris Yeo to A (Fast Jet) Squadron; Duncan Ross to B (Heavy Aircraft) Squadron; and Rob Tierney, Simon Thornewill, Terry Creed and Rob Humphries to D (Rotary Wing) Squadron. I think that Neil Sellers ended up involved with MRCA, which eventually became the Tornado. So that left Vic Lockwood, George Ellis and myself to head to pastures new. Vic and I were posted to the Experimental Flying Squadron at the RAE at Farnborough and George to the Aerodynamics Flight at RAE Bedford-Thurleigh. The latter appointment was usually reserved for the RAF graduate test pilot with the most active brain cells; neither Vic nor I could compete with George in this respect!

My arrival date at Farnborough was slated to be 22 December, ten days after the McKenna Dinner. That threw Mo and I into a frenzy. We had to obtain three competitive quotes for the removal, make journeys to Farnborough to take over our OMQ and check out the local area, as well as packing everything – and just a week before Christmas! When things just got too much, and as I had done throughout the course, I would contact Ted Steer in the ETPS Ops Room and enquire as to whether there might be a single-seat Hunter sitting around doing nothing. One day there was, so I presented myself for briefing and authorisation and spent a very happy hour in my favourite aeroplane and element, flying a Hunter F6A at 420kt and 250ft on a bright, clear late-November afternoon. I also flew the Canberra again, this time with Mike Vickers putting me through the rigours of an Instrument Rating Test (IRT) so that I could turn up at Farnborough fit to fly at night, in cloud and in poor weather.

Although some days were busy we all found it difficult to 'wind down' to a normal sort of life once more. The sixteen-hour days of study, preparation, flying, report writing and just thinking were over. So were the parties; although some farewell dos were happening. It was weird to be once more available to bathe the kids, read them stories, put them to bed, to sit down in the evening to watch TV and even do some cooking. Vic Lockwood reckoned that he would install a desk and anglepoise lamp in an understairs cupboard in his new house, so that when he got ETPS withdrawal symptoms he could retire to his cubbyhole and write a report about it! Then the last day finally dawned. The night we had awaited so long: The McKenna Dinner. It was to be a Mess Dress or Black Tie stag event. Our ladies would be invited to spend the evening at the 'White House', the rather grand OMQ occupied by OC ETPS. Naturally our erstwhile schoolmasters saw the whole thing as just another test exercise so there was a briefing, which we all attended. Some of us were allocated a guest to greet, accompany to the anteroom for pre-dinner drinks and ensure that they found their place at table. I was delighted to discover that my charge was going to be Chris Wren, the celebrated and very gifted cartoonist who attended all McKenna Dinners to produce a cartoon of the prizewinners and significant personalities for later publication in *Flight* magazine. Chris Wren had become a bit of a hero of mine when I first discovered his brilliantly conceived and executed cartoons in the likes of *Punch* and *RAF Flying Review*, as well as *Flight*. From a very early age I had been a bit of an artist and won prizes at my schools. I had learnt cartooning and Wren's style was a big influence on much of my drawing. Over the past year I had kept an open diary of our course and I still have it today; it has within it many of my own works, but its star insertion is a copy of Chris Wren's submission for the Christmas 1975 issue of *Flight*.

The day seemed to drag. But by 7 p.m. I was spruced up, in my best RAF bib and tucker, heading up the road with a few of the guys. We arrived to be herded into a room where we were to await our allocated guests, who would be brought to us by those who had 'volunteered' to do so. Officially the event was to start at 7.30 p.m. with dinner at 8 p.m. It was not long after 7.30 p.m. that a dapper, moustachioed elder gentleman was headed my way. I introduced myself and escorted him to the large anteroom where aperitifs were being served. After we had taken ours, I asked him about his career, how he had started and why he majored on aircraft and flying. Someone had obviously told him of my artistic bent so he became the inquisitor for a while. After ten or so minutes I thought that I'd acted the star-struck apprentice for long enough and I invited Mr Wren to meet some of the other graduates. As I headed towards a knot of our overseas colleagues I found that progress became interrupted by folk he had met before. Each greeting took time and, before I knew it, we were being invited to process into dinner. I had searched

the seating plan for my guest's position at table and escorted him to it before
finding my own. Our senior guest that evening was no lesser figure than the
Chief of the Air Staff, Air Chief Marshal Sir Andrew Humphrey. I'd never
seen a real-life CAS before, let alone heard one speak or shaken his hand! The
president of the dinner was, as is the custom, the OC ETPS, or, for the evening,
'The Headmaster'. During the third term this duty had been transferred from
the newly promoted Air Commodore Alan Merriman to the very capable
shoulders of Gp Capt. Mike Adams. After everyone was in place and grace
had been said, we sat down to enjoy what might be the best dining-in night
we had experienced so far. But before a knife or a fork was lifted there was a
special ceremony to come. We were all invited to look at a particular corner
of the room, where high up on the picture rail was a camera, along each side

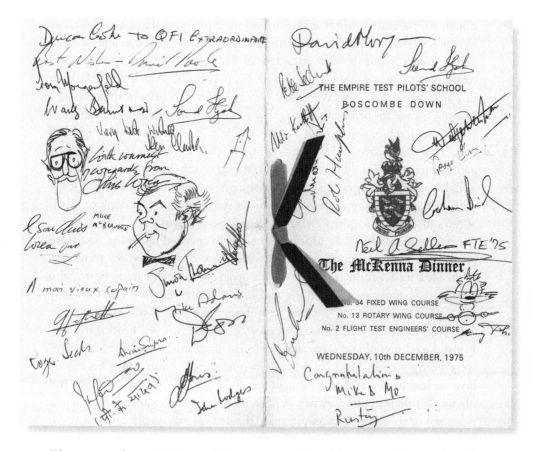

The cover of our McKenna Dinner menu, signed by many there and with
Chris Wren's cartoons of himself and of me. (Author's collection)

of which stretched an array of flash units. At the instruction, 'SMILE!' there was a blinding flash and we and our cheesy grins were frozen for perpetuity. As the song goes … 'Flash! Bang! Wallop! What a picture; what a photograph!'

The meal passed in the usual way with silver service, ample wine and convivial chat. The food, company, ambience and sense of celebration were all there. It was a night to remember. At the conclusion of the eating, following toasts to Her Majesty the Queen and 'all the heads of state here represented', and there were lots of those, it was time for the Headmaster's speech. Mike Adams was attired with what is known as the 'titfer', a rather well-worn schoolmaster's mortar board, in order to give his report on the class of '75. The 'titfer' had been acquired nefariously by some ETPS students in the dim and distant past.

Chris Wren's cartoon for *Flight* magazine of the 1975 McKenna Dinner. (Author's collection)

At the end of his speech, which made many non-too-flattering allusions to some of our number, the CO invited Sir Andrew to present us with our graduation certificates. This took some time, with each of us making our way to the centre of the top table when our name was called. Then it was the prize giving. None of us except the winner of the McKenna Trophy (for the best overall performance on the course) knew who had won what. The McKenna winner knew because it was he who had to give the response and thanks on behalf of the graduating courses.

US Naval Aviator Tom Morgenfeld was that man. George 'Mad Dog' Ellis, he of the deerstalker hat, waistcoat and watch and chain, was the runner-up, taking possession of the Patuxent Shield, which had been given to ETPS by its sister school over the pond – the US Naval Test Pilot School (USNTPS) based at Naval Air Station Patuxent River in Maryland. But it was Chris Yeo who won the prize for the most prizes! He took home the Sir Alan Cobham Award as the best pilot and shared the Hawker Hunter Trophy for the best Preview with our great Dane, Svend Hjort. Rob Humphries won the Dunlop Trophy as the best FTE and Terry Creed the Westland Trophy as the top Rotarian. But the biggest cheer went up when it was announced that the erstwhile Italian Starfighter pilot turned whirlybird driver, Bruno Bellucci, had won the Edwards Award, given by the other stateside test pilots' school, for the most improved student.

Sir Andrew spoke great and good words; the only part that I still recall nearly forty years later is his introductory sentence: 'If you wake up one morning and find that you have become the Chief of the Air Staff ...' That was something that was not likely to happen to any of the gathered company! Later, after port, cigars and liqueurs, we retired to the anteroom where postprandial chat continued and got progressively louder. The new graduate test pilots downed much beer and many silly jokes were told.

So that was that. I, along with all those folks, some of whom would stay friends for life, had passed the most demanding flying course that the RAF could devise. We British officers would have the miniscule characters 'tp' added to our entries in the relevant service lists. Those letters and our certificates were the total extent of the recognition of our ten months hard labour. But that didn't matter. We knew what we had achieved, so did our families. And much of what I had been able to achieve in 1975 was down to the support of my long-suffering wife. She had typed all my reports, except the Preview, which was typed by the lovely HQ Typing Pool girls on base. Mo had also taken back a lot of the domestic duties to allow me the time to do my 'homework' on most evenings. She had been a tower of strength in many ways and helped to keep my feet, not literally of course, on the ground.

What had we learned? Well, lots of maths, physics, Greek, test techniques, grammar, syntax, paragraph structure and how to fly about ten disparate types of aircraft. But the most important thing was that there was now a new way to work. We had to be objective, gathering evidence to build a case for improving effectiveness and safety and we had to do it with unwavering honesty and integrity. So bring it on!

For the final entry in my chronicle of the 1975 ETPS courses I wrote the following, in the school's recommended style for the summary to a flight test report:

The Summary

There was a requirement for certain, selected members of the human race to attend the 1975 courses at the Empire Test Pilots' School (ETPS). The aforementioned persons became members of Nos 34 Fixed Wing, 13 Rotary Wing and 2 FTE courses from February to December 1975.

The ETPS courses were thoroughly tested over a period of ten months, one week and five days, in variable weather conditions, and were found unacceptable due to excessive and extensive pilot workload (HQR 9).

Recommendations are made that the aforementioned human beings be forever prevented from having to undergo such a course again and that they are awarded the accolade that they so richly deserve: that all men will know that they are banned from all further ETPS courses. It is also recommended as essential that the courses be reduced in length by ten months and one week and consist only of rehearsals for the McKenna Dinner.

PART 2

TESTING TO LEARN

12 FARNBOROUGH

In the mid 1970s the RAE was a large government-funded aerospace research organisation that operated as a part of the UK Ministry of Defence called the Procurement Executive; henceforth referred to as MOD(PE). This title is an anagram of the word 'MOPED' and I would soon come to realise that there was a significance relating to the speed at which things got done within the organisation. The MOD(PE) head offices were in central London and I wondered what the man in the street there would make of someone announcing that they worked in 'procurement'.

I was headed for the Farnborough arm of the RAE, which was the biggest of the nationwide locations from where it managed its wide variety of research projects. The other main RAE sites were at West Freugh[13] in southwest Scotland, Aberporth in west Wales and at Thurleigh, near Bedford, in the English Midlands. The RAE site at Farnborough was originally a large, open area of heathland known as Laffan's Plain and Cove Common that stretched about 3 miles west from the Farnborough to Aldershot road. By the end of the nineteenth century the British Army had, under the direction of the Royal Engineers, developed the use of hydrogen filled balloons and set up their headquarters at the nearby military garrison of Aldershot. But by 1905 the activities there needed more space than was available within the garrison. In the search for more elbow room for his large, floating charges, the beady eyes of the OC, Col J.E. Capper RE, looked northwards and found Laffan's Plain and Cove Common wide open and waiting.

---

13 Freugh is pronounced something like 'Frooh' with a Gaelic gutteral embellishment for which there is no easily written expression.

After the move and the construction of a huge hangar[14] the unit became known as the Army Balloon Factory. But balloons were not going to be the only output of 'the Factory'. Capper was joined at Farnborough by two pioneers of British aviation: Samuel Franklin Cody and John William Dunne. Both were given honorary military ranks and encouraged by Capper to pursue their individual efforts to design, build and fly an aeroplane. It was the eccentric, American born, 'Colonel' Sam Cody who was the first to succeed. On 16 October 1908 he took his large biplane to the top of a slight rise at the eastern end of Laffan's Plain and took off in a westerly direction; he flew less than 300 yards. It was the first officially recorded sustained flight in Britain of a heavier-than-air, powered, man-carrying aeroplane.

However, only a few months later, with typical lack of vision or foresight, the War Office dismissed Cody and Dunne from military service and withdrew all funding for future aeroplane development. The generals believed that there was no military future for the flying machine. Oddly, Cody and Dunne were allowed to keep their aeroplanes and pay for their own future development, but they were not allowed to keep the engines! It only took three years for the military bigwigs to change their minds and in 1912 the first Military Aeroplane Competition took place. Much to the chagrin of his former employers Cody won first prize!

During those three years the Balloon Factory had evolved into the Air Battalion of the Royal Engineers and then, on 13 April 1912, that became the Royal Flying Corps (RFC). By now many private aeronautical companies had been set up and were thriving. Names like Avro, Sopwith and Bristol were building relatively successful aircraft, many of them copied from foreign designers such as Wright and Farman. But the military ethos was maintained at Farnborough where the RFC had its HQ and the civilian-managed Royal Aircraft Factory was tasked with designing, building and testing aeroplanes for purely military use. The first Officers' Mess for the use of the RFC was built on that raised ground from where Cody had launched himself only four years earlier.

With the outbreak of the First World War the RFC HQ was absorbed into the War Office in London and the Factory's output was now tested and delivered to France by RFC aircrew based nearby, on the eastern end of Laffan's Plain, at what was officially known as South Farnborough, or more colloquially 'the Park'. Many of the Factory's designs are still well known to aviation buffs: FE2, BE2, RE8 and SE5a to name (or should that be enumerate?) but four. They all flew and fought alongside their civilian-built

14 Still preserved on the site today and a Grade 1 listed building.

counterparts, such as the Sopwith Camel and the Bristol Fighter, during the horrific conflagration that was 'The War to End All Wars'.

During that conflict the Army had provided personnel for the RFC and the Royal Navy had formed its own flying arm, known as the Royal Naval Air Service (RNAS). Both of these forces had spent most of the war in support of their respective parent services. It was a senior RFC officer and pilot, called Hugh Trenchard, who proposed a resounding case for an independent air arm, with the vision of carrying out strategic bombing in any future armed conflict. His arguments were accepted and on April Fools' Day 1918 the Royal Air Force was formed. This had two immediate effects: Trenchard became the first head of the RAF and promoted himself to Air Marshal and the Royal Aircraft Factory could no longer continue to use its RAF acronym so it became the Royal Aircraft Establishment – RAE.

With peacetime came a clearer definition of the establishment's function. It was no longer to be a factory turning out military aeroplanes but to expand its experimental role to become a centre of expertise in all things aeronautical. The RAE continued to be headed by a scientific civil servant, known as the Chief Superintendent, but the wartime staff of over 5,000 was reduced to 1,380. The RAF continued to provide experienced pilots to both advise and fly the research projects.

Between the two world wars the RAE built a formidable reputation in many areas of aeronautical research. These included the definition of all the parameters that affected an aeroplane during a spin; development of engine superchargers; and research into structural loads and the often-fatal phenomenon of 'flutter'.[15] Research into high altitude flight led to the formation of the RAF IAM, co-located at Farnborough. Part of that initial aeromedical research led to flights in 1936–37 up to the amazing height of 54,000ft, with the pilots dressed like deep-sea divers!

During this inter-war period three breeds of government employees staffed the RAE: scientific civil servants, civilian skilled technicians and craftsmen and military officers. Most of the latter were RAF pilots who were specially selected for their experience and outstanding levels of skill. Many of these first-class aviators would lose their lives while expanding the envelope of collective aeronautical knowledge in this still relatively little known science. In order to allow the RAE to concentrate on pure research and development (R&D)[16] the testing and evaluation for service of aircraft offered to the War

---

15 Flutter happens, usually at high speeds, when control surfaces start to oscillate violently and divergently, more often than not leading to structural failure and total loss of control.

16 R&D was sometimes known as 'Risk and Disaster'!

Office and Ministry of Aviation became the province of the aforementioned A&AEE, which was based at Martlesham Heath in Suffolk.

At the outbreak of the Second World War the A&AEE sensibly retreated westwards from Suffolk to the large airfield of RAF Boscombe Down in Wiltshire. At RAE Farnborough the work expanded and accelerated to support the war effort. There was an influx of the nation's leading scientists and versatility and effectiveness were the watchwords for their work. As in all wars, money became no object and bureaucratic procedures were minimised. Whereas at Boscombe Down the work concentrated on bringing specific aircraft types, armaments and equipments up to scratch for service use, Farnborough was taking a much more in-depth approach to the testing of allied aircraft types with a view to performance improvements across the board. Another RAE role soon became the evaluation of captured enemy aircraft types, while the newly-formed RAF IAM expanded its work in survival at high altitude and under ever increasing G-forces; for which a man-carrying centrifuge was built.

Amongst the RAE's important, and often ground-breaking, contributions to the war effort were the gyro-stabilised bomb- and gun-sights, an automatic dead-reckoning navigation aid and a huge growth in the understanding of ballistics, fluid dynamics and aircraft structures. Core research into flight at high subsonic speeds was just one of the many very high-risk areas into which the RAE's pilots had to tread. For instance, in early 1944, Sqn Ldr Tony Martindale was flying a Spitfire in a dive when, at 0.9 Mach (about 600mph) and 27,000ft, the propeller shattered. The reduction gearbox flew off the front of the engine and the resultant collateral damage covered the windscreen in oil and coolant. However, Martindale found that he still retained control of his injured steed and with consummate skill he glided the 20 miles back to Farnborough where he carried out a faultless forced landing. By doing so he brought back all the data and, most deservedly, earned himself an Air Force Cross. There were many more instances of similar calm, skill and expertise shown by service pilots at the RAE during the Second World War.

Although in 1945 there was a concomitant downscaling with demobilisation, the work of the RAE in the fields of jet propulsion, high-speed and high-altitude flight continued almost unabated after the end of hostilities. International collaboration, particularly with the Americans, had blossomed during the war and continued well into the peacetime era. The coincidence of the vast amount of data on flying at high altitude and high speed accrued by the RAE with the performance of the new jets, the Gloster Meteor and the de Havilland Vampire and Venom, led, in 1945, to the re-formation of the RAF High-Speed Flight, under the command of RAE test pilot Gp Capt. 'Willie' Wilson. And it was he, leading from the front in a Meteor, who established a

new world speed record of 606.4mph (975.9 km/h) off the English South
Coast on 7 November 1945. Research into the jet engine led, in 1946, to the
creation of the National Gas Turbine Establishment in woodland at Pyestock,
adjacent to the RAE Farnborough site. The early 1950s saw specially built
research aircraft flying from Farnborough to test a variety of powerplants
provided by industry. This research led to some weird and wonderful flying
machines being seen in the 1950s Hampshire skies. Such as the world's first
turboprop powered aircraft, a modified Meteor. Or the Short Sperrin that had
its four jet engines in two vertically mounted pods on each of its wings – did
Petter get his idea for the Lightning's engine layout from this? Then there
were Canberras fitted with the new Rolls-Royce Olympus engines or rocket
packs in their bomb bays that zoomed to incredible altitudes. On 28 August
1957 Canberra B2 WK 163, piloted by Mike Randrup, flew to over 70,000ft
and held the world altitude record for about eight months.[17]

The mid 1950s brought about a huge spurt in aerodynamics research.
There were the three diminutive, triangular-winged aircraft built by Avro for
research into the delta-wing (and forerunner of the formidable Vulcan nuclear
bomber). The stalky-legged Short Brothers SC1 for exploring the possibilities
and problems of vertical TOL (eventual forerunner of the Harrier). The
Handley Page 115 slender delta to look into the low-speed handling of such
wings (a forerunner of Concorde). The Fairey Delta 2 supersonic research
aircraft was another. But these exotic and immeasurably valuable aeroplanes
flying over and around the burgeoning urban development encroaching ever
closer to the airfield at Farnborough was not tenable. Fortunately that air-
minded visionary Sir Stafford Cripps had proposed, in the late 1940s, that
a national aeronautical establishment be created in the wide open spaces of
Bedfordshire, centred on three wartime airfields that were close to each other
north of the town of Bedford.

By 1955 Cripps' vision of the 5-mile long runway and collocated wind
tunnel site had dimmed somewhat, but the airfield at Thurleigh now had a
10,000ft runway and two sites for aircraft operations as well as technical and
scientific support buildings. So it was to there that the erstwhile Farnborough-
based Aerodynamics Flight decamped. Meanwhile RAE Farnborough took
oversight of activities at Bedford as well as ownership and responsibility for
the support of missile testing in the Cardigan Bay Test Range in the Irish
Sea, with sites at Aberporth and Llanbedr on the west Welsh coast. Also
under its umbrella was the airfield at West Freugh in south-west Scotland,

17 At the time of writing WK 163 is still airworthy and will feature again later in my tale.

with its bombing ranges in Luce Bay, south of Stranraer. There were other sites around the British Isles for specific aerospace research work, all coming under the oversight and management of the Chief Superintendent at RAE Farnborough.

By the 1960s RAE Farnborough was a busy place and the organisation was still operating much as it had done in the past, with functional 'flights' manned by service test pilots and commanded by a squadron leader, or RN or Army equivalent. Work now included much more R&D in the field of electronics, including HUDs, navigation systems, automated flight controls, high frequency radio communications and the development of electro-optical devices. In 1968 a decision was made to move the ETPS out of Farnborough, where it had resided since 1947, back to its birthplace, Boscombe Down. This decision was another symptom of management's concern over the amount and type of flying activity going on over and near the densely populated areas in and around Farnborough and Aldershot. Nevertheless, the risks inherent in that situation were still exercised every two years, and had been since 1948, when the Society of British Aircraft Constructors (now SBAC) held its six-day air show.

By the mid 1970s the 'sharp end' of RAE Farnborough – its flying units, air fleet and the aircrew who operated and managed them – were organised along the following lines. At the top of the pyramid was the Commanding Officer Experimental Flying, invariably known as 'COEF'. He was a RAF group captain and test pilot. At the time that I arrived Gp Capt. Reggie Spiers was settling into this particular hot seat, having just taken over from his predecessor, Gp Capt. 'Polly' Parrat. Gp Capt. Spiers was an avuncular man with a look of a 1930s huntin', shootin' and fishin' country squire. But his appearance belied his background as a fighter test pilot at Boscombe Down and the CTFI at ETPS. 'Uncle Reggie', as I would soon learn that most of my colleagues called him (not to his face of course), was a great raconteur and had a very ready sense of humour. I would also soon discover that he was a formidable after-dinner speaker, with the ability to deliver the most humorous oratory with mellifluous ease. He did, much later, admit to me that he actually prepared his speeches meticulously and was always quite nervous; it never showed. He also had a wonderful collection of scale model aeroplanes that he had crafted with all the detailed care of a trout fisherman making artificial flies.

As COEF Gp Capt. Spiers was responsible to the senior airman in the MOD Procurement Executive for the safe and effective conduct of all flying from any of the RAE sites. He was also responsible to the Chief Superintendent RAE for the efficient use of resources under his command and control in support of the overall scientific effort. In effect COEF was the

RAE's Chief Test Pilot. In command of all the flying activities and airfield support facilities at Farnborough was another test pilot, this time of wing commander or equivalent rank. He was also COEF's deputy and his job equated to a combination of a squadron commander and OC Operations Wing rolled into one. At my arrival through the hallowed portals of 'the Factory' this post was being filled by Wg Cdr David Bywater. He was a man with a lot going across his desk and always seemed to be very busy. He did, however, 'keep his hand in' by flying regularly with the various flights under his overall command. I had seen him at Boscombe Down before I had started my test pilot course, but only in passing.[18] He was presiding over a Board of Inquiry into the loss of a Jaguar during a flight test sortie; I had been impressed by his youthful looks and abundance of blonde hair!

Both these senior men had their offices in the prominent, white-painted control tower situated right alongside the main runway and so could exercise a great deal of first-hand supervision of their subordinates and their flying. The RAE flying units based at Farnborough in 1975 were: the Experimental Flying Squadron (EFS) with three flights – A (Aircraft Systems), B (Radio and Communications) and C (Weapons Systems) and an independent Transport Flight, which provided air transport around the main RAE sites. Also based at Farnborough were the Meteorological Office's Research Flight (MRF), who operated a much modified Lockheed C-130 Hercules and a Canberra PR3; there was also the flying element of the IAM, which had its own two-seat Hawker Hunter T7. A squadron leader or equivalent commanded each of the flights; the IAM aircraft was operated within the EFS, but the project pilots for all IAM trials were medical officers who were also fully trained military pilots. In 1975 the RAE Farnborough aircraft fleet included such types as Hunter, Buccaneer, Canberra, Comet, Andover, BAC-111, Devon, Puma, Wessex, Gazelle and Sea King. As I drove east to start work on EFS C Flight, I wondered if I would get to fly all of these.

13 SETTLING IN AND DROPPING FISH

For the third time in my thirteen years in the RAF I had found myself moving house and settling into a new job just a few days before Christmas. Overall

---

18   See the final chapter of *Follow Me Through*, The History Press, 2013.

it was our eighth move in ten years of married life. No wonder service personnel get so used to what is said to be one of life's most stressful events. I suppose that the stress is still there, but somehow subdued by familiarity; although doing it in winter just ahead of Yuletide doesn't help!

I reported for duty at the rather downbeat-looking buildings of the EFS on Monday 22 December 1975. They were situated on the south side of the airfield, near a wooded area in which was the huge green tank that had held the de Havilland Comet fuselage in the 1950s investigation into the Comet's in-flight disintegrations. The squadron buildings were all single-storey, with a mixture of wartime and more modern adapted portacabins. There was an adjacent double hangar and various aircraft parking areas very close by. Before 1968 this area had been the flying end of ETPS.

First I met my new flight commander, Sqn Ldr Richard 'Rich' Rhodes. He was a largish chap with a broad smile and welcoming, 'hail fellow well met' air. He took me to the office I would share with the flight's other two pilots, Flt Lt Ian Frost, inevitably known as Jack, and Flt Lt Terry Adcock. Both were test pilots and ex-Lightning pilots; Rich Rhodes also fitted into that category. The navigators on C Flight shared another office in the same portacabins and they were Flt Lts Mo Hammond, Vic Avery and Ian Hail. The latter of this trio of directional and positional consultants made it possible on many days for Frost and Hail to be widespread over much of the UK, even on warm and sunny ones!

Vic Avery had been on No. 16 Squadron with me in the 1960s. Before that he had been a member of the ETPS staff at Farnborough. This led to an amusing story that he told me later. At Farnborough there was a fleet of cars that acted like free taxis for staff that needed to move beyond walking distance around the site. We on EFS used their services a lot to go from our rather remote location over to the 'Factory' for meetings, or to the western 'squadron' area where many of our aircraft were based. Most of the drivers were friendly ladies, not of a tender age. When Vic had arrived back at Farnborough in 1975, after an absence of at least seven years, one of these ladies collected him from his quoted location to return him to the squadron HQ. 'Oh, hello, sir,' she said brightly, 'I haven't seen you in a while. Been on leave?'

I was allocated a locker in the aircrew changing room, given the usual pile of books on the local flying regulations to read and told to make sure I'd signed in the appropriate place to certify that I had done so. Some things about life as RAF aircrew never change! In slower time I met some of the other aircrew on the squadron. A Flight was commanded by test pilot Sqn Ldr John Bishop, who was not only an ex-fighter pilot but an accomplished pianist who could frequently be found practising his scales and arpeggios in the Officers' Mess. I used to think of him as an aviating Beethoven! The other A Flight test pilots were Flt Lt Harry Maclean and, like me, newly arrived from

ETPS, Flt Lt Vic Lockwood. Yet more ex-Lightning pilots! Four helicopters were included within the A Flight 'Order of Battle' and were manned by three RN pilots, two of whom were test pilots. B Flight was commanded by its sole tp, Sqn Ldr Pete Smith, a small, bird-like chap who nearly always had an air of eager busyness about him. Having all the multi-crew transport aircraft under his wings he had command of a multitude of pilots, navigators and air engineers to help him. Among them was a real gentleman, Flt Lt Ken Mills, one of a slightly older generation than all of us eager young tps. Ken was unswervingly considerate to everyone, an accomplished transport aircraft pilot and captain and a man who crafted and flew the most beautiful large-scale flying model aircraft that I had ever seen. Ken would often invite us 'jet jockeys' to learn the art of handling heavy aircraft as occasional co-pilots. He would eventually check me out on the Comet. However, the real backbone of the EFS organisation was the Ops Room staff and its formidable, but softly-spoken overseer, Mrs Penny Lawrence.

Having settled in I then had to fly three check flights in the Canberra T4, Buccaneer and the Hunter T7, plus a familiarisation flight in the co-pilot's seat of the Andover. This illustrated that common EFS practice was not to stick rigidly to our flight boundaries and that we would be called on to help out with manning other aircraft types when the need arose. This applied to all the 'back-seat' crew as well.

By the new year of 1976 I was a fully paid up and certified member of Weapons Flight. So bring on the weapons! But because I had only flown a handful of hours on the Buccaneer it was decreed, quite wisely, that before I could start dropping things from it I needed a bit more training. This included an arrested landing at Boscombe Down. The experience was nothing like as exciting as I had thought it might be. I flew a normal circuit, with all the changing of hands and high levels of visual and mental activity that I described earlier, plus the selection of the switch to drop the hook; its green light came on when it was fully deployed. So that meant calling, 'Finals, four greens.'

All I had to do now was to aim to touch down a couple of hundred yards before the arrestor cable. I felt and heard the rumble from the aft end of the aircraft a micro-second or two before the wheels hit. I throttled back, lowered the nose and kept my toes well clear of the brakes. Then there was a definite retardation, but not as strong as I had imagined. I put my feet firmly on the floor so that I would not brake, which could cause the arrestor cable to tangle. If this happened I would have to send a crate of beer to the fire section, who had the job of rewinding it! At the end of the travel there was a slightly disconcerting small backwards movement – again it was important not to brake or the aircraft might tip onto its tail (although the hook itself should stop that). The fire crew were, by now, fully in charge and one of them signalled for me to raise the hook. And that was it, all over – no problem! On top of that I also had to fly a Buccaneer sortie in the dark and take a trip up to the main place that I would be dropping things from Mr Blackburn's bomber – RAE West Freugh. But more on that later.

But before I would be sent to Bonnie Scotland I would have to earn my stripes on other trials. The first of these would turn out to be our 'bread and butter' work over the next couple of years: the Stingray torpedo project. Our dark blue brethren call torpedoes 'fish', hence the piscatorial nomenclature of this chapter of my tale. Our role in this was to take a 'fish' to Cornwall and drop it into the sea on a range near the Lizard peninsula. So, early one morning I walked out to Canberra B(I)6 WT 309, sitting waiting for me in an eye-catching red and white livery. In the back would be one of the navigators, on this occasion Vic Avery, and an RAE FTO, on this occasion Mr Peter Lear. Peter worked in the Air Armaments Department of the RAE and was the senior FTO for the Stingray project. His deputy in this endeavour was no other than Mrs Mavis Lear, his wife. They were a well-matched pair of short, middle-aged people who would have looked equally at home in boots and anoraks as members of the local Ramblers' Association.

Over the next three years I would take my turn in spending a day out at the seaside on what would become a very familiar pattern of work. Fly one of the two Canberra B(I)6s, WT 308 or WT 309, loaded with a torpedo to the range, drop it and then land at nearby RNAS Culdrose, where another torpedo would be loaded. A quick fifteen-minute flight would get that one wet and then, if there were more ready, it was back to Culdrose to be reloaded. It was unusual to drop more than four in one day. But after the last one had been dispatched it was back to Farnborough.

The FTOs liked not to fly too high so a transit at between 6,000 and 10,000ft was the norm. When Mavis was down the back it was common for her to pass this time knitting, usually socks or gloves for Peter. On one occasion, on a lovely summer's day, I had chosen to fly at the lower end of our usual altitude band. After a while I heard Mavis ask me: 'Mike, do you think that we could climb up a bit?'

'Certainly,' I responded. 'How high do you want to go?'

'Oh, just until we get above this turbulence,' she said, 'I keep dropping stitches in the bumps.'

These trials were undoubtedly important. What we were doing was expanding the dropping envelope for the torpedo, progressively dropping them from higher altitudes and speeds. The 'fish' at this stage were not 'runners'; they were recovered to examine their structural integrity. It was hardly demanding work, but I didn't have to write a report within ten days and it was always, as Wallace and Gromit would have it, a grand day out. The drop conditions were relatively easy to achieve: speeds in the range of 150–180kt and heights from 500 to 1,000ft.

However, on one my early outings to Cornwall as I floated past Boscombe Down I looked down at the airfield and wondered why I had been put through all that brain-burning work the previous year just to be back in a Canberra again; by now I had over 1,500 hours on type. On that first Stingray test sortie, on 21 January 1976, I dropped a weapon from a Canberra for the first time since my final flight on No. 16 Squadron at RAF Laarbruch on 20 April 1967. On that occasion it had been at low-level in the dark and I had released the Mark 106 practice bomb on my navigator's call, as he had been using the very accurate Decca Navigator to achieve the correct release-point. And there was another irony; the torpedoes were also dropped on instruction, but this time from the Range Officer. This remote control would be common to most of our weapons trials – hence the rather paradoxical lack of aiming systems in any of our aircraft.

14 DROPPING BOMBS

Apart from delivering prototype and developmental torpedoes to their watery fates we only occasionally dropped anything else from our two venerable Canberras, although my logbook shows that we did occasionally drop 1,000lb parachute-retarded bombs on Larkhill Range in Wiltshire, but I cannot remember why! There was also something called the LSPTV, which stood for Low Speed Parachute Test Vehicle; this we occasionally dispatched earthwards at RAE's bit of Larkhill Range. My logbook also reminds me that we occasionally dropped Marine Marker Buoys and even fired SNEB (French: Société Nouvelle des Etablissements Edgar Brandt) air-to-ground rockets, but the latter not frequently enough for me!

The rest of the weapons R&D was carried out using our Buccaneers, invariably flying on the ranges at West Freugh. Two of these range areas were on land, to the south-east of the main runway at West Freugh, and the other was in the watery expanse of Luce Bay, the arm of water stretching south-east to the end of the Mull of Galloway. The land targets were open areas and not specific points within them. One was a grass rectangle a few hundred yards long and half as wide; this was known as the Soft Target. The other was another rectangle that had been excavated and then filled and resurfaced to mimic a runway surface; this was known as the Hard Target. One army officer once asked, in all seriousness, whether it was called that because it was difficult to hit!

The airfield at West Freugh, south-west of Stranraer on the Galloway peninsula, had been built on the site of a First World War Naval Airship Station. In 1937 it was reactivated as a training base and retained that role throughout the Second World War. The original triangular pattern of runways was modified in the 1950s when the RAE started its flying operations there. One runway was put out of use, the short north-west/south-east runway was retained and the north-east/south-west runway was extended to give it a length of 6,000ft. Sadly, the prevailing local winds tended to follow the north-west-south-east orientation of Loch Ryan and Luce Bay so West Freugh was renowned for its strong crosswinds for aircraft that had to use the main runway. In those conditions it was normal for Buccaneer landings to engage the Rotary Hydraulic Arrestor Gear (RHAG); the airfield was never too busy and the fire crews seemed to greatly enjoy having their days enlivened by having to go out onto the airfield to release the 'Banana' and reset the RHAG. Hence the need for me to experience one earlier on Boscombe Down's long runway before I was launched to 'the Freugh'.

The three special-build Buccaneer S2Bs, used solely by C Flight, spent most of their time at West Freugh. They were painted in a rather bizarre and very distinctive dark green, yellow and white colour scheme. This was apparently scientifically designed to give both maximum visibility on the high-speed cameras and the pattern was of known dimensions so enabling accurate post-flight analysis of distances travelled by weapons in any particular time. The distinctive trio came off the production line at Brough in succession, so they were given consecutive military registrations: XW 986, 987 and 988. These 'specials' had no radar in the nose; this was replaced with a test instrumentation and telemetry package. The in-flight refuelling capability had been removed and there were stations for no less than thirty-two cameras on the airframe. Four of these could be carried on special pylons near the wingtips. The whole photographic shebang was controlled by the back-seater from a specially installed panel in his cockpit. Sitting in the front one did not notice much difference from the operational jet, except that there was no refuelling probe getting in the way and no bombsight; I thought that a bit strange for a weapons testing aircraft.

At West Freugh, along with all the scientific civil servants, ground crew, air traffic control and range personnel, was a resident Buccaneer crew. These two lived locally and they were there to carry out all the routine flights that repeated weapons development trials demand. At the time that I was on EFS they were two Specialist Aircrew squadron leaders, pilot Bob Newell and navigator Jim Boyd. We test pilots would only be required to fly trials sorties when something new was being flown, a significant envelope expansion was required or when the carriage, release or jettison of a new or experimental weapon was being tested. Also one of us would go to West Freugh when Bob went on leave. Two of the three C Flight Buccaneers were continually based at West Freugh, the third would often be at Farnborough for deeper servicing or to provide continuation training to keep the four Buccaneer-qualified test pilots current.

More often than not our time at West Freugh meant going there and staying for a few days, often a full working week. That meant staying in a local hotel or B&B. When I made my first such trip I stayed in the hotel in Stranraer that the other pilots used. It was hardly salubrious. I remember that the very Scottish and rather Spartan bar had a bare light bulb hanging down from the ceiling. When this was illuminated drinks were at half-price. Also in true Scottish style it didn't come on often or stay illuminated for long! When I got back to Farnborough I expressed my disappointment in the nominated hostelry and said that I would branch out on my own on my next sojourn up north.

The next time I arrived at West Freugh I found another Buccaneer there. This turned out to be from HSA, at HOSM. It was crewed by the CTP, Don Headley and his FTO, Nick. It was still less than a year since I had first met Don during our ETPS visit there and it was good to renew our acquaintance. We were both in Bonnie Scotland to carry out trials on the ranges, but the weather forecast for the week was not good. In fact it had already precluded any flying on that Monday afternoon.

We got to chatting and drinking coffee, as aircrew do, and the topic of where I was staying cropped up. I told Don the saga of my previous stay in the 'red light' district of downtown Stranraer and said that I was going to try to find somewhere else. I asked him if he knew of anywhere. He told me that the company aircrew always stayed at the Crown Hotel in Portpatrick, a picturesque harbour town about 10 miles west of the airfield. I then told Don and Nick that I had enquired about official transport to my overnight accommodation and had been told that it would only be provided to Stranraer and nowhere else. When I had asked the man on the phone why, he gave me the usual civil service answer – 'Because it is.' Don said that I was not to worry about that because good old HSA allowed them to hire a car and that it had already been delivered for their use. He invited me to go with them; he said that there was sure to be a room at this time of year and in this weather. And sure enough there was.

Every day of that week the weather was dire, with at various times low cloud, fog, driving rain and howling winds – right across the main runway as usual! So we drove in and out each day hoping against hope that the Met Man had got it wrong. Each evening was spent convivially in the Crown Hotel where good food and fine ales were in plentiful supply. My room was charming and cosy. However, one night I was woken by a tremendous hammering on the window. I was on the first floor so I was surprised. Then it happened again. I arose and drew back the curtains just in time to see a wall of water heading my way! A ferocious storm had blown up and was driving huge waves into the harbour – only yards from the hotel – which had nowhere to go than across the road and over the Crown. The weather finally lifted on Friday afternoon, just sufficiently for us each to get airborne and wend our way home! Before I went again I spoke to senior management at West Freugh who agreed to change the transport policy to include Portpatrick as an appropriate destination. Result!

When we did fly weapons trials at West Freugh they could come in a variety of forms. The most common were those concerned with the development and refinement of that terrible battlefield armament – the cluster bomb – officially known as BL 755. These bombs were designed for use against armoured and soft-skinned vehicles. The main body of the weapon contained a large number (I've forgotten how many) of bomblets that had high-explosive, shaped charges so as to release a supersonic streak of white hot metal that would make holes in most things. The development work that we were involved with was mainly concerned with increasing the speed and lowering the height at which the bombs could be released. This would have the effect of reducing the exposure of the delivery aircraft to enemy anti-aircraft fire. But, in turn, this meant reducing the time intervals for the bomblets to be released from the cluster weapon itself.

One of the many problems induced by this was collisions between bomblets during their short flight. If they hit each other in such a way as to activate the explosive a high-speed shot of liquid steel could hazard the aircraft or other bomblets. And too many of these premature explosions would reduce the overall effectiveness of the bombs. One day I was at West Freugh to carry out one of these tests, which had been designated 'high-risk'. We got airborne, carried out a couple of 'dummy rums' so that all the folk with the high-speed cameras could get their eye in and then went round for the 'live' run. The way that the weapon release was activated, to make sure that it happened at exactly the right spot, was via a 'magic eye' in the underside of the aircraft sensing when we passed over a narrow infrared beam. All I had to do was to make sure that the speed and height were correct for the particular release condition and that the Master Arm switch was on. We had four bombs on board and would be dropping them as two pairs over the Soft Target. All went well and after landing we went to see the boffins. The senior man, Johnny Aldridge, immediately invited us to view some of the high-speed film. 'Particularly this bit,' he said mysteriously. However, I soon saw to what he was directing my attention. A collision had occurred just after the first set of bomblets had emerged from the bomb and then a bright yellow-white line appeared on the screen. By pausing the film one could clearly see that the trajectory of the shaped charge had passed just under the tailplane. Had it hit the latter we may have instantly lost control and at 480kt and 200ft that would not have been amusing. I was glad that we did not have to fly another one of those sorties that week. It was later decreed that we had exceeded the desired limits of speed and height, which were both altered to give less chance of a repeat.

One day, in 1977, I was sitting at my desk at Farnborough, minding my own business, when my boss, Rich Rhodes, strolled in with a pink folder and dropped it in front of me. It was a classified file on the JP 233 project. Initially known as the Low Altitude Airfield Attack System or LAAAS, this was a concept initiated by Hunting Aviation Ltd and then taken up as a Joint Project (hence the 'JP') between the UK and USA. 'There's a meeting in Building T55 at 10 a.m. this morning and I'd like you to attend. Report back what you learn,' he said.

'OK, Boss.'

'And make sure you take your pass – that place is where all the secret stuff happens.'

I went along, clutching my pass and a notepad, was allowed in and found a seat in the conference room. The presentation told us that the JP 233 was a multi-mode weapon, which would be carried in pods and included two types of munitions, each of which would be retarded by a small parachute. One was a 26kg penetration device that would create deep craters in hard surfaces and the other was an anti-personnel mine, preset to explode at random intervals. The thinking behind this complex weapon system was that it would deny the use of an enemy's airfields by making big holes all over the runways and taxiways and then deterring folk from going out to fill them in. I listened attentively to the technical stuff and began to wonder how on earth we were going to test the individual bomblets before we put them in what appeared to be huge pods and sorted out the release mechanisms, which included an explosive ejection device for each munition.

Eventually the time came for questions. I had noticed that there had been scant attention to the fact that the aircraft delivering this awesome weapon had to fly straight and level across an enemy airfield at low altitude for the considerable amount of time it would take for all of the thirty cratering bomblets and the more than 200 mines to leave the pods. Up went my hand. One of the presenting team spotted it.

'Do you think that it is operationally viable to expose the delivering aircraft to the concentrated enemy firepower that it will undoubtedly encounter over

---

19   See Chapter 29 of *A Bucket of Sunshine* by this author, The History Press, 2012.

a Warsaw Pact airfield?' I asked. I remembered asking the same sort of question when my 1960s low-level strike/attack squadron changed from a stand-off nuclear weapon delivery system called LABS to an attack profile that required us to fly low and fast right across those same Warsaw Pact airfields.[19]

The answer was at best indirect, at worst woolly. However, someone there reported me back to management because I was later called to appear before the Wing Commander who, with a wry smile, told me that I was to confine my thoughts as to how to test things and leave the operational thinking to the folks who were paid to do that. I think that he realised that my motives were pure but that he was constrained by direction from much higher up.

Notwithstanding the 'rocket' I received, JP 233 provided us, the boffins, ground crews and the aircrew at West Freugh with hours of endless fun. The prototype munitions had first to be tested, their effects quantified and the optimum speed and height for delivery determined. To do this the boffins came up with the Four Tube Rig (FTR). This was, as its name prosaically suggests, a container with four tubes, arranged in a square that would be the launcher for four of the catering bomblets. It was decided that one of these boxes would be put into the Buccaneer's rotating bomb bay, with all the firing electrics connected to a panel in the rear cockpit. The Hard Target had its origins from this trial and machinery went out there to reconstruct areas of representative airfield surfaces.

The problems started early in the trials process. If the sub-munition failed to leave an FTR tube but stuck halfway out then there was a danger that the now potentially live bomblet could explode in-flight and structural damage would ensue when the bomblet's now protruding nose hit the fuselage as the bomb bay rotated closed. The big problem was that with such a small munition it was difficult for the range personnel to determine whether the bomblet had not been ejected or was a 'dud'. The final answer was a pragmatic one. The end of each tube would be covered with a high visibility disc. If the number of explosions observed did not match the number released then the bomb bay would be left open and a slow flypast be made over the range or air traffic control towers for observers with high-powered binoculars to see whether any high-visibility discs were still showing. The final catchall was that – if in doubt land with the bomb-bay door open! Later in the trial process we had to start thinking about carriage and release of the JP 233 sub-munitions from the large pods that would represent the operational load for the Tornado (then still called MRCA). Carrying two of those monsters on a Buccaneer from a 6,000ft runway, even with the minimum fuel load, was going to be a challenge. Normally our take-offs at West Freugh were done without the use of the BLC mechanism or 'blow'. But that option did exist and was still used at very high weights. The problem with using blow was that the take-off run was a bit longer because there was less thrust from the engines as a lot of the air that would have given the required power was being used to get more lift out of the wings. A corporate aircrew solution was proposed. We would set the flaps and droops to the usual 'blown' setting of 30/20/20 but turn the BLC off. At a predetermined point in the take-off run, predicated by the aircraft's weight, headwind and temperature, the blow would be switched on. This would therefore give us the best possible performance off the 6,000ft runway at West Freugh for the higher than usual aircraft weights. The problem was that there were potential handling problems related to this technique that would need examination. Call in the company! I left the RAE Weapons Flight before this conundrum was resolved, so lost track of the outcome!

In late 1977 we received paperwork for the trials that would be required for the UK's first Laser Guided Bomb or LGB. The whole system was known by the codename Pavespike/Paveway and had been in use on the other side of the Atlantic for some time. For instance the LGB had been very successful in cutting communications and supply links during the Vietnam War, especially over bridges. The average accuracy of the LGBs used there was 23ft as opposed to more than 400ft for unguided bombs. They had their limitations, usually caused by cloud, mist or fog obscuring the seeker's view of the laser spot designating the target. Moreover, the actual designation method could also be an operational limitation. If the target was to be illuminated from the ground then that meant having personnel close by and good ground-air communications. If the target was to be illuminated from the air, either by a third-party or using a self-designation system, then vulnerability to anti-aircraft defences became an issue, especially as the ideal delivery was to be made from medium altitude.

In its early form the UK LGB was a standard-issue 1,000lb bomb with bits strapped to it that allowed it to seek and track a laser and then move four fins at the rear end to make the bomb fly to the point of laser light reflecting from the target. Our job would be to first carry the weapon and ensure that it did not cause any untoward handling difficulties and then release it. The first drop would be a totally inert, ballistic drop with no attempt at guidance, the second drop would have a pre-programmed flight guidance protocol to check the ability of the fins to steer the bomb and the third delivery a drop onto a laser-illuminated target to see if the bomb would actually do what it said on the label. Further developments of delivery profiles and envelope expansion would come later.

On Wednesday 8 February 1978 Pete Hill, who had replaced Ian Hail, and I strapped into Buccaneer XW 988 at Farnborough to fly to West Freugh for the first UK LGB trials. Ian 'Jack' Frost was the other test pilot involved and he took the low road to Bonnie Scotland in a Devon of Farnborough's Transport Flight. On the following day two Buccaneers were out on the line waiting for us to get aboard and do the business. The distinctive shape of an LGB was hanging menacingly from the starboard inner pylon of Ian's aircraft. My job that day was to fly 'chase', that is to fly in formation with Jack, film the bomb release using the two movie cameras on the port wingtip pylon and, they said, 'Chase the bomb down as far as you feel it is safe to go'! I'd never flown formation on a bomb before!

I had noticed that the two aircraft were not parked in line next to each other, as might usually be the case. This odd arrangement was soon explained when I was asked to get into the cockpit half an hour before we were due to man-up and close the cockpit canopy. On the left-hand side was a neat rectangle marked out in black grease pencil. This represented the field of view of the wingtip cameras and was there to help me position my aircraft for the best air-to-air coverage of the morning's historic event.

About thirty minutes before we were due to get airborne the four of us, Jack and his nav and me and Pete Hill, walked out together. We didn't often get the chance for formation flying in this business, unlike American test pilots whose philosophy seems to be to chase absolutely everything. But flying close together is like riding a bike, once you've got the hang of it the basic skills never leave you. Nevertheless, when you haven't done it for a while there is a raised sense of awareness and a frisson of excitement. We started up together and taxied out to Runway 24. We had decided not to take off in close formation so I let my brakes off fifteen seconds after Jack had departed from just ahead of my left wing. Jack had a small amount of handling to perform just to ensure that carrying the LGB was essentially identical to carrying a normal 1,000lb bomb. Once that was done I closed up until I had 988 nicely framed in the black rectangle on my canopy. We changed radio frequency, checked in with the Luce Bay Range Controller and climbed to the drop height of 12,000ft. After flying a full pattern under radar control we turned outbound to the north-west for the 'hot' run. As the ten-second countdown started Pete started up the cameras and I moved out a little just to ensure that if the strange-looking bomb did anything odd I wouldn't be in the way. At the controller's count of 'zero' off it came. A clean separation and off I set to follow it down. It flew a typically normal ballistic path, slowing down only slightly but as the angle and rate of descent increased and we passed 8,000ft I thought discretion the better part of valour and pulled up and away. I tipped the left wing down and saw the splash just short of one of the several raft-mounted targets in Luce Bay. Well, that was that. The first release of a LGB in the UK.

Of course, by definition, that was the beginning. My turn the following day was to release number 2 with its pre-programmed flight control inputs. This one had a special radar reflector so that the range could track it with the radar as well as observe it with their high-powered optical telescopes and high-speed cameras. It too behaved impeccably. Number three was released by Jack and I watched using the tripod-mounted ex-German U-boat binoculars from the air traffic control tower. This time the range illuminated the target with a laser, the bomb did what it was supposed to do and removed the laser reflector from the top of the mast on the raft. There were cheers from the scientific team but moans from management because that meant that they would have to keep replacing the rather expensive reflectors as the trials went on! In fact, I believe the question was asked as to whether the boffins could make the bomb miss!

But there was a lot more to weapons trials than just hurling the things at the ground (or sea). The total package of development included carriage and jettison as well as release. Some of these tests made us test pilots actually practise the test techniques we had learnt at ETPS – and have to report on the results! They also brought with them some challenges to our abilities to handle the Buccaneer correctly.

For instance I walked out to my colourful jet one day to find what looked like a dustbin, painted in black and white quarters, hanging on one wing. On the opposite side was an inert 1,000lb bomb. The dustbin was a special store designed to fit on a bomb station in tandem with another more conventionally shaped bomb. My job was to fly this thing around to find out how fast we could go before its drag became too much of a control problem, and to take notes of the fuel flow for performance data. The prediction was that the drag would become so much that I would run out of rudder trim at about 350kt. The 1,000lb bomb was there to try and balance the asymmetric weight; however, the bomb was actually twice the weight of the 'dustbin'. We got airborne and flew round the range areas at incrementally increasing speeds. When we got to 350kt indicated airspeed, far from running out of trim, everything was neutral! So much for the theory!

Every now and then we were allowed to use the full airworthiness envelope of the Buccaneer, as opposed to the in-service limits. In effect this allowed us to fly at a maximum indicated airspeed of 610kt, instead of the service maximum of 580kt. Although only 30kt more one soon found out why it had been set there for everyday use. I did my first low-level excursion at that speed over Loch Ryan and Luce Bay. In addition to an even greater increase in the cockpit noise level, I noticed that there was a definite tendency for the aircraft to go out of balance directionally and, following the advice in the Aircrew Manual, I used judicious inputs of rudder trim to make sure that the tail kept following the nose exactly. It wasn't easy and then at the bottom end of Luce Bay I started a right turn. That was to fly around the Mull of Galloway and then head towards the plum duff pudding shape of the island of Ailsa Craig, ready for the next run. As I rolled gently into the turn the nose just kept going straight on and, along with the hairs rising on the back of my neck, a loud noise added to the cacophony already prevalent in the cockpit. I pushed gently on the right rudder pedal and things came back to normal; it took a bit longer for the hairs on the back of my neck to do so!

Quite often the first step for some new weapon that the boffins were researching was the aerodynamic and structural properties of their latest shape. So strain gauges were fitted and we went off gathering the data. We always started in the middle of the flight envelope as defined by wind tunnel or computer-derived fluid dynamics calculations. Not the most exciting test flying admittedly but every now and then something would get one's attention, such as the day I was asked to do a series of test points on an experimental external store. One of the points was a 3G-force while rolling at about 30° per second at 10,000ft and 300kt indicated airspeed. I thought that this would be right on the edge of the Buccaneer's own flight envelope so I approached this test carefully. Sure enough as I made my first attempt the nose pitched up and the roll-rate increased beyond what I had demanded. It was the beginning of a departure from controlled flight. I moved the stick forward but it kept rising. I then remembered a bit of advice that Don Headley had given me.

'If you ever get the nose coming up on you, move the stick forward *and* hit the trim switch in the same sense.'

I did that and the aircraft recovered. Jim Boyd, in the back, was very pleased when I said that we were not going to repeat that particular test point!

Another demand that needed some thinking about were the tests for negative G. Zero was easy – a parabolic pushover from a climb would do it; it also worked for −1G. But more (or should it be less?) than that was trickier. It meant doing an inverted turn and if the boffins wanted more than a few seconds of it, that was fairly uncomfortable. It also usually meant that the cockpit filled with all the detritus that had built up in the bottom!

Sometimes it was speed that was wanted, usually for drag purposes, but on one occasion a new experimental frangible nose cone for an in-service rocket pod, called SNEB, needed to be hot-soaked by flying it at 600kt for twenty minutes. This coincided with the return of one of the Buccs to West Freugh. It was an interesting flight and we set a new Farnborough to West Freugh record transit time! We had to fly as low as we could to get the maximum thermal effect. I decided that 1,500ft would do the job. Any lower than that could mean the mother of all bird strikes!

Another feature of working at 'the Froo' was the daily closure of the airfield for one hour at lunchtime. Coupled with the often very slow appearance of our steed from the hangar, not helped by the insistence of the folk to do everything in duplicate, we often had to get airborne with just enough time to make a couple of runs on the range before ATC shut down for lunch! Then we were still overweight for landing, especially when there was a crosswind (which was most of the time!). The Buccaneer does have a fuel dumping facility but that would take time and stop the nice folk in ATC and Fire Section from getting their midday repast. So a much better idea than polluting the area with kerosene was to use it up in the normal way by passing it through the engines.

So, when the weather was suitable we used to call the nice people who controlled the UK Low Flying System and book ourselves into the Scottish bits. Then it was down to 250ft above ground and speed at 420kt and giving the man-in-the-back some ad hoc navigation to do. I flew this way over most of the Highlands and Islands marvelling at such sights as the seaside distilleries on Islay, the columns of Fingal's Cave and once, flying low over the Isle of Skye, passing between a tall needle of rock and the mountainside it was rooted on. One sparkling blue winter's day we were flying along the Great Glen, there was a good covering of snow on the mountains, the visibility was unlimited and barely no wind to ruffle the surface of the lochs. It was beautiful and lifted one's soul. It was then that a thought that had knocked on the door of my mind actually entered, made itself at home and has stayed with me ever since: *It's amazing! And I get paid for doing this!*

It was during the LGB trials that something occurred that would bother me for the rest of my time in the test flying business. At one point we had four Buccaneers at West Freugh, all doing overlapping bits of the Pavespike project. The company's aircraft, with dear old Don Headley and Nick, were doing tests to look at the carriage of multiple LGBs, our two machines were doing the release and guidance tests and then a Boscombe Down crew turned up in one of their Buccaneers to look into the handling aspects. It struck me that this compartmentalisation of roles was causing expensive duplication. We were all qualified test pilots and it could have been much more cost-effective if Weapons Flight had been given the whole package to test and report on. It wouldn't be the first time that I felt the need for someone to rationalise the whole test and evaluation process. But at this stage I was still a 'Junior Joe' and, as I had been reminded earlier, I should get on and do my job and let those who are paid to do so resolve these higher issues!

15 NOT ONLY OWLS FLY LOW AT NIGHT

A large area of R&D interest at the time was involved with giving strike/ attack aircraft the capability to fly safely at 250ft above the ground in the dark. One way to do this was to use Terrain-Following Radar; this equipment had been developed for the MRCA and would be refined for operational use by the RAF's Tornado force once it was in service. The problem with the use of any radar device is that it sends out electromagnetic waves ahead of the aircraft, which can be detected by any suitable receiver and so give notice of its imminent arrival – very useful knowledge to the opposition. Thus Terrain-Following or Terrain-Avoidance Radar is known as an 'active' system. What the operational ivory towers were looking for was something 'passive' that could not be so easily detected.

Seeing in the dark, as if it were daytime, is the province of inter alia the owl and the feline members of the animal kingdom. We humans can adapt to darkness, but imperfectly. I had found that I could fly as low as 250ft at night in my Canberra over north Germany if there was a full moon and little or no cloud, especially if there was a covering of snow. But it was risky because slender masts and dark, tree-covered up-slopes were difficult to discern. What we needed were better eyes.

The scientists had already produced two systems that had potential for giving aircrew those better eyes. One was Low Light Television (LLTV) and the other was Forward-Looking Infrared (FLIR). There were also prototype Night Vision Goggles (NVGs) that used the same technology as the LLTV to enhance the night light levels to a useable amount; however, in 1976 NVGs were in their infancy and definitely not suitable for fast-jet pilots to use. Because of the cooling requirements and the state of electronics in the FLIR systems of the mid 1970s that kit was not ready to be installed in small fast jets either; however, FLIR was being trialled in larger aircraft where there was more space for all the gismos. But more on that later.

At Farnborough there was a very special two-seat Hunter T7 – military registration WV 383 – known as 'Hecaté'. This name was painted on the side of the nose and is that of the ancient Greek goddess of, among other things, the moon and the sky. Images of Hecaté show her carrying torches, indicating her ability to see in the dark. WV 383 had been used as a trials aircraft at Farnborough for many years before I first got my hands on her. Much of the R&D for HUDs had been done in 383, especially for the cancelled TSR2. Hecaté still had two HUDs in front of the pilots and the one on the right-hand side was still being used for the continued exploration of different types of symbols, the layout of the visual presentation and other esoteric research aimed at optimising the operational utility and safety of HUDs.

But the other obvious item was that the right-hand instrument panel had been replaced with a small TV screen and, in order to give the right-seat occupant the best view of this screen, the top 3 or 4in of the right-hand control stick had been sawn off! The TV screen was there to display the picture seen by the LLTV camera mounted in the nose of the Hunter. That picture was also overlaid with essential flight information such as speed, height and heading. So the job of the pilot sitting in the starboard seat was to try to fly the aircraft in the dark at a selected low altitude and speed, along a pre-planned route and avoid hitting the ground or any obstacles. The man in the other seat was there to taxi the aircraft out, get it airborne and land it (the wheelbrakes were not operable from the right-hand seat). Once settled down en-route the 'safety' pilot would hand over to the assessing pilot to fly the majority of the sortie, most of which would be at low level. The safety pilot would then monitor (ever so closely) where the aircraft was going and be ready at any time to take over and climb to a safe altitude. The real irony was that the best information as to what was really going on outside could only be gained by looking at the TV screen! Most of the time it was too scary to look out of the cockpit windows because all you could see were vague, dark shapes and odd lights flashing past below.

I first flew Hecaté in the dark on Wednesday 17 March 1976. Harry Maclean and I were briefed to fly two identical sorties on a route from Farnborough to the West Country and back. On the first flight I would occupy the left seat as 'Safety Pilot' and Harry would fly as the assessing pilot. Then we would reverse roles for the second sortie; this would give the scientists two opinions, one of them from a newcomer to this dark art. The minimum altitude at that time was 500ft above ground level at a cruising speed of 360kt. The final aim of the trial programme was to work down to 250ft and speed up to 420kt.

Having flown the Canberra in the dark a few times the previous month I was deemed to be 'Night Current' so I flew the Hunter at 2,000ft until we passed into an area of the UK's Low Flying System about 15 miles west of Boscombe Down. Then I handed control to Harry and he got his head down on the TV screen and descended to low level. I kept a good eye on the height, speed and our position relative to the planned track over the ground. I could tell that Harry had done this before; although concentrating hard he was talking smoothly into the voice recorder when needed and didn't appear at all stressed. Things were a bit different on my side of the cockpit. The light levels were on the marginal side for the magic kit to operate at its best and completely unuseable by my own visual system. It was as black as the ace of spades outside and my uneasiness was only exacerbated by the illuminated bits of the countryside flashing by beneath us feeling far too close for comfort! At one point Harry exclaimed – I thought that I would need to take over and climb – but it was a momentary 'blindness' caused by the headlights of a car coming over a rise in front of us. Bright lights like that caused a large, bright flare on the screen that could temporarily take out most of the visual cues that were helping Harry avoid the ground.

Other than that the trip went well and I had now seen the route and some of the problems that had to be overcome. An hour or so later it was my turn.

I settled into the right-hand seat and let Harry take us to the start point of the low-level route. During that short transit I had watched the small screen and familiarised myself with the presentation of the flight information symbology. At the appointed juncture I heard, 'You have control,' so I grasped the top of the rather odd, stubby stick and started a gentle descent to 500ft on the radio altimeter. As I levelled off and concentrated on getting the speed right, holding the altitude and trying to follow the route, a strange feeling came over me. I vocalised this for the benefit of the boffins who would listen to the voice recording after the flight.

'I have a peculiar internal conflict going on in my head,' I said. 'One part of me is saying "this is a simulator that I'm flying by looking at a TV screen" and the other is screaming, "no it isn't – the ground out there is real!! Get a grip!!"'

After a few minutes this internal tension diminished and I started to become accustomed to this rather odd form of flying and navigating in the dark. Then I came to a corner. When I banked and started to turn in the required direction for the next leg of the route the view ahead, in the direction of the turn, shrank to very little. The horizon was now laid at 45° across the screen and a spot on the ground was coming into view only briefly before we were over it. The dangers of turning towards rising ground became very obvious. Fortunately the route had been surveyed and we could compensate for this by climbing a little, even though we would only see what we were climbing over for a few seconds beforehand. The rest of the trip went well and by the end of the thirty minutes I had flown at low level I was feeling much more comfortable.

I would spend many more hours in 'Hecaté' helping the A Flight guys with their LLTV R&D. Some would be memorable. Such as the night when I flew with John Bishop while he carried out a landing at Boscombe Down with no runway lighting; in fact no airfield lights on at all. The Air Traffic Controllers took some persuading to turn everything off, but they did in the end. Of course the last bit was the hardest bit. The LLTV gave a very good view but its position in the nose well ahead and below the pilot's normal eyeline required a bit of interpretation. But JB did a good job and we touched down in an acceptable manner not far from where we should have. We are pretty sure that this was the first ever, lights out, safe, night landing made by a UK fast-jet aircraft.

As we went into the summer of 1976, which became famous for its very long heat wave and drought, a new route was devised for the LLTV trials. This was done to explore another potential limitation that was similar to what we had found when turning. It was this: if the hills and valleys were bigger and deeper than those in the south-west of England then the pilot's forward view of the top of the next piece of rising ground was limited by the field of view of the camera and the size of the screen. Descending across a wide, deep valley all that you could see was the opposite hillside unnervingly rushing towards you, leading to a strong temptation to raise the nose so that you could see the ridgeline and a bit of sky. This of course would bring the aircraft away from the ground and so lose the advantages of flying at low level. To achieve the necessary topography the new route was in Wales. After it had been devised and planned we first flew it by day with a filter over the camera lens so that we could assess the utility of the route before we tried it in the dark. We could also make changes if we found that the route was either too challenging or not demanding enough. But there was a knock-on effect that became a limitation in itself. To be able to fly to Wales, travel round the route and return, predominately at low level, we needed more fuel than for the Devonian routes. So we had to put four fuel tanks on the Hunter's wings, in lieu of the two that 'Hecaté' normally carried. However, during the hottest days of that golden summer of '76 the jet was too heavy to get safely airborne from Farnborough's runway! So then we had to leave the outboard tanks empty and cut the route short! Irony rules – OK?

Thankfully, most of the time we could get airborne safely with the fuel load necessary to fly the full route. On 28 and 29 June 1976 I flew four consecutive sorties in WV 383 once in the right-hand seat and the other three as 'safety pilot' to Vic Lockwood. On the last of these the overlaid symbology on the TV screen stopped working but we decided that, as it was daylight and that I had a good view of what was going on, Vic would continue to fly using the screen and I would monitor our height. However, at one point Vic started descending as we came over a wooded hillside in one of the many Forestry Commission areas in Wales. After a few seconds I invited him to ease up. He did so. What had happened was that we had flown over a 'nursery' area for new conifers that were only a few feet high. Vic had inadvertently interpreted these mini firs as trees of a normal height and instinctively descended to get closer and make them appear 50ft tall! In fact this was a very useful outcome as it emphasised that a display of height above the ground was essential and that then became a 'no-go' item.

The LLTV research programme developed further during the late 1970s. The acquisition and implementation of a HUD that could show both the flight-related symbols and the TV picture[20] meant that we no longer had to fly around in the dark looking at a screen just above our knees, a very unnatural posture, but we could rather sit back in the seat and look straight ahead. A much nicer arrangement, although giving the safety pilot a means of independently seeing what was really going on outdoors would have to wait!

---

20 Such HUD technology was known as 'raster/cursive' and became very important for future developments in the display of FLIR.

16 VARSITIES

In early July 1976 we were sweltering under the unrelenting sun of that record-breaking summer. At home we were sharing bath water and throwing the washing-up water on our garden. And still no sign of rain. Then 'the boss' called me into the sauna cunningly disguised as his office.

'Good news. I've been told that the flight's establishment of aircraft is going to increase by three.'

'Great,' I prematurely responded, 'what are we getting – Jaguars, Harriers, Lightnings?'

'No, Varsities,' he said.

A stunned silence followed, which he interrupted with a grin. 'And the really good news is that you are going to be our Varsity specialist. As you are now RAE Farnborough's Canberra guru and the Varsity is really a Canberra with propellers it'll be right up your street.' Although, with my 2,000+ hours on English Electric's jet bomber, I had to agree with his logic but I hadn't seen myself as an expert on 1940s piston-engined, twin-prop trainers! While this 'good' news was sinking in I was told that arrangements had been made for me to go to Pershore in Worcestershire, where the Radar Research Squadron was based, and where there was a Varsity ready for me to learn to fly. That happened on two very busy days in the middle of July. As is so often the way in the R&D world I wouldn't actually fly a Varsity again until the following February!

So what is a Varsity? In 1948 the Air Ministry issued a requirement to the UK aircraft industry to propose a twin-engined pilot and navigation trainer as a replacement for the Vickers Wellington T Mk 10 and the Vickers Valetta. Perhaps, therefore, it was no surprise that the Vickers Aircraft Company came up with the winning submission. The Varsity was a development of the military Valetta and the civilian Viking that they had already built and were successfully in service. The main differences were that the Varsity had a tricycle undercarriage, rather than a tailwheel layout, with a wheel under the nose. Moreover, the company had added a ventral pannier under the already rather rotund fuselage; this lower protuberance housed a small, glazed, prone position cabin for a student bomb-aimer and his instructor and, behind that, a bomb bay that could carry up to a couple of dozen 25lb practice bombs. There were hydraulically operated bomb doors over this part.

The Varsity was bigger than a Canberra at about 68ft long, with a wingspan of around 95ft and the top of its tail reached 24ft into the air. It was equipped with two big, round Bristol 'Hercules' 14-cylinder radial engines, each driving four-bladed, variable pitch propellers giving a total motive power of almost

4,000hp. That was sufficient to take its 15-ton weight to a maximum speed of around 200kt in level flight and up to an altitude of over 25,000ft. We, however, would be generally operating below 10,000ft and cruising at 130–160kt. The overall impression of the Vickers Varsity was one of bulk. In RAF service it had picked up the rather rude sobriquet 'the Pig'.

The entry and exit for all who would sail in her was via a ladder, carried on board, let down from the door aft of the wing on the port side. The flight crew, usually of a pilot and navigator for our trials, or two pilots and a nav for training sorties, would then make their way forward to the bit with forward-facing windows, where there was a rearward-facing navigator's station behind the two pilots' seats. The instrument panels were pretty conventional for the era and the central console had a wondrous collection of levers that were there to control the engines: rpm, throttles and fuel cocks. The flying controls were manually operated from a control yoke and rudder pedals and the usual set of three trim-wheels fell easily to hand.

Starting the engines was a challenging procedure because one needed more hands and fingers than the good Lord had provided. As well as operating the throttles there were switches on the roof panel to manipulate in a set sequence. After turning the engines over without fuel and ignition on (to ensure that any oil pooled in the lower cylinders was first expelled), the ignition switches were selected 'ON' and the booster coil, for that added electrical *oomph*, was pressed. This usually resulted in a wonderful sequence of pops and bangs, accompanied by clouds of white smoke from the engine's exhaust, before the Hercules finally settled into a rhythmic rumble. For those of us with little or no experience of big, round motors (and actually that was all of the C Flight test pilots) it was to be an extraordinary experience getting to grips with our new steeds.

Eventually all three Varsities arrived at Farnborough from the various places where they had been operated by civilian contractors; I never did discover the politics behind the move of them back under direct RAE control and finance. That was well above my pay grade! The three were WL 679, WL 635 and WJ 893. The first two were equipped with two different Forward Looking Infrared (FLIR) systems and the latter was employed on highly classified trials connected to the development of Polaris missile guidance systems. We also regularly 'borrowed' RRS's Varsity, WF 379, for training purposes. Once I had converted all of our pilots to type I flew 679 most often.

But why the Varsity? The Varsity was of sufficient size and, although being phased out of RAF service to be replaced by the Jetstream turboprop, it had an adequate performance for the job and was still relatively cost-effective. Its design made it rugged and had given it a very long and sustainable fatigue life. In the early days of the infrared research, using WL 679 as an FLIR trials vehicle, we aircrew just flew the kit and its attendant boffins around the sky while they gathered lots of data on objects and landscapes while playing around with the various settings that controlled the FLIR. Of course it was much more scientific than that, involving esoteric language and technical terms describing the characteristics of the system and its capabilities. The relatively early system in the Varsity was capable of seeing through light mists and thin clouds, but anything that blocked light in the 8–12 micron wavelength could prevent images being identifiable. The detector was a rotating scanner and the system required cryogenic cooling. That and the array of control and recording gear had driven the need for an aircraft with a cabin big enough to take all of that equipment and up to five scientific operators and observers.

But before getting to the trials, there are a couple of incidents that I remember from some of those training sorties. Flying the big beastie became fun after one had got used to the antiquarian ambience. The controls felt heavy at first but one soon adapted to that and the stability and handling were much as one might expect from an aircraft of its size and age. We practised stopping an engine in flight, at a safe height of course, including feathering the propeller; always a rather strange sight when one looked out of the window at the stationary prop. However, carrying out that drill had to be done slowly and methodically, as it was all too easy to cut off the fuel to one engine, feather its prop and then turn off the ignition switches to the other engine!

Handling with one engine at zero thrust in the circuit pattern was no more challenging than in the Canberra, indeed the forces needed on the rudder were just a shade less, even when going around from an aborted approach. However, there was one rather academic but nevertheless entertaining item in the repertoire and that was a glide approach to land; a very unlikely event for real – with both engines 'failed'. This was flown from a 1,500ft downwind leg and, after a level turn onto base leg the throttles would be closed. The landing gear was already down and mid flap selected. Then when one was certain that the aircraft would land about one third of the way down the runway, full flap was selected and the nose lowered to keep the speed at about 110kt. The ensuing attitude was very nose low and the rate of descent concomitantly high. The glide angle was now way above 10° and from both inside and outside the old bird looked like it was doing an imitation of the Space Shuttle that was to come later!

The first memory involved the braking system. Like most aeroplanes of its era the Varsity had hydraulically operated disc brakes on the main wheels. Unusually though, these had two means of operation: toe pedals on the rudder bar and a handbrake on the control yoke. The latter was also the means of locking the brakes on for parking, but the toe brakes gave a much smoother way of operating the brakes during landings and taxiing. In fact, if you were standing outdoors when a Varsity taxied past it sounded like a runaway concrete-mixer, with the brakes screeching and those big engines making rumbling noises via the exhausts! I converted 'Jack' Frost to the Varsity in March 1977 and, as expected, he coped very well, falling into the same nostalgic trap as everyone eventually did. However, some time later Jack had to land on the shorter north–south runway at Farnborough and decided to use the hand-operated brake lever. Sadly he was over-enthusiastic with his application and burst all four tyres!

The other memory was to do with the lack of sealing around the multiple Perspex panels that made up the 'glasshouse' pilots' windscreen. When it rained the water dripped in all over one's lap and legs; anything written in grease-pencil on one's kneepads was soon obliterated. One time I was converting two rather elderly ex-military pilots at RAE Llanbedr on the Cardiganshire coast, because they were going to be flying a Varsity there for some esoteric radar trials. On one of these training flights we had to get airborne in the rain. As we climbed away from the airfield the redoubtable Mr Ainsworth looked across the cockpit at me and said, in his northern accented voice, 'Eeee, it's just like being back in a Wellington again.' We should have been wearing Wellingtons!

17 WHITE HOT TECHNOLOGY

Llanbedr was also the location of a week-long 'high-risk' FLIR experiment that could easily have been dreamt up by the Ministry of Silly Trials. Apparently there was an urgent need to get detailed data on the infrared signature of an aircraft flying at high speeds that had been unobtainable from ground based cameras. So on 3 April 1978 C Flight navigator Flt Lt Sean Sparks and I, accompanied by three boffins, headed west to Llanbedr where we would meet up with Flt Lt Keith Hartley, an A Squadron test pilot from Boscombe Down, flying a single-seat Jaguar. The week would be spent with Keith aiming his aeroplane at us to achieve the closest possible miss distance within the fixed field of view of our FLIR. Llanbedr was chosen because it was close to Aberporth Range, which was equipped with highly accurate radar and employed controllers who were used to such manoeuvres.

It didn't start well. We had not long been on the ground at Llanbedr when a camouflaged Jaguar arrived overhead going at a fair lick. It made a tight turning break to slow down and land on the southerly runway. Unfortunately there was a strong westerly wind blowing; we had landed on the south-west facing runway – but that was far too short for Jaguars. Keith touched down but did not use his braking parachute, which is large and effective on the Jag, but can be difficult to handle in strong crosswinds. He then had to taxi quite a long way from the other end of the 7,500ft long runway to be parked near our aircraft. By the time he got there the brakes and wheels had obviously over-heated because, as he moved the last few feet to a stop, there was a soft 'thud' and the Jaguar tilted to the right. The starboard tyres had deflated as the heat sensitive fusible plugs in the wheels had 'blown'. The ladder was then put up to the cockpit and as our fighter pilot descended there was a repeat performance from the port tyres! Oops! Fortunately our first range slot wasn't until the following morning so there was time to get the problem fixed while we briefed.

It was a memorable week. The range controllers did an outstanding job and it was fascinating to look out and see the small smoking dot appear out of the distant blue sky and then rush past us – *very* close at times! Every pass would have been reportable as an Airmiss in other circumstances. Hartley did a great job adapting his passes to give the boffins an excellent collection of all-round views of his jet by the end of the week.

We stayed in a local hostelry each night. One evening, after dinner, we were imbibing a post-prandial *digestif* with some of the natives when one of them asked, 'Are you 'ere to fly them pilotless aeroplanes then?' Llanbedr was the home base for the UK's only remotely operated target drones; a small jet-engined aircraft called the Jindivik.

On the way back to Farnborough I received a valuable lesson in limited aircraft performance. The weather was good so Sean had planned our return at low level (250ft) and we were straight into the UK Low Flying System after take-off. After about twenty minutes he gave me a change of heading for the next leg. I turned onto it and found myself soon increasing power to climb up a hillside, well more of a mountainside. After a short while I had applied maximum continuous power and the airspeed was continuing to fall. When it got down to 120kt I admitted defeat, dropped a few degrees of flap and turned right away from the rising ground so that we could accelerate back to our planned cruising speed.

'I'm afraid you'll have to do some ad hoc replanning, Sean,' I said. But that didn't put him off his stroke; he had already worked out a new route! I like navs like that.

After a few months and in conjunction with the scientific powers it was decided to imitate the LLTV Hunter and look at using FLIR as a piloting aid, especially in the dark. This brought an interesting little project my way. I had to redesign the right-hand instrument panel so that a TV screen, for viewing the FLIR image, could be installed. There was insufficient funding to allow cursive script to be superimposed on the screen, *à la* Hecaté, so I was tasked with coming up with a design to put sufficient flight information on the rather meagre amount of space left around the screen. Thus I spent many happy hours with the RAE's flight instrument folk and trade catalogues searching for instruments that were small enough to fit but clear enough to read easily. In the end we got, as is usual, a fairly happy compromise between size, readability and cost. So it was that we started a whole new phase of night flying, with two pilots up front and a less happy navigator with his back to the direction of flight at the desk behind us. At first it seemed that the boffins couldn't stop their data gathering but it soon became apparent that now that we could see where we were going the terrain avoidance aspect and the collection of pretty infrared pictures went hand-in-hand. We also started to learn about the temperature 'gates' and whether the imagery was best viewed with the hot bits white or black. The consensus seemed to be that white-hot was good for finding 'targets' at some distance but black-hot seemed to give a more three-dimensional look to the terrain.

One trial that we flew was aimed at looking at high-tension wires of the National Grid. This was to determine if the heat present in the N-thousand volt cables would be detectable on the FLIR and therefore could be avoided. Another target and intelligence related query was about fuel refineries. Could the FLIR see which tanks were full or empty, or even partly full? Was it possible to see which pipelines were operating and which were not? So we came up with an epic route that flew west all the way to the oil terminal at Milford Haven in South Wales, following as much of the National Grid as we could. The answer turned out to be yes to all the questions asked! However, the avoidance of power lines at high speeds would not be feasible as the resolution of the system was such that you could not see the thin white lines on the screen until you were about a nautical mile from the wires; at 420kt that is less than ten seconds away!

We were satisfied that we could safely fly at low level on the FLIR and this was reported back up the line. However, we did not have any other method of giving the 'safety pilot' an independent monitoring aid; he still had to look at the screen as well. This facility would come later and make this very high-risk flying a bit less so!

While the two Varsities, WL 679 and WL 635, both carried FLIR equipment, albeit of different types and origins, we had another aircraft that, among other things, was exploring the use of airborne FLIR – Canberra B(I)8 WJ 643. Having flown about 600 hours in this mark of Canberra during my first tour it was great to climb back on board what felt like an old friend. However, this airframe had not been built originally as a B(I)8 but as a B2 and then converted. It had been with the Ferranti Company based originally in Scotland and then transferred in the early 1970s to RAE Farnborough. By the time I had arrived there 643 was used for research under the auspices of the Flight Systems Department and not the Air Weapons Department for whom we on C Flight did most of our flying.

The bomb bay of 643 was filled with digital computers suspended from the bomb racks and the aircraft's main role was in deriving algorithms for the correct control of moveable, harmonised sighting systems, like lasers and electro-optical equipments such as FLIR. The trials went under the acronym of LOSSE – Line of Sight Stabilisation Equipment. A Hughes FLIR turret had been acquired from the USA; it was identical to the one fitted to USAF Boeing B-52s. The turret was mounted under the front fuselage.

The aeroplane's colour scheme was rather eye-catching: white upper surfaces and light grey beneath, with royal blue flashes dividing the two and, just to give this unique aircraft an even better chance of not being run into by someone else, dayglo red panels at the nose and tail. The pilot's cockpit was also more exotic than the operational models that I had flown in Germany. It was fitted with an HUD that allowed the pilot to view the world outside overlaid with the usual flight parameters and a symbol that showed him where the FLIR was looking.

As the B(I)8 had only two crew positions the other was occupied by a civilian FTO and for the LOSSE project he was a very personable young man called Pete Spencer. He had undergone all the survival and emergency procedures training for his special role as 'the man without a bang seat'. This mark of Canberra had only one ejection seat and that was for the 'driver, airframe' sat above and behind the FTO under the slightly offset, fighter-style canopy. Poor old Pete had to wear a dreadfully heavy and restricting special flying suit that all B(I)8 navigators had to fly in; it had an integral parachute harness and an emergency oxygen bottle in one of the leg pockets.

When the B-52 FLIR turret was fitted we did a lot of low-level flying, often in co-ordination with military vehicles to test tracking and various methods of indicating possible targets to the pilot. Tracking was also of interest so that the stability of the system could be analysed and, when necessary, improved. One interesting anomaly that we uncovered one day was that Pete was picking up hotspots that were not military vehicles. It was my job to home in on them and see what they were. The two most common such 'hotspots' were haystacks and cows, both of which were much warmer than their surroundings!

On another occasion we were flying back to Farnborough when we were asked to follow one of our Buccaneers around the instrument pattern. We were about 3 miles behind it and Pete said that he had locked onto the Buccaneer using its hot jet exhaust. The FLIR had two fields of view so a magnification of about five could be achieved. On that setting it was easy to identify the aircraft type. Pete was still telling me that he could see the aircraft even after I had lost sight of it as it descended into cloud. Eventually it did disappear from his view as the cloud thickened. This experience gave us the idea that we should set up some sort of trial in which we could examine the use of FLIR as an air-to-air identification and aiming aid. So we did. It was successful, especially in the head-on mode, which was one of the areas of concern for medium-range, missile-equipped fighters where positive visual identification was a major factor in the rules of engagement.

Later a Ferranti Laser was installed in 643 and was harmonised with the FLIR and a daylight TV through a clever system of moveable and steerable mirrors in the nose. This part of the LOSSE programme would eventually lead to the successful production of a thermal imaging designator that would be known as Thermal Imaging and Laser Designator and see operational service in the First Gulf War.

But first, of course, we had to fire the laser from the aircraft. This brought lots of angst to the safety folks and there followed many meetings to decide where we could safely do this and what the hazard to the crew, range personnel and casual passers-by might be. In those days the more powerful lasers were not eye-safe and could cause severe damage to the human ocular kit. The upshot was that we would be given a special area within the restricted range zone at RAE West Freugh and stringent procedures would have to be put in place to make sure that nobody was anywhere near the area into which we would be firing the laser. This included the beach at the north end of Luce Bay, which was a favourite dog-walking spot for the locals. We would also have to wear special goggles throughout the flight. These proved to be cumbersome and of dubious optical quality. I thought that they were a greater flight safety hazard than the rather questionable chance of a stray reflection from the laser swiping me in the eye. As soon as the firing was completed and the system powered down I pulled them off for the rest of the flight.

These wretched things turned up again when we started the Paveway LGB trials that I've already described. Bob Newell's comments on the goggles after his first flight with them on were totally subjective and unprintable!

18 PLAYING WITH THE NAVY

June 1977 brought us the Queen's Silver Jubilee. Some of us were domestically involved with arranging a street party where our Married Quarters were located – St Michael's Road. This created some very welcomed interface with the civilian neighbours around us. On the Big Day it all went off very well and much food and drink was consumed well into the gloaming of a June evening.

At work our chief boffin, Terry, had a Jubilee trick up his sleeve. In keeping with historic practice there was to be a gathering of ships from all over the world for the Royal Review at Spithead, in the Solent. Such reviews of the British Naval Fleets had taken place in this area of water between Portsmouth Harbour and the Isle of Wight since the forteenth century. This presented us with an opportunity to look at a wide range of vessels with the FLIR and build up a catalogue of such images.

On Thursday 23 June we received a clearance to fly over the ships as they were gathering and being positioned according to the complex plan that some clever, and no doubt very senior, naval person had drawn up. We arrived late in the evening and stayed until after dark. We flew around at about 1,000ft while the boffins did their thing down the back. The RN was controlling the airspace from the aircraft carrier *Ark Royal*. After a while I asked our scientists if the view of an approach to the *Ark Royal*'s deck would be of use. After all it would perhaps be a way of making a covert visual carrier landing or an attack and it might be worth recording. '*Ark Royal* this is Nugget[21] 51.'

After a short delay, '51 – go ahead,' came the response. I'm sure that I caught the sound of a coffee cup being suddenly put down.

'We'd like to set up for an approach to your deck. Would that be acceptable?'

Another pause. 'I don't see why not, but we haven't got the deck illuminated.'

'Nugget 51, that's not a problem, with our kit we can see everything we need to.'

Then '51, what's your wingspan?'

'95ft. Why?'

'In that case there's not enough clearance between the deck centreline and the superstructure.'

'Oh, I'm not coming below 150ft, so don't worry.'

'OK, 51, in that case you are clear to make your approach.'

So I went over the *Ark Royal* and turned outbound to about 4 miles from the ship and then turned back to line up on the deck. When my nav, Mo Hammond, reckoned we were at 3 miles I started a descent at 110kt with a modicum of flap down but the undercarriage up; that was because the nose wheel came down right in front of the window through which the FLIR watched the world go by.

Looking across at the screen I maintained a 3° approach path and held us on the centreline. It was easy to see everything I needed to make a steady approach. At 150ft I applied full power and climbed to pass over *Ark Royal*'s

---

21 'Nugget' was a long-standing collective callsign for RAE pilots.

deck at 250ft. This was probably going to be the only time that I would make an approach to an aircraft carrier.

The Jubilee Fleet Review took place on the afternoon of Tuesday 28 June and we were given permission to fly over the Fleet in its final positions. We arrived and flew around as quietly as we could. I checked in on the radio and our man on *Ark Royal* was there again.

'Welcome back Nugget 51,' he replied. 'I hope you are not going to do another approach to our deck, because the Queen is downstairs having dinner.'

'In that case we won't,' I said.

We often worked with ships. An epic trip was set up for us to get a lot of images of a ship – HMS *Blake* – exercising at sea. *Blake*, with its sister ship HMS *Tiger*, was to be the last of the RN's cruisers and had been present at the Jubilee Fleet Review five months earlier. There was a regular maritime exercise held off the Moray Firth and it was in this that we would participate with our flying museum piece equipped with its futuristic technology. I had to arrange a detachment to RAF Lossiemouth, and we had to fulfil a requirement to fly sorties by both day and by night, but not stay for more than three days. This led me to devise a pattern of trials whereby we could get images almost round the clock without putting myself and my navigator, Flt Lt Sean Sparks, outside the 'Duty Hours' rules. Wednesday 30 November dawned clear and frosty. Everything was planned, the boffins had all turned up on time (not always a regular event) and the aircraft was loaded. Sean and I looked at the en-route weather, which proved to be sparkling – an anticyclone was positioned over the UK giving nationwide winter sunshine. 'Let's go up at low level,' I suggested.

'Why not?' responded Sean.

So we got out the necessary maps and drew lines to get us from Farnborough to Lossiemouth with the maximum use of the UK Low Flying System. We gave the boffins the news when it was too late for them to get off!

The trip went well. It was great to be floating along at 250ft and 150kt on such a glorious day. As we came over the last of the snow-covered Cairngorm Mountains I maintained 2,500ft and called Lossiemouth Approach asking for a visual approach from a run-in-and-break. Sean had already looked at the Lossiemouth information given in the Terminal Approach Procedures book and had pointed out that it stated that run-in-and-breaks were not to be flown lower than 1,000ft and at a speed not exceeding 420kt. He also told me that we were not to fly over the environs of Lossiemouth town.

'OK,' I said, 'but I'll trade a bit of height for speed on the break!'

So we turned onto the centreline at about 5 miles from the runway and I called, 'Nugget 51, initials.'

'Nugget 51 you are cleared for the break – circuit clear,' came the response from the man in the tower.

At about 1 mile I put the nose down slightly and managed to build the speed up to 210kt, just half the locally laid down limit. When I turned left onto the downwind leg I climbed from about 500ft (again about half the local limit) and, without touching the power the speed dropped nicely to below the undercarriage-lowering limit and I selected some flap. I could see Lossiemouth town ahead but we hadn't yet reached the nearest dwelling so I dropped a bit more flap, reduced power and turned smartly left onto a close final turn. Soon afterwards we were rolling down the runway and receiving our parking instructions.

'Nugget 51, taxi to three-quarters hard,' came the mysterious directions.

'Say again?' I replied.

'You will be parking between numbers 3 and 4 hangars, 51. Just turn left there and go straight ahead.'

Like a good pilot I did what I was told. But as we proceeded I could see that we were going to pass between the control tower and some buildings. I wasn't entirely sure that I could get through unscathed. I advised the controller of my concern. 'What's your wingspan, 51?' he asked politely.

'95ft,' I replied.

'Stop!' came the response.

I obeyed. There was then a pause while, no doubt, somebody was dispatched to find out just how wide the gap actually was.

'OK, 51, turn left there and we'll let the marshallers know that your parking arrangements have changed.'

'Roger' I replied and waited until a man with red table tennis bats directed me into a big enough space for our rumbling flying machine. When we had parked and were disembarking a young airman turned up who said that he was looking for the aircraft captain. I owned up.

'Wing commander ops wants to see you right away, sir. Please follow me,' he said, adding, 'He seemed a bit peeved, sir.'

It was nice of him to give me a bit of a warning and I asked Sean if he would like to come and provide a bit of moral support. Being the nice chap that he was he readily agreed. We followed the airman to the open door of the wing commander's office. We were instructed, not invited, by a loud, gruff voice to enter.

There followed a long, loud and continuous diatribe that included comments about coming too low on the break, flying over Lossiemouth town and having holes dug in his airfield. Mentally I accepted the first, denied the second and was totally at a loss about the third. The wing commander went on to complain about Boscombe Down and its way of doing things and closed with an instruction, not an invitation, to leave his office and, I imagined, the unsaid thought that we were not to darken its threshold again.

Outside and out of the said senior officer's earshot I asked Sean what he thought of that. 'He must be having a bad day,' opined my nav, 'but what was all that about holes being dug in his airfield?'

'Beats me,' I said.

Later on we discovered that another trials aircraft, a Puma helicopter from RAE Bedford, was sharing the same trial with its FLIR. It turned out that their system was mounted in a turret that was lowered through the cabin floor when in use. If the electro-hydraulic system that raised it failed then the only solution, to avoid damaging hundreds of thousands of pounds' worth of white-hot technology, was for the helicopter to land over a hole deep enough to avoid ground contact. The Puma pilot, Alistair, from the RRS, had apparently sent all this information to Lossiemouth in advance. But when he had arrived, some hours before we did, there was no hole. Alistair was a straight-talking Scotsman and had obviously upset Wingco Ops with his demand for spade-equipped ops staff to get out on the grass and get digging! It was done but it did stretch the wing commander's patience to breaking point. And then we arrived and broke it completely! Ah, such is trials life and life's trials.

All after that went well, but we did get tired. On the third sortie, when we had got airborne at 1 a.m., we flew about two hours 'on task' with HMS Blake. When, finally, the word came from the boffins in the bowels of the aeroplane that they had got enough data recorded I climbed to 2,000ft, selected the autopilot on and headed back to Lossiemouth. The radio was very quiet and I told the controller that I would head towards the extended runway centreline and make an approach to land using the ILS. No more run-in-and-breaks, just the quietest straight-in approach that I could make. It was very dark and very quiet with just the gentle drone of the engines in the background.

The next thing that I was aware of was my head snapping upright. *I've been asleep*, I thought. *I wonder for how long?* I was about to tell Sean and looked across the cockpit only to find him in a somnolent posture! I looked at my watch and decided that it could have only been a minute or two. Good old 'George' our very mature autopilot had kept us on heading and height. But it was a worrying event. I turned the small louvers that let cold air into the cockpit to open and directed them to blow into my face, disconnected the autopilot and gave Sean a nudge. I didn't let on that I had nodded off too. We flew again later that day having spent a few hours in bed trying to sleep while the local jets tore the sky asunder.

Another foray with the Royal Navy involved a submarine; this time in the English Channel. It was a hazy day but there was a very high priority on this adventure. Questions were being asked as to whether FLIR could detect the wake of a submerged submarine, due to the heat generated by the engines and propellers. We had been given a position and time for our rendezvous and set off south from Farnborough to be there. The brief was that the sub would start on the surface and then make a slow submerge while we flew around to see whether we could see the wake. As we neared the RV position on the heading given by the sub we could see nothing ahead in the water. Varsity 679 had a Low-Light TV camera alongside the FLIR and the boffins could display either on our screen up-front. Outside the visibility was not good so I asked for LLTV, which often penetrates mist quite well. But to no avail, nothing in the water ahead. We went back to the FLIR display. The nav, Mo Hammond, said 'One minute to go.' I wondered whether the Navy had done one of their favourite tricks again – mixing up time zones and being an hour out.

'Thirty seconds,' said Mo.

'Wait a mo, Mo,' I said. 'What's that hotspot there?'

'Not sure.'

As we watched the spot grew bigger and out of the window I could now see the bulk of one of Her Majesty's underwater boats rising impressively out of the water. Spot on time and spot on position. Well done, Navy! The trial went well but the answer to the question was 'No'.

19 AND THE ARMY

But it wasn't all playing with the dark blue – the khaki became our targets as well. Someone somewhere, probably from the Ministry of Silly Trials again, wanted FLIR imagery of a Main Battle Tank (MBT) firing its gun. Could the shell be seen and tracked? So we were dispatched to the Army firing range at Lulworth Cove on the south Dorset coast. An MBT was being sent there especially for the trial. We arrived a little ahead of the planned time to be greeted with 'Ah, hello Nugget 51, I'm afraid that there's going to be a bit of a delay.'

No further information being forthcoming I responded with the usual aircrew question, 'How long?'

'Not sure, old boy. We're trying to find out what's going on ourselves. Apparently the tank transporter has had a bit of a problem.'

We decided that we would follow the road out of the range to see if we could spot it. Within a very short time we had spotted a long truck at an odd angle and an MBT lying upside down next to it. We informed the range officer. He was not best pleased. It was soon obvious that our MBT was going to remain on its back, like a stranded turtle, for more time than we had fuel to wait. So we took a few infrared pictures of the underside of the said armoured vehicle and hightailed it back to base. *There won't be many air-to-ground infrared images like that*, I thought. The trial eventually happened but someone else flew the slot. However, I did see the recordings and the shells were very easily visible. What use that knowledge was I never really grasped!

The Army had an annual exercise on Salisbury Plain called Exercise Phantom Bugle – soon known to us as Phantom Bungle. We were to be allowed to fly over the exercise during set periods by day and by night. So the planning went ahead. In order to maximise the data that we could gather the trials protocol brought with it a requirement to fly at the periods just around dusk and dawn. This was because of a phenomenon known to the boffins as 'thermal crossover'. This was when there was a waning of thermal contrast in the terrain due to the cooling down or warming up of the landscape. This effect made it harder for the FLIR to give a sharp and definitive image to the scenery and so much harder for an operator to interpret what he or she was seeing; this was of particular interest for us up front using the images to avoid hitting the ground.

This in turn meant that the plan involved getting airborne at around 4 a.m. for the dawn slot and not landing until after midnight for the dusk one. It was at this point that I learnt that we would therefore have to detach to RAF Lyneham at the far end of Wiltshire, home to the RAF's Hercules Tactical Transport Force. I queried why we could not fly out of Farnborough and was told that it was because of a local working agreement between, of course, the management and the unions. It turned out that any member of a trades union who was still on the premises after midnight had to be paid until 8 a.m., and at an elevated rate. Apparently management were not going to be paying anyone anything if they were not actually doing something for it!

The next time I was strapping into an aircraft I chatted to my two ground crew, who were, like all their colleagues, civilians. I asked them whether what I had heard was true. They confirmed it.

'But do you realise that if the unions had not insisted on this blanket eight hours of extra payment and if we flew from here next week and were not detached to Lyneham you'd all get about another three hours at time and a half? Instead you're going to get nothing.'

I didn't think any more about it until I got a call from the group captain's PA who asked me to go over and see him. I complied as quickly as I could, as you do. I was shown into the great man's office. 'I've just got back from a Board Meeting and heard that you have been stirring up dissension in the ranks. Apparently some of the ground crew have been giving the shop stewards a hard time over the ban on working after midnight. What did you actually say, young fellah me lad?'

I told him and didn't spare him my opinion that the men had been given a bad deal by this arrangement.

'Yes, I see. Well, I have to order you to desist in any future interference between the ground crew and their union masters. As a serving officer it's not your place to get involved in civilian working arrangements. Understood?'

'Yessir,' I replied with a suitably hangdog expression.

'Right that's it, you can go now. By the way, strictly *entre nous*, I do tend to agree with you.'

So the following week we set off for Lyneham, with a bevy of boffins, two ground crew and Sean Sparks as our directional and positional consultant, aka 'nav'.

We arrived at Lyneham on Tuesday 11 July after having flown for a couple of hours back and forth over the exercise areas on Salisbury Plain chasing tanks and other assorted militaria. After landing we were parked amongst the Hercules, for once feeling relatively small. As we were offloading our bags for onwards transport to our accommodation a Land Rover turned up with a young airman in it. Memories of our reception at Lossiemouth resurfaced.

'Could the aircraft captain please come with me?' asked the youthful driver politely.

Sean offered to come with me but, being pretty certain that we had not done anything remotely approaching naughty, I declined and asked him to take charge of getting everyone to the accommodation. I was taken to the rather grand building that announced itself with a large nameplate as Station Operations. Inside I was guided to – yes, you've guessed it – the office of Wing Commander Operations. 'Come in,' he said. 'The Station Commander has just been on the phone rather angrily demanding to know "What on earth is that Varsity doing here?" I told him that you were from Farnborough doing some sort of trial with the Army on Salisbury Plain, but he was still not very happy.'

My puzzled look gained more information.

'Last week we took delivery of a Varsity from RAF Training Command that was due to go to the Fire Section's Practice Ground. We had heard that this was the last of the RAF's Varsities so we put on a bit of a ceremony; you know, flags and fizzy wine and that sort of thing. We even had the RAF News come and take photographs. So it was a heck of a surprise that, less than a week later, you turn up in a perfectly serviceable and obviously still in use Varsity with RAF roundels on it!'

I didn't have the heart to tell him that there were still another three flying. 'Well, strictly speaking, sir, the Varsity you are going to burn may well be the last that the RAF operated. Ours is not RAF, it is part of the Ministry of Defence Procurement Executive's fleet. I think that you can reassure the Station Commander that he hasn't jumped the gun,' I said as reassuringly as I could.

'OK, thanks. How long is yours going to be flying?' he asked.

'Oh, years yet,' I said with a mischievous grin.

'Get out,' the wing commander rejoined – with a grin of his own.

A bit like the exercise with HMS *Blake* this trial brought with it some very unsociable hours and our fatigue was not helped by us being housed in temporary accommodation far too close to the taxiways and main runway to be conducive with sleeping during normal working hours. Messrs Lockheed's C-130 Hercules is a fine beast and rugged transporter of all things military, but it makes a phenomenal amount of noise moving around on the ground.

Despite this we flew over ten hours of productive FLIR data gathering and we all learnt a lot more about the system's capabilities. The one part of the trial that I still vividly remember was when we had arrived at dawn and the main force of Chieftain tanks were barrelling across the plain like the Russian hordes coming through the Fulda Gap. The problem was that no one could see them. There was a shallow but thick layer of fog. But as we flew towards the wide line of tanks the FLIR was picking up lighter coloured lines in the fog from the heat of the tanks' exhausts warming the air stirred up behind them. Visually I could still see nothing but a white layer below us, but on the FLIR I was able to home in on a few tanks by following their warm wake.

Sure enough as we closed in on them the white hotspot of the engine compartment glowed on the FLIR. If I had been armed with an infrared missile I could easily have taken them out, despite them being totally obscured by the fog. Result!

As always in defence-related science, as soon as someone invents something that might become an effective threat then someone else (often from the same company) invents a countermeasure. So it was with FLIR. Because the infrared radiation can be blocked, dependent on the wavelength being used, the best countermeasure would be to produce a shield of something with elements of that size: in this case 8 to 13 microns.[22] One of the ways of making a hot target disappear would be to immerse it in smoke with particles of the right size.

Thus it was that in the summer of 1977 I was summoned to a meeting in the office of Mr Terry Hallet, the RAE's Air Weapons Department trials co-ordinator of all things FLIR.

'We're going to have a look at whether a tank can hide itself from FLIR in a cloud of smoke,' he announced.

Not using mirrors as well, I thought, but said nowt.

Terry continued, 'Next week a Chieftain MBT will be positioned in Long Valley and we are going to fly shallow-dive attacks at it, as if we were an infrared missile and see what the effect of the smoke canisters will be.'

'Well we won't have to go far,' I said. 'That'll give the navs an easy job for once.'

This was because the Long Valley Military Vehicles Trials and Test Area was literally over the fence from Farnborough airfield.

We had a chat about speeds, angles of dive and minimum heights. When I enquired about the latter the answer was, 'How low can you come?'

'I'll have to ask but I expect that 100ft could be allowed,' I replied, more in hope than expectation. When I got back to the office I talked over the trials protocol with 'he who must be obeyed' and he said that he would put up the request for a minimum pass distance of 100ft to higher authority. So that was that.

Some days later Terry rang me to say that the tank would be available on Thursday 4 August. 'Right I'll set it up; just let me have the times when you know them,' I said. Come the day our boss, Sqn Ldr Rich Rhodes, had gone away so 'Jack' Frost was acting as the flight commander and was about to authorise me. We went through the trials procedure and checked that we had been authorised to fly our 'attacks' to a minimum of 100ft. He duly signed me off and Mo Hammond and I went off to meet the boffins at the aircraft over the other side of the airfield.

We got airborne on our planned time and by dint of a left turn found ourselves immediately over Long Valley, with its network of sandy tracks, scrub and fir trees. The weather was perfect. The tank was in position and we made a few practice runs to ensure that everyone was happy with all the parameters. Mo was calling out the heights from the radio altimeter in 50ft increments as we descended on our 8–10° dive. His voice got higher as we went below our usual minimum of 250ft! When we were all happy we instructed the tank commander to deploy his smoke canisters. These were explosively ejected in a circular pattern around the tank, landing at a radius of about 30ft. We turned in for our attack and, sure enough, we could not see the Chieftain, either visually or on the FLIR. Any tracking device would have been useless and as there was virtually no wind the tank remained hidden until well after we had passed over it.

The brief was for three lots of smoke to be used so we went round again for another attack. The smoke from the first event was now spreading out and, as the tank ejected its second salvo, this added to the obscuration. This time I looked at the FLIR screen and saw what looked like one of the dive-bombing targets I used to drop bombs on from my Canberra. Selecting white for hot showed a ring of bright objects in a circle on the ground. Although the Chieftain was not visible, even though its engine was running and therefore hot, I knew exactly where it was – in the centre of that ring of white dots. These were the hot smoke canisters. The third run made it even more obvious. I pointed this out to the folk in the back and there was the odd 'Oh, yes' and 'How about that?' Back to the drawing board, boffins!

When we got back Jack and I were told to report asap to the group captain's office over in the control tower. Apparently he was not aware of the trial and its peculiar flight profile so close to the airfield and the wing commander, who had signed it off, was not there. Apparently his PA had come into his office and found 'Uncle Reggie' standing on his chair trying to see why our Varsity, one of the priceless trials aircraft under his charge, kept diving below the distant tree line. His enquiries had tracked down the culprits and we were summoned to explain. Once we had explained he was somewhat mollified, but it was interesting that on the second such sortie about a week later, the wing commander accompanied me to experience it for himself!

20 OTHER HOTSPOTS

In concert with all the FLIR and electro-optic work there were ongoing attempts at giving pilots a view of what their systems were 'seeing' without having to redesign cockpits. The first one of these that I came across was a Honeywell device that effectively put a miniature TV tube onto the pilot's helmet. It was one of the very early Helmet-Mounted Displays or HMDs. The TV tube was fixed to the right-hand side of the helmet and poked around to place a little, circular screen in front of the pilot's right eye, so giving him a monocular view of whatever the TV or FLIR was seeing. It was all very odd at first, the helmet was much heavier than usual and felt like it was trying to tilt to the right with the off-centre weight of the tube. Then it got worse when I was told that high voltage electricity was running through the cable up the back of my neck and alongside my right cheek. Goodness knows what the Health and Safety folk of today would make of it.

We flew with this contraption on our heads in one of the Canberras, but it was difficult to make much use of it in its original state. What was needed was

22 The micron or micrometre (symbol: μm) is a unit of length equalling 1×10^{-6} of a metre; that is, one-millionth of a metre or one-thousandth of a millimetre, 0.001mm, or about 0.000039in.

some sort of connection between the pilot's head movement and the electro-optic seeker. However, all these things were being worked on and I spent many hours in a simulator over in the 'Factory' area with a monocular sight, which did not have a picture in it but a miniaturised HUD. The simulator, which had a single seat 'fighter' cockpit and a visual display of the outside world on a screen, fed by a model of the terrain on a continuous belt passing under a TV camera. It was actually quite realistic despite its lack of sophistication.

This research crossed over into the LLTV work that we were doing and the boffins were trying to give us the ability to look away from the conventional displays in front of us and look towards the way we were travelling during those steep low-level turns in the dark. The monocular HMD had a patch of flight information, modelled on a HUD, which meant that we could still see the important parameters like height, speed, heading and the aircraft's flight path. The idea was to eventually incorporate the LLTV or FLIR image within the display.

But several problems soon came to light. The first I discovered was that after flying for about twenty minutes in darkened 'night' conditions, the monocular display suddenly went out. 'The display's failed,' I called. 'No it hasn't,' came a prompt reply from outside. There followed a short reprise of the pantomime – oh yes it has – oh no it hasn't – before the lights came on and the run was stopped. 'Ah, it's back on,' I said. 'Must be a loose connection.'

Everything was checked and we decided to do another session. After about fifteen minutes it happened again. 'Close your left eye,' came the dubious suggestion. I did and the display miraculously reappeared. In the end the medical wizards up at the IAM diagnosed something called Binocular Rivalry. In brief it meant that if the visual input to one open eye was vastly more than into the other, the brain could not compute the result and, after trying very hard, it would shut down the feed from the optic nerve of the highly active eye. Hence my experience that the HMD had failed.

A second problem arose because the miniature patch of flight symbology was not always pointing where the aircraft was going. Within it there was a tiny, stylised winged circle that represented what was called the aircraft's velocity vector; that shows where the aeroplane is going at any instant in time. However, if the velocity vector is no longer related directly to the flight path vis-à-vis the outside world it means very little. So we had to play about with different ways of displaying the velocity vector and finally decided that it should be fixed in space along the aircraft's axis. That meant that when we looked away from the forward view, say up and right while turning, we no longer saw the velocity vector but we could recapture it when we next looked ahead. However, one day I was doing a very demanding exercise at high speed and very low level and was moving my head quite a lot. I had just rolled out of a turn and descended into a valley trying to follow the navigation demand when I crashed. 'What happened?' came the disembodied voice from the desk outside.

'I dunno,' I replied.

Then I realised that I was sitting there with my helmet right back on the seat's headrest. I had tried to make the velocity vector go up with my head and not the stick! Sheepishly I owned up. 'That's a really useful result,' came the response. I suppose it was.

Away from all this esoteric stuff came a requirement for us to fly a Buccaneer to Eglin AFB in Florida for trials with a new piece of Electronic Counter Measures (ECM) kit called Skyshadow. This was built by GEC-Marconi and was a wing-mounted pod. At the time none of our Buccaneers had an in-flight refuelling facility. However, there was one in the MOD(PE) fleet and that was Buccaneer S2 XN 975. It was due to come to Farnborough for HF radio trials in May 1978 and following those it would be earmarked for the fitment of the ECM pod and flown to Florida for about one month's work. I was to be the pilot.

This was all well and good and I was a very happy bunny. Somewhat hesitantly, in fear of losing a month's flying in Florida, I did point out that, unlike the rest of the fighter pilots on EFS, I had actually never done any flight refuelling; well, not of the sort in question. Although I had consumed many a cardboard sandwich from a cardboard rations box in my time! 'Well, it's about time you learnt,' came the rejoinder from the boss. 'Get onto the FR School at RAF Marham and fix yourself a course.'

So I did and went there to learn all the technicalities of the way that kerosene can be passed safely from one large flying petrol station to an aeroplane in need. After the two-day course I felt well up to having a go at inserting my probe into a basket. It had been agreed that before we set off westwards I would get a couple of sorties on the tanker over the North Sea in 975 with one of the more experienced guys in the back to tell me what I was doing wrong! The aircraft arrived in late May and I flew three of the HF trials sorties myself. Then the aircraft was due to detach to RAF Laarbruch to continue the trials at low altitude in Germany. Flt Lts Terry Adcock and Mo Hammond had drawn the long straw for this particularly arduous detachment. On 14 June, while Rich Rhodes was away and I was standing in as flight commander, I received a call from the Ops Room to tell me that the radio folks had lost the signal from 975. I told them not to worry too much, but that we would call Laarbruch operations to see if anything was amiss.

Within about half an hour we were told that the aircraft had crashed. Not long after that we received the good news that Terry and Mo had ejected and landed safely with only minor injuries. It transpired that they were flying at about 500ft and suddenly Terry spotted a helicopter right in front of him. It was slightly, but not a lot, higher so he pushed the nose down to fly under it. But then the ground came up fast so he pulled the stick back – a bit too hard. The Buccaneer didn't like that at all and it departed rapidly from controlled flight, so our boys did the only thing that they could – eject. Ironically the helicopter saw the whole thing and landed near the downed aviators and took them to hospital! There must be some sort of moral there!

So that was the end of Buccaneer SMk2 XN 975 and my detachment to Florida. By the time a new way of doing the trial had been found I was long gone! I never did do flight refuelling – although I *nearly* did many years later.

21 OVER THE POND

By April 1976 I had never visited the United States. So it was a very pleasant surprise when Rich Rhodes informed me, with one of his usual beaming smiles, that we were going to spend a couple of weeks together working in the USA. We would be based at the plant of the US aerospace company Martin Marietta, where the main business activity was the production of Minuteman missiles; however, we would be using a co-located flight simulation facility. But first we had to get there. In those days the RAF ran its own transatlantic airline. It was called No. 10 Squadron and it operated a fleet of Vickers VC10s in the grey, blue and white livery of RAF Transport Command. The squadron was based at RAF Brize Norton in Oxfordshire and its graceful but noisy airliners flew to destinations worldwide, as well as to the USA. Now Rich and I were going to put our lives in the hands of a gallant VC10 crew who were going to fly us from Brize Norton to Washington Dulles Airport. One of the anomalies of being forced to use the RAF airline instead of searching out a good deal via a travel agent was that, despite not starting our trial until the following Monday, we had to travel out on the Friday as the VC10 schedule to Washington was only twice per week. This meant that we would be spending two nights in a Washington hotel before travelling to Florida on the Sunday. The economics of this were beyond me.

When we arrived at Brize and found our way to the very utilitarian 'departure lounge' I noticed that our aircraft was having quite a lot of freight loaded. I soon learnt that we 'talking ballast' would be sharing the cabin space with a pile of boxes, aircraft spares and other oddments all secured to the cabin floor by straps, turnbuckles and nets. Speedbird service it was not. The other anomaly that we discovered on locating our seats was that they faced the back of the aeroplane. This, apparently, was deemed to give better survivability in the case of a crash. Once we had settled in the captain gave his usual introductory chat during which he announced that the biggest of the wooden crates under the aforementioned netting was an original copy of the Magna Carta which was going to the USA on loan as part of their bicentennial celebrations – 200 years after they had escaped from the rigours of the British monarchy.

The seven-hour flight passed tediously, although my first views of the Greenland icecap and the wastelands of north-east Canada were interesting and awe inspiring. Over New York City I was even able to see Manhattan through the haze and pick out the green postage stamp of Central Park among the skyscrapers.

We finally landed at Washington Dulles Airport and, as we taxied to our allocated slot, a long procession of black and white police cars fell into echelon port formation. We were then told that we were to remain seated until the Magna Carta had been unloaded. Being a bunch of service personnel the only upshot was a low murmuring; I suspect that if we had been the usual mix of today's airline passengers there would have been uproar and mutiny!

Eventually we were allowed out, but then came another novelty. On leaving the VC10 we stepped directly into what seemed to be a large, airy and sunlit room with rows of seats arranged down the side and up the middle. Once this room was full, a man in a uniform walked from the end closest to the aeroplane through the assembled crowd to the other. There he got into a small cabin and proceeded to drive the whole shebang across the tarmac towards the main terminal. As we rolled along between the serried rows of commercial airliners the driver adjusted the height of our mobile lounge so that when we reached the door of the terminal we could walk straight off into the lower reaches of the building. NATO Travel Orders in hand we followed the more knowledgeable towards the entry point of 'The Land of the Free'. As we rounded a corner I saw on my left a huge African American figure, dressed in a black uniform and prominently supplied with a gun, handcuffs, truncheon, radios and badges – a real American cop.

'Now I know I'm in the USA,' I said to Rich.

After completing all the arrival formalities and collecting our baggage we had to find out how we got from the airport to the hotel. Then came an announcement in a rich American baritone, worthy of a trailer for the latest Hollywood blockbuster:

'Ground transportation is now leaving for downtown Washington. All aboard!'

We soon learned that this was repeated at monotonously regular intervals. However, it had given us the clue as to what signs to look for. Sure enough there was a large arrow with those unambiguous words Ground Transportation written upon it. Following that we came across the next verification of our transatlantic location – a large silver Greyhound bus, being driven today by an undoubtedly close relative of the policeman we had seen earlier.

Fares paid, destination announced and we were on our way. The journey into DC was an interesting replay of a multiplicity of background scenery to many of the movies that I had watched. Everything was so different from the UK: the styles of houses, water towers, farmsteads and the slat-sided tobacco barns. As we reached the more urban areas of the capital and the houses crowded closer together the differences with the Old Country got smaller.

Soon we were driving down the side of the Potomac River and had pulled into the environs of the Twin Bridges Marriott Hotel – our home until Sunday. It was then that I realised that it was still mid afternoon and I was going to face another new experience: jet lag. So when I had settled into my room, I took a shower and lay on the very large and very comfortable bed and, quite quickly, fell asleep.

Rich roused me in time for us to institute our own Friday evening 'Happy Hour'. After all it was now 5 p.m. local time, although my body knew it was just coming up to bedtime. After sampling my first ever Budweiser beer, with a dish of 'chips' to hand, I made my mind up to push on through the rebellious biological clock signals and enjoy my evening. There was a nice restaurant, a well-stocked bar and the Queen was paying. What was there not to like?

I eventually gave in to the aforementioned insubordinate body clock at about 10.30 p.m. and wandered off to my room. I would sleep the sleep of the righteous until breakfast time now. Not a bit of it. At 4 a.m. I awoke with a box of birds in my head. *What is going on?* I asked myself. *Body-clock-wise I didn't get to bed until about 4.30 in the morning – I surely should have slept until at least 10.30? So what time is it now in the UK?* A short pause while my addled brain calculated. *Rats! It's the equivalent of 10 a.m.!* So now I had to lie there for another three hours before I could legitimately get up and move around the place. I could now see why folk got so worked up over jet lag. It is a real nuisance and, as such, has generated quite a lot of work to overcome its effects on those most affected, namely the air transport pilots and aircrew.

Our weekend in Washington was spent as tourists. We ascended the needle of the Washington Memorial, the views through the letterbox windows at the top were awe-inspiring and as I looked out towards Washington's National airport,[23] across the Potomac, I was sure that I could feel a very slight sway under my feet. The Lincoln Memorial, the Reflecting Pool, and the Jefferson

---

23 Under legislation signed by President Bill Clinton the airport was renamed Ronald Reagan Washington National Airport on 6 February 1998, President Reagan's 87th birthday.

Memorial were all on the schedule. We discovered the hop-on-hop-off tourist buses to move us around as well as the 4.6-mile stretch of the newly opened Washington Metro. The latter was impressive with huge canopied stations and large bore tunnels. Being so new (it had opened only two months earlier) the rolling stock was sparkling clean and comparisons with the London Tube were inevitable. 'Yes, but how do you think this will all look in 100 years time?' was a fair rhetorical question. There were still many more miles to be constructed and put into service, but what there was was certainly impressive.

At one point we needed to find a gent's convenience and we discovered one not far from the Washington Memorial. As we entered someone pushed at a cubicle door to reveal a gent sitting in mid evacuation. When he reached out to shove the door shut a small revolver clattered onto the tiled floor.

'Yes, we are certainly in the United States,' said Rich.

After a good day taking in all the sights and actually remaining safe we returned to our hotel to pass another evening fending off the jet lag with food and drink. The agenda for the following day, Sunday 30 May, would be breakfast, checkout, cab to National Airport and our flight to Orlando, Florida.

All went to plan and we arrived to a steamy sunset in Orange County, Florida. Our hotel was on the Orange Blossom Trail and was more than adequate for our needs. The jet lag was receding a little by now and having met up with the two BAe boffins joining us for the trial we helped things along with king-sized steaks and Californian Merlot. And so to bed.

By now I had read my way into the background for the trial. It was a tri-national US-Anglo-French project called Sabre. At least that was the name of the air-ground missile that would form the central part of our assessment and work. This was a modified version of the highly successful, laser-guided version of BAe's Rapier SAM, which would be redesigned to be carried by single-seat attack aircraft such as the Jaguar, Mirage or Harrier. The French bit was the TV and laser pod to be used as the missile guidance system; the French aerosystems company Thomson-CSF had supplied this to Martin Marietta so that they could simulate it correctly. The whole project was a response to a requirement for a more accurate method of attacking enemy armoured vehicles from the air. The rationale being that the use of bombs led to the need for multiple sorties to kill one tank. Moreover, the tank had to be overflown, so increasing the exposure of the delivery aircraft to enemy action. It was felt that a laser-guided missile could increase the likelihood of stopping more tanks with fewer sorties and give a safer stand-off capability. In cold technical terms: improve the kill probability. An added advantage was that the much lighter weight and slimmer profile of the Sabre missile meant that more of them could be carried than the conventional laser-guided or cluster bombs, another factor in improving the KP. Our job was to test the system's utility and make recommendations to those in the appropriate ivory towers as to moving forward to flight trials.

The next day we boarded the hire car furnished by Hertz and paid for by BAe and drove to the Martin Marietta plant about 5 miles to the south-west. Once we had checked in we were directed to the simulation and laser-range facility, where the managing director of our trial met us. Briefings and a first look at the flight simulator followed and by coffee time we felt ready to start. The flight simulator was modelled loosely on the cockpit of the Fairchild Republic A-10 Close Air Support aircraft. However, we were told that the flight dynamics had been modified to allow us to fly at speeds up to 500kt; something impossible in the rather ugly, straight-winged A-10, which soon gained the nickname Warthog from its aircrew. The A-10 was then still in final operational test and evaluation and would enter USAF service the following year.

By the end of that first day both Rich and I had 'flown' an hour or so each and had got to grips with the cockpit layout and the operation of the total system. The task was to fly repeated attacks on a wide spectrum of model targets and launch and track a missile to its target during a low-level pass over the 'battlefield'. The simulator was set up with a model diorama, which was viewed by a miniature TV camera that 'flew' over it in response to our inputs from the cockpit. We viewed this Lilliputian world on a large screen outside the cockpit through a fairly conventional HUD and we saw the simulated seeker of the TV/laser pod on a small display high up on the instrument panel, just to the right of and below the HUD; we called this the Chin-Up Display.

The basic principle of operation was as follows. As we flew towards the area where there would be targets (usually tanks) randomly positioned we used the pod TV in a wide field of view mode to look for the targets. We could move the seeker with a button on the throttle. When we found a target, the field of vision could be narrowed down with another switch and then the target centred with the button. At this point a button on the stick was used to initiate what was called 'contrast edge lock', which kept the cursor that indicated where the laser would illuminate the target, locked to the body of the tank. Then another button on the stick was pushed to launch the supersonic missile. As long as the clever digital technology kept the laser locked on a few seconds later the missile would arrive and its shaped-charge explosive would put the tank out of action. Sadly this bit of the process was not simulated.

As the trial progressed we were able to refine the 'switchology' to reduce both the pilot's mental workload and the number of errors we made in using the various buttons on the throttle and the stick to complete the task successfully. Every now and then we had found that we had launched the missile before we had locked the laser to the target, or locked the laser onto the target but then omitted to launch the missile by pressing the wrong button. After a few days we sat down with the rest of the team and came up with a scheme that rationalised the previously somewhat random layout of the switches and buttons of the Hands On Throttle And Stick system.

Because there was just the one cockpit and the mental demands of more than two one-hour sessions each per day started to lead to induced errors we did find ourselves with some spare time. However, I was starting to pick up on the American work ethic. It seemed to me that one was expected to be *at* work from 8 a.m. until whenever the boss said 'quit', but not necessarily *doing* any work.

One day I decided to take a walk outside and found a sandy track leading down through some scrub and pines. It was, of course, sunny and very hot. Being around lunchtime the threat of the daily thunderstorm had yet to materialise; that happened at 4 p.m., as regularly as clockwork. As I strolled along the bright yellow trail I first heard and then saw hawks and buzzards circling around in the vivid blue above my head. Looking down I then spotted strange elongated curved depressions in the sand. They reminded me of something that I had seen on TV or in a book. It then came to me – sidewinder snake tracks. I started to walk a little more briskly and with a much firmer stride. I had read somewhere that snakes are very sensitive to ground vibrations and that they will tend to slither away unless you confront them. After seeing more of the 'S' shapes in the sand I decided to loop around and head back towards the simulator building. Anyway the daily delivery of burgers for lunch had probably arrived by now. Sure enough, when I was munching my way through my 'hold the mayo!' burger one of the company guys asked me where I had been. When I told him he was visibly shocked and warned me quite sincerely never to go out there again on my own. 'That's real bad country – no-one goes moseying about in those woods – you take a truck!'

On the other hand when we did go to the company restaurant ('Chow House') for lunch we discovered that quite nearby, in one of the many lagoons on the site, lived a huge alligator. People apparently often went to feed it, probably with burgers and doughnuts, and they had given it a name – Herbie or Walter or something of that ilk. I never saw the creature but it was reputed to be at least 3m long and quite docile. I supposed that it might be if its diet was mainly from the Chow House! It was there that Rich spotted a sign over a line of microwave ovens that he wanted to take back to put in our crew room, for the advice of the more mature members of B Flight. It read, 'If you have a pacemaker please do not stand near these ovens'!

When we went to the head honcho's house for a meal he reinforced my view of the American work ethic by telling us, quite proudly, that due to this project he had only been able to take one weekend off since the beginning of the year – that was in five months! I noticed that his wife said nothing. On the other hand we, much against the British work ethic, had by then worked six days straight so it was a very pleasant surprise when we were given free tickets to Disneyworld and told to take a day out. Martin Marietta had an allocation of these because they had designed and built the monorail that transports people from the vast car parks to the gates of the Magic Kingdom. So on the following day we set off, like four kids to Walt Disney's version of Utopia.

It was like a childhood dream come true. I had often wondered what it would be like and, on the whole, the experience did not disappoint me. I've always maintained you can either grow up or you can be a jet pilot – you can't do both! It was hot but not overcrowded. The queues were bearable and my favourite 'ride' was the Haunted Mansion. However, the Runaway Mine Train and Space Mountain were pretty awesome too. Much of the place is filled with money grabbing tourist tack, but it is done in very clean and friendly surroundings. We also visited Sea World where much was being made of the bicentennial celebrations, with frequent references in the commentaries at the Killer Whale and Dolphin enclosures to the evil, Redcoat Brits! We let it run off our collective backs, just as we had when splashed by the Orcas.

On another day the simulator was unserviceable – someone had talked about a large snake being found under the floor amongst all the cabling – as a result it was agreed that we could take the rest of that day off. So we set off on the one-hour's journey to Cape Canaveral to visit the Kennedy Space Center. That turned out to be even better than Walt's Magic Kingdom – but in a very different way. The scale of the place was awesome. After we had parked the car we naturally headed towards the enormous Vertical Assembly Building – the VAB – which in those days the public were allowed to walk through. The freshly painted Stars and Stripes on the outside was the world's largest painted flag, put there to celebrate the bicentennial. The stars are each 6ft across, the blue patch is the size of a standard basketball court and the stripes each as wide as a single carriageway road. On the right side, opposite the flag was the specially designed red, white and blue Centennial Star; that has now been replaced by the NASA logo. The VAB is so big that it forms its own clouds inside and huge birds of prey circle its upper regions, soaring at 500ft above the ground.

When we set off from the car park I remember thinking that it didn't look that far away. But as we strolled on, with the other visitors, the distance did not appear to reduce – the big white shed just got bigger and bigger. Then I spotted the people who were about to enter through the huge open doors – they looked like ants entering an upturned shoebox. It was another fifteen minutes before we were in that position, open-mouthed with our 'wow-meters' at full deflection. There was not much inside because the Apollo Mission Saturn V rockets were no longer being assembled; the programme had come to an end four years earlier and the Space Shuttle programme was still several years in the future. The VAB covers an area of 3 hectares (8 acres) and its interior space makes it the ultimate cathedral of the scientific age.

As if that was not enough we then made our way outside to view the Mobile Launch Platform mounted atop the world's largest tracked transporter – The Crawler – and a Saturn V Apollo rocket laid on its immense side. It was all totally mind-blowing. The final part of our visit was to stand at the back of the Launch Control Room while a simulation of the events of the last minutes before the release of a typical Apollo mission took place. The audio sequence of the many controllers giving status reports and the final echoing, 'Go,' 'Go', 'Go' from each console to the Launch Director's prompt was only outdone by the chest-shaking roar of the simulated launch itself. What a programme that must have been to be a part of!

But it was soon 'back to earth' for us. Back in the simulator Rich and I became quite good at the tasks we were presented with. So much so that later and later acquisitions of the various targets were simulated by the simple expedient of defocusing our view of the 'outside' world until we were at a given distance from the targets. This gave us a sensible minimum flight visibility for our recommendations.

In the final analysis the calculated average error of the simulated missiles that we launched after the system had been optimised was amazingly small at around 18in. This compared very favourably with that for any bomb, including laser-guided ones. There was a big presentation up in London on the Sabre project to those with the operational and financial clout. Rich went up and reported back that there was much negativity from the Harrier Operations folk about 'Our guys rushing about at low level looking at a TV screen in the cockpit.' My impression of all the Harrier pilots that I had met was that they could walk on water and that this system offered them a realistic chance of being a much more effective close air support force. Ours not to reason why …

22 BECOMING A 'TRUCKIE'

A 'Truckie' is the not so polite but very descriptive sobriquet that non-transport pilots give to their passenger and freight carrying colleagues. RAE Farnborough had its own small airline, a flight of three de Havilland Devons and three crews of a pilot and navigator each. They occupied what was known as 'A Shed', which was just opposite the control tower, in the base of which was a small passenger waiting room.

The number of aircrew on the RAE Transport Flight was such that it was de rigueur for other aircrew to be checked out on the Devon and so become what were known as 'Guest Artists'. The number of these had to be limited so that all could maintain sensible currency and that the supervisory load did not become too large. Two of these guest artists were always COEF and OC Flying so the other slots were taken up by invitation of OC Transport Flight from those who had volunteered and who had plied him with sufficient ale at Friday Happy Hours.

Eventually, in July 1977, I was invited to join the hallowed ranks of the local 'Truckies'. My part-time status, quite correctly, did not preclude me from passing through, or rather over, the same hurdles that all RAF transport pilots had to negotiate: conversion to type, instrument and night ratings and RAF transport pilot categorisation tests. We guest artists would only be awarded C Category, which I believe meant that we could not fly as captain with nominated VIPs. That was OK by me!

The conversion and route familiarisations went hand in hand. Two sorties with an instructor, covering the entire required training syllabus, were followed by several route familiarisations as co-pilot and then an IRT and, finally, the Categorisation Check Flight. It was all very correct and proper, unlike the very brief conversions to type I had become used to in the test-flying world. But that was just as well because I would be carrying precious scientific people around the country on national aerospace research business. They might not have been fare-paying passengers but they still deserved the best service that our tiny airline could give them.

The de Havilland DH.104 Devon C Mk 2 was a military version of the de Havilland Dove commuter airliner, one of Britain's many successful post-war civil designs. The Dove was a response to the Brabazon Committee report that called for a British designed short-haul feeder for airlines. It was powered by two de Havilland Gipsy Queen engines, each giving 400hp, and standard accommodation was for eight to eleven passengers. The aircraft had been produced in large numbers for a variety of nations worldwide. Surprisingly Doves and Devons were built over a period of no less than twenty-one years from 1946.

Access to the cockpit was through the passenger cabin, which had single seats on each side, and the entrance door was between the wing and the tailplane on the left-hand side. Once in the rather comfortable pilot's seat, which was a bit of a squeeze in the tiny cockpit, everything fell easily to hand. The overall impression was one of neatness, however the centre console was a bit hedgehog-like with a multiplicity of levers arranged vertically below the instrument panel. Starting the engines was relatively straightforward, electrical power being provided by a plug-in, mobile 'trolley-acc' with its bank of batteries. The usual piston engine tricks of priming first and gentle warming up afterwards applied, as did the checks of rpm, oil pressure and magneto-drop before take-off, along with operation of the propeller pitch controls.

Taking off was a straightforward exercise and the Devon lifted easily into the air with only a light pull on the control yoke at the correct speed. It was usual not to retract the undercarriage until the speed for safe control of the aircraft following an engine failure had been exceeded. Before that speed the action in the event of an engine problem would be to land immediately and try to stop on the remaining runway. Personally I found this the hardest thing to get used to. For many years in jets I had retracted the lading gear as soon as I was sure that there was air between the wheels and the ground.

One very rarely had to climb to a great height in the RAE's Devons because most of the routes were flown at around 2–3,000ft clear of cloud and at a cruising speed of about 140kt. The Devon was a delight to fly in this mode: light on the controls and easy to trim. As to the approach and landing, nearly always completed visually, that was easy too. There were no large trim changes to cope with and the engine handling was conventional. In fact the very nice longitudinal stability and control made it possible, in the right wind conditions, to make very smooth touchdowns in just the right place.

The routes were varied and some overseas flights were called for; I went to Alderney in the Channel Islands and to the French Navy's airfield at Landivisiau in Brittany. However, the Transport Flight aircrew snapped up most of the further flung destinations long before they were offered to us 'guest artists'.

The standard route, flown three times daily and five days per week, was from Farnborough to Bedford and return; always known as the Bedford Ferry. The first of these departed Farnborough at 8 a.m. and the round trip took just over an hour. Thus it was possible to fly a Bedford Ferry and be in the EFS crew room ready to start a normal day there by 9.30 a.m. Some folk weren't too keen on starting their day at 7 a.m., but if you wanted to fly regularly, which was often not the case with trials aircraft, then it was a great way to 'keep your hand in'.

The Bedford Ferry route was normally flown at heights not above 2,400ft and the route went overhead the old Miles Aircraft Company's airfield at Woodley, just to the east of Reading. There was a VOR (VHF omnidirectional range) beacon at Woodley, much used by airliners flying into and out of the London Heathrow Control Zone. In fact our track took us along the western edge of that zone, into which we were not allowed to stray, and we worked that part of the route with Heathrow Radar. It was very interesting to watch the airliners either departing or arriving to land at Heathrow right over our heads; they were supposed to be at or above 2,500ft as they went over the Woodley VOR.

But on one very hot day in that amazing summer of 1976, when I was flying north on the midday Bedford Ferry, the nice man at Heathrow called me and asked me if I could see a Boeing 747 to my right. I was at 2,300ft at the time so my nav and I looked out towards London. We were both looking above the horizon and we could not see a Jumbo Jet. I told the controller. He said that it was now in our 2 o'clock position and below us. We were now closing in fast on the Woodley VOR and then I spotted it. The 747 must have been 500ft below us, its nose was very high and, at least to me, it did not appear to be climbing. I told the Heathrow controller that we would orbit in our present position, about 3 miles south of the VOR, while the struggling Jumbo had gone further west. As we completed that orbit we saw the light blue and white airliner passing from right to left ahead of us, its nose still unnaturally high and apparently just hanging in the sky. I wondered what was wrong and whether the passengers were aware of the predicament they were in. I never heard any more about it but I did wonder if the light aircraft operating from and around the grass airfield at White Waltham, about 5 miles west of Woodley, found themselves a bit too close to a huge aeroplane passing through their circuit! Other regular routes included destinations such as Cranfield (for the then Aeronautical College), Boscombe Down (for A&AEE), Gloucester-Staverton (for Smiths Industries), Bristol-Filton (for Rolls-Royce or BAC), East Midlands (for Rolls-Royce Derby) and Warton in Lancashire (for BAe). Then there was the West Freugh Ferry. I think I recall correctly that this epic trip was flown three times a week and was a 'grand day out'. Depending on the passenger requirements en-route destinations between Farnborough and 'the Freugh' could include stops at RAE Aberporth and RAE Llanbedr, as well as including some of the places I've already mentioned.

The best part of the day out to the Freugh was that we stopped for lunch, taken in the RAE canteen there, and the favourite dish of the day was a bridie. This was the Scottish response to the Cornish pasty and was usually enormous, covered in rich gravy and served with heaps of neeps (turnips) and mash or chips. Except on Fridays when fish and chips were on offer. I soon found that if I wanted to stay awake and alert on the long flog home I had to persuade the bonny ladies that served us to give me a smaller portion!

Life as a part-time 'truckie' was a real bonus that I had not expected, let alone known about, when I was posted to Farnborough. Mostly it was a sinecure and a good way to keep up the hours tally per month. However, one trip in the Devon is permanently etched on my mind. It was on 16 November 1978, my last month of flying at Farnborough. Flt Lt Sean Sparks and I had flown a Buccaneer together earlier in the day and even in that solid aeroplane it had been pretty bumpy at low level. A front was approaching from the west with increasing north-westerly winds, lowering clouds and rain forecast for the evening and night. After landing the Buccaneer we made our way together to Transport Flight HQ to do the evening Bedford Ferry; Sean was a categorised guest artist nav as well.

Being November we arrived at Bedford in the dark and the wind was really picking up. Once we had exchanged passengers we got airborne and headed home. I soon began to hope that there was an adequate supply of sick bags down the back because we had to fly at our usual 2,000–2,400ft and the turbulence was becoming quite violent. When we arrived at Farnborough the wind speed and direction was at and occasionally above the Devon's crosswind limit for a landing on the main runway. However, I gave it a go. But as we came down to the last 100ft before touchdown the drift angle and the turbulence coming off the hangars upwind of the runway threshold was getting very silly and unmanageable.

I went around and told the local controller that I would have to use the short north-westerly runway, which was not very well lit. I told Sean to keep an eye on the airfield in case we got blown away too far from it and I concentrated on flying as accurately as I could as we passed over the well-illuminated areas of suburbia that surrounded the RAE. When I turned back towards the airfield with the landing gear down and locked and the first selection of flap down I could just make out the runway and headed down what I estimated was a 3° glidepath. The turbulence and drift angle were much improved, but the wind was now blowing at 30–35 knots and it seemed to take us ages to get to the runway. I did not use any more flap and kept a good 10kt of speed in hand for air pockets. We touched down firmly and virtually stopped immediately.

While I taxied back to our parking spot Sean unstrapped and went to see what the passengers looked like. There were no overt signs of illness and some of the select few who had been through it with us seemed quite enthusiastic – probably the effects of relief that they had survived!

I ended my tour having flown 120 hours in the Devon to destinations all over the UK. I thoroughly enjoyed being a 'truckie'; although I still didn't want to do it for a living.

23 A MISCELLANY OF WORK AND PLAY

It was soon apparent that a test pilot at Farnborough was fair game for anyone around the place who wanted someone to sit in their simulator, play with their special piece of kit or simply be a guinea pig in whatever was their latest test programme. Most of which did not involve getting airborne. A lot of which did involve being 'wired for sound' with electrodes to measure all sorts of bodily parameters while one was undergoing the tests.

On trials that required this rather intimate monitoring of one's heart rate, temperature, breathing rate and similar data the aeromedical team would turn up at the squadron and apply the sticky little pads, wires and electrodes before we donned our flying kit. For most of us it was not a big deal but for poor old 'Jack' Frost who, like Esau of ancient biblical history was 'a hairy man', it was something of a trial before the trial! The medics had to shave off small squares of 'fur' from Jack's torso before they could apply their instrumentation; he looked like a ragged rug afterwards! But the best bit was Vic Lockwood's loud protestations to the proposition that a rectal thermometer be used during one of the high-G trials! I personally think it was a wind-up.

Work in which I got involved included experiments on voice-activated systems, refining a pilot workload measurement scale (comparable with the Cooper–Harper numerical scale used for aircraft handling qualities) and a variety of aeromedical trials into survival at high-G levels. Other trials run by the IAM involved measuring visual acuity and the use of an advanced flying helmet with protection against nuclear, biological and chemical weapons and their effects.

I also took part in the development of HMDs in the combat simulator at BAe Warton. I had very briefly 'flown' this device on the ETPS visit in 1975. But this time I would spend several hours in the combat simulator, during one-day visits over a period of months, evaluating HMDs and HUDs. Most of the HUD work was aimed at helping pilots in extreme manoeuvring flight keep track of where they were in relation to the horizon and the HMD work was aimed at giving the fighter pilot continuous displays of his aircraft's potential energy, fuel state and weapons status through a small display in front of his right eye. It was really fascinating stuff and I was sharing the work with a pilot from the Air Staff Requirements branch at MOD. He was an ex-Lightning pilot called Sqn Ldr Dave Carden. To get to Warton he used to drive to Farnborough and I would fly us up there in one of Transport Flight's Devons. I let him be co-pilot and do most of the flying; quite a change from his last steed! An odd thing was that neither he nor I had used HUDs operationally and here we were setting standards for the future! Fresh minds and fresh eyes, I guess.

The cockpit in the combat simulator was a generic fighter design and mounted on a stand about 8ft from the floor, with wooden steps up one side to give access for the pilot. There was a platform alongside the cockpit and sometimes the scientists would kneel alongside while we did our work, watching over our shoulders. The projector that provided a schematic simulation of the earth and sky was mounted above and just behind the cockpit at the centre point of the dome-shaped structure. Although unsophisticated, the visual impression was strong and unlike many other simulators the cockpit was not furnished with a motion system. However, there were devices to simulate increasing G loads: shoulder straps that tightened and a seat cushion that inflated and a 'greying' of the projected scene as the G level increased. As there was no change in the textured matrix that simulated the ground there were voice height warnings at 10,000 and 5,000ft and every 1,000ft below that.

The lack of cockpit motion was more than overcome by the very strong sensation of movement endowed by the very wide field of view. In fact one day I was in the simulator, 'fighting' one of the model aircraft projected onto the earth–sky background, when I was told that some visitors were going to enter and watch me. They came in and were conducted up onto the platform. We set the fight in motion again, and as I pulled up and rolled a couple of the visitors very nearly fell off, such was the strength of the optical illusion of motion! After a couple more manoeuvres one of them suddenly departed looking ashen and a bit green around the gills!

Back at Farnborough, two lady scientists in a lab on the main site were doing the voice recognition work. Their research had reached the stage of trying to refine the equipment so that the error rate in response to a voice command was sufficiently low as to make the system's credibility acceptable. It was centred around the sorts of commands pilots would make in flight and in combat situations to activate weapons, radios or ascertain critical information. When one had spoken a word from the list provided then the system would respond by displaying that word on a screen. One day when the pollen count was at its height I sneezed. The screen came up with the word 'FUEL'! But the trials progressed to a stage where it was flown in a Phantom fighter at Boscombe Down. One particular area of interest was what the effect of stress or speaking under high G might have on the recognition of words. One of the ladies told me later that the Phantom crew had seemed to have forgotten that the system was recording as they discussed the characteristics of various senior personages back at their base!

The pilot workload rating scale trials came in the form of sitting in a fairly simple simulator, 'flying' a series of tasks, which became increasingly demanding, while someone made one do mental arithmetic. A measure of our workload was the time that it took us to come up with an answer. We were then asked for our assessment of our workload on a scale with which we were provided. These tests invariably brought on a headache and a great thirst for a pint or two of the amber nectar. Thankfully they often took place at the end of the working day when one could swing by the Officers' Mess on the way home.

The aeromedical trials were the best fun, although an element of sadomasochism would be needed to call them that! Throughout my tour there was a lot of work going into the configuration of the cockpit of the next generation fighter, still called AST-403, but eventually known as Eurofighter and then Typhoon. One of the requirements was for the pilots to be able to sustain a force of nine times that of gravity (9G) for up to thirty seconds. The most obvious solution was to start with the seat being installed at a reclined angle. With the pilot's body in a semi-prone position the vertical heart to head distance would effectively be reduced and allow a greater G threshold to be sustained. Of course this arrangement had to allow enough display surface above the pilot's legs for the flight instruments, engine parameter and navigation displays. The use of a large field of view HUD would be essential. There would also be a need to use the normal anti-G trousers, always called a G-suit, to squeeze the legs and lower abdomen to prevent too much blood flowing down, away from the brain. Without that the pilot could quickly lose consciousness – black out.

To this end the IAM's centrifuge was fitted out with a reclined seat and we gallant guinea pigs had to climb aboard to see how much G we could sustain, with and without the G-suit operating. Various reclined angles were to be trialled starting at 30° and going in stages up to 60°.

When I did my first 'flight' in the centrifuge it was to establish a baseline for my performance. The seat was set at 30° and I was wearing my G-suit. I achieved a steady thirty seconds at 7G, above which my peripheral vision closed in markedly. This was discovered by the doc, who sat in the rotating centre of the twin arms of the centrifuge, watching me on CCTV, as well as my response to lights that came on randomly towards the edge of my visual field. When I saw them come on I had to push a button clutched in my sweaty little hand. As my vision faded, called greying-out, the lights stayed on because I could no longer see them. All the while I was breathing in a special way, tensing my stomach muscles and 'bearing down', sometimes quite noisily.

When the doc slowed the huge whirling dervish towards a stop, a very strange thing happened. I had a very strong feeling that I was tumbling over backwards. I knew that this was impossible but I couldn't stop the feeling. It wasn't at all unpleasant and I had no nausea, unlike some of my colleagues.

As the trials progressed and the seat angle became more inclined a new problem arose. The increased force of gravity was compressing our ribcages and making it very hard to breathe deeply enough. However, at 60° it was possible to hold 8 or 9G for thirty seconds, but the pain was almost unsustainable. The next trick that the medics came up with was graduated pressure-breathing. This increased airflow through the oxygen mask, which helped with the breathing problem; however, that brought with it another predicament: a danger of over-inflation of the chest cavity and yet more pain!

So the next trick was a vest that inflated along with the G-suit and held everything in balance. With this arrangement and a 60° reclined angle most of us managed the 9G threshold without blacking out. But it was physically very taxing. On top of that some folk were suffering with nausea every time that they rode the centrifuge. Luckily I wasn't and I learnt to play a game during the deceleration of trying to convince my mind that I had indeed completed a small loop in my seat!

The 60° seat seemed to be the solution for the G, but it brought all sorts of ergonomic stoppers for cockpit design. In the end it was realised that a 30° seat could be used and so allow a sensible arrangement of the cockpit because, as the envisaged fighter's AOA would increase as more G was pulled, then that angle, which might be up to 30°, would confer the same benefit as we had found at 60°. It was the total angle between the vertical and the pilot's body that mattered most.

There were some test flights coupled to this research and these really did push the sadomasochistic boundary! The IAM had its own aeroplane: two-seat Hunter T7 XL 563 and they always had a medically qualified pilot on their staff, invariably known as the 'Flying Doctor'. In my time this post was occupied by an RAF squadron leader called Mike Bagshaw and a USAF Lt Col called Dave Root, who had been the aeromedical specialist at Beale AFB where he was attached to the SR-71 Blackbird and U-2 squadrons. Dave had come up with a way of measuring the real stress levels on pilots during high-G air combat and had invented a demanding flight profile to test this. He briefed several of us on this new trial and its flight profile, but it was when he got to the bit about taking blood immediately before and after each flight that we started to regret having said yes!

Apparently there is a protein or enzyme (or one of those things) in the blood that can indicate the level of physical stress, even if the subject (for that is what we were) doesn't necessarily feel stressed in the classic sense of the word. The problem is that once the cause of the physical stress is removed things quite quickly revert to normal. Hence the need for blood letting no later than immediately after we had dismounted from the Hunter's cockpit. This sample would then be compared with the one taken immediately before we had boarded XL 563.

Each pilot had to fly three sorties on, if at all possible, consecutive days. The flights consisted of a departure to the west to get into clear airspace and then a series of high-G manoeuvres up to the aircraft's limit of 7G. Then a dash back towards Farnborough with two low-level 6 to 7G turns over the airfield before landing and a high-speed taxi to our dispersal area. Sure enough as one descended the ladder there was a medic with a needle!

The ETPS Courses of 1975. Front row, left to right: Sgt Hatschek (Adjutant), Terry Heffernan (FTE Tutor), Peter Sedgwick, Walt Honour, Duncan Cooke, Graham Bridges (FW Tutors), Wally Bainbridge (CTFI), Alan Merriman (OCETPS), John Rodgers (CGI), Peter Harper, Tony Bell (RW Tutors), Brian Johnson (AGI), Mike Vickers (QFI), Vic Little (QHI), Wedge Wainman (Systems Tutor), Bill Anderson (Clerk); Second row, left to right: Len Moren, Terry Colgan, Terry Jones (air engineers). Students: Me, Gerard Le Breton, George Ellis, Rob Humphries, Svend Hjort, Udo Kerkhoff, Simon Thornewill, 'Rusty' Rastogi, Duncan Ross, Bruno Bellucci, Mark Hayler, Ted Steer (Ops Officer); Back row, left to right: Students: Neil Sellers, Tom Morgenfeld, P.K. Yadav, Edward Küs, Terry Creed, Roger Searle, Vic Lockwood, Jerry Lambert, Chris Yeo, Rob Tierney, Dave Morgan. (OGL (A&AEE))

The CGI – Wing Commander John 'Chalky' Rodgers in action with the rolling chalkboard behind him. (Author's collection)

Officers' Married Quarters in Bawdsey Road, Boscombe Down. (Author's collection)

Pre-Summer Ball drinks
on 4 July 1975. Tom
Morgenfeld and Simon
Thornewill watch Vic
Lockwood trying to find
his mouth! (Author's
collection)

OC ETPS about to
commit aviation in the
vintage Blackburn B-2
with Chief Test Pilot
Don Headley. (Author's
collection)

One of many photographs from the infamous Danish Viking party. Svend Hjort, Tom Morgenfeld and me having a welcome break from report writing! (Author's collection)

Buccaneer S2 XV 337 in which I flew the final sortie of our Preview exercise. (OGL (A&AEE))

Buccaneer S2B XW 987 of C (Weapons) Flight at RAE Farnborough. (OGL (MODPE))

C Flight personnel in 1977. Left to right: Mo Hammond, 'Jack' Frost, Rich Rhodes (OC), Pete Hill, Jerry Fisher, me, Sean Sparks. (Author's collection)

C Flight Canberra B(I)8 WJ 643 airborne on a LOSSE sortie. (Author's collection)

Me, about to start up Hunter F6 XG 290 at Farnborough. (Author's collection; photo by Peter Gilchrist)

'Jack' Frost releases the first UK laser-guided bomb at West Freugh. (OGL (MODPE))

The team of the Air-to-Air FLIR trial at RAE Llanbedr in April 1978. Left to right: me, Tim Bowmer (FTO), Fred Mayhead (Trials Leader), Keith Hartley (Jaguar Pilot), Penny Wright (FTO), Paddy (Team Support), Sean Sparks (Nav). (Author's collection)

Varsity WL 679 passes 100ft over a tank during the infamous infrared trial in Long Valley, Hampshire. (OGL (MODPE))

Me flying Buccaneer 2B (Special) XX 897 over the RRS complex at RAE Bedford. (Author's collection)

The rather ugly nose of Canberra SC9 XH 132. (Author's collection)

Comet XW 626 with the front half of the ill-fated AEW radar. (Author's collection; BAe Photograph)

Me flying Canberra B6 XH 568 in formation with Comet XW 626 during its transit from BAe Woodford to RAE Bedford on 13 June 1980. (Author's collection)

I lead a formation of four RRS Canberras on a multiple target trials sortie. (OGL (MODPE))

Foxhunter Radar trials vehicle Buccaneer XX 897 airborne. (Via Norman Roberson)

RRS Canberra SC9 XH 132. (Via Norman Roberson)

RRS Canberra B6 XH 568, with a Varsity in the background. (Via Norman Roberson)

The ETPS fleet, April 1981 (The single-seat Hunters had gone but the Hawks had not yet arrived). (OGL (MODPE))

ETPS Lightning
T5 XS 422. (Via
Allan Wood)

The ETPS line
in mid 1982.
A Hunter T7
can be seen in
the foreground,
with Hawks
in evidence
beyond. (OGL
(MODPE))

A still from the
video of an
inverted spin in
ETPS Hunter
T7 XL 612,
flown by me,
chased by John
Thorpe. (OGL
(MODPE))

Me, about to fly in a Hawk with Lt Col Panato, Commander of the Italian Air Force Test Centre, during his visit to Boscombe Down. (OGL (MODPE))

Captain Debertolis returning the favour during my visit to the Italian Air Force Test Centre with a flight in a Aermacchi MB-339. (Author's collection)

in the front seat of a Jaguar is OC ETPS Wing Commander R. Hargreaves, about to fly with USAF Captain Jay Jabour in July 1982 – when that idiot gets off the ladder! (OGL (MODPE))

Jock Reid looking relieved that I didn't frighten him too much during my checkout in the Hawk! (Author's collection)

Me and Captain Thomas of the French Test Pilots' School about to fly the Nord 262, October 1981. (Author's collection)

Me manning the
Ground Pilot's
Station for an ETPS
spinning sortie.
(Author's collection)

One of the
Argentinian Pucarás
arrives by air. (OGL
(MODPE))

The rebuilt airworthy RAF Pucará in flight. (OGL (MODPE))

A photograph of Robert Finch's painting of Lightning T5 XS 422 which he gave to Allan Wood following our 1,000mph flight. The inscription reads: 'For Allan – as a reminder of your flight in XS 422 on the 25th of April out of Boscombe Down, flown by Squadron Leader Mike Brooke, RAF.' We will both never forget that flight! (Via Allan Wood)

The three flights were flown in a specific sequence: the first with no G-suit, the second with a G-suit and the third with G-suit, pressure-breathing and the inflatable vest. Needless to say it got easier to stay awake as the trial progressed! And I think that Dave's analysis of our blood samples proved the theory right.

I even picked up my own IAM trial. It was the assessment of a new flying helmet; always known to aircrew as a 'bonedome'. This one was a bit like the full-face covering motorcycle and racing car drivers' helmets. It had a hinged bar at the base that contained the oxygen mask and the two-tone visor came down and locked into place so enclosing the head totally. This sort of design had been seen before and in this form was known as the High Speed Anti-Blast helmet. It had a mark number, which I think was 6. My job was to fly with this device on my head and assess its use. Two advantages were seen for the helmet: it would give full face protection in the event of a high-speed ejection and the use of a filtered air system would endow it with a good level of anti-NBC[24] protection when that was appropriate.

Having been issued with my shiny white 'spaceman's' titfer, much to the amusement of some of my colleagues, I spent several hours sitting in as many appropriate cockpits as I could. Sadly that wasn't many at Farnborough. What I discovered was that the lower part of the helmet obscured the view of much of the equipment on the cockpit side panels, to the left and right of the pilot. This was particularly bad in the Buccaneer. By then we had been allocated the use of a single-seat Hunter F6 and that was not much better. A lot of items that required numbers to be read, such as when setting radio frequencies or selecting multiple-choice switch positions, were nigh on impossible to achieve without error and too much attention being diverted from the paramount task of flying the jet.

Then came the flight trials, again with Lt Col Dave Root in Hunter XL 563. Once I had got the Hunter moving the very first thing that I noticed was that I could barely hear the engine. It wasn't until then that I realised just how much I relied on the note of the engine to judge how much power I was using to move the Hunter on the ground. That was important because too much power could wreak a certain amount of havoc behind the aircraft and was not good for the health and safety of the ground crew and their equipment. As well as looking where I was going, I now had to keep an eye on the rpm gauge.

In the air things were better and in the Hunter T7 there was not much on my lower left or right that I needed to use or look at in flight. Two small problems did crop up during the flight trials. Both happened when I was

24 Nuclear, Biological and Chemical.

flying with the helmet in its NBC configuration. For this the visor needed to be sealed to the helmet, so avoiding the possible ingestion of any nasties, so a large rubber device was pulled over the whole helmet, which overlapped the recessed rim of the visor by a few millimetres; inevitably this arrangement became known as 'the Condom'. However, I now had to fly being unable to raise the visor. This gave me a problem for clearing my ears in response to the pressure changes during climbs and descents; I could not do the usual thing of pinching my nose and blowing down it to pop my eardrums back into place. Yawning and swallowing are alternatives, but they don't always work. Something was going to have to be done.

The other problem came to light (if that's the right term!) when we flew at low level under a large and very dark cumulonimbus cloud. The tinted part of the visor, about the upper two thirds of it, was now too dark for me to be able to continue to fly safely. I handed over to Dave until the light conditions improved. How this problem would be overcome was not at all clear (pun intended). And what about flying at night?

Other problems included misting of the visor, for which filtered air had to be provided and blown into the front of the helmet, the inability to take in-flight refreshments and blowing one's nose. When I wrote my report I had no alternative to declare the Mk 6 HASB flying helmet unfit for purpose – in Test Pilot's talk – unacceptable. The boffins at IAM mulled it over and finally decided to cancel any further development.

There were quite a few Hunters at Farnborough, but one of them was very special. So special that it had a unique Mark number – T12. It also had a unique colour scheme – all emerald green with white 'go faster' stripes; hence it was known universally as 'the Green Hunter'. It was actually a modified F6 Hunter, tail number XE 531, which had a T7 cockpit grafted on, but it still had the bigger engine of the single-seater, giving it better performance than the other two-seat Hunters. On board the Green Hunter was a complex analogue computer system that was electrically connected to the right-hand pilot's flying controls and the surfaces that they operate; this was known as Fly-By-Wire (FBW). The left-hand set of controls was connected to those same control surfaces in the conventional way. The Hunter had hydraulically operated lateral and longitudinal controls, whereas the rudder is manual (if that's the right term!). The research that this magic machine was under-taking was to do with the shaping and prioritising of control laws for the next generation of aircraft. There was also an alternative control to the usual stick; a very strange device on the right side of the cockpit. We called it the ashtray because it looked a bit like one. One placed one's fingers in the recess at its back edge and then used them to control the aircraft in both pitch and roll.

I flew this wonderful machine only a few times; it was really the preserve of the A Flight guys, but every now and then they wanted a wider opinion of how the jet flew after yet another change to its FBW control system. I found the handling of the Green Hunter always exemplary, especially in turbulence and on the approach to land. I particularly liked using 'the ashtray' – real fingertip control for everything, including aerobatics and high-G turns. However, there was one 'gotcha' that the man in the left seat had to watch for. Because the top of Hunter's stick is slightly angled (to allow a better view of the compass) it is easy, when holding the stick well back, for a bit of right aileron to be applied. When we did touch-and-go landings it was necessary to hold the nose wheel off the ground with a good dose of back stick, so giving rise in this jet to a problem.

Because the roll control law was what was termed as rate-demand any small amount of displacement would demand a small rate of roll. But with the main wheels on the ground no roll rate would be forthcoming. So the feedback loop would then demand more aileron and until full, aileron was applied. There was no indication of this to the man in the right seat, who was quite busy anyway, but if the man in the left seat looked down he would see that his control column was now fully deflected, because it was connected mechanically to the control surfaces. If nothing was done then everyone would get a severe shock once the Hunter lifted off and immediately tried to roll at a high rate very close to the ground. Hence during these touch-and-go landings the safety pilot had to watch the top of his stick and advise his companion if anything untoward started to happen.

Although based on an analogue computer the Green Hunter produced a wealth of data that related to and formed much of the UK research into FBW that followed using a digitally controlled FBW Jaguar and then BAe's EAP (Experimental Aircraft Programme) research aircraft, which was an immediate predecessor of the Eurofighter. Sadly the Green Hunter met its end a few years later when the engine failed immediately after take-off; although the test pilots ejected one of them was seriously injured when he descended into the fireball.

On a lighter note, one day, I got a phone call from OC Flying, Wg Cdr David Bywater, asking me to go and see him. When I reached his office he showed me a colour photograph of a Nimrod painted in a bizarre red, white and blue colour scheme. This monstrosity – the colour scheme not the Nimrod – had emanated from HQ in London with the instruction that all MOD(PE) aircraft were to be henceforth painted in a similar manner; apparently high visibility was behind it. The basic scheme was that the whole empennage, the outer part of the wings and the nose were to be painted Post Office red and then the rest of the upper surfaces white and the lower parts navy blue.

'I think that this looks really ugly and will detract greatly from the natural lines of our aircraft.' opined the good wing commander. 'You're a bit of an artist, Mike, could you draw me a more aesthetically pleasing scheme, but using the basic arrangement of colours?'

'Yes, I think so, sir. I certainly agree that this design does no favours for the aeroplane's looks. Where did this come from? I thought that the latest thinking was that an all-black colour scheme was the best high visibility scheme.'

'I think it came from boffins at the Royal Radar Establishment in Malvern. But we'll have to go along with it as our lord and masters have so decreed. However, I think that a bit of adaptation will be acceptable. I'll worry about that; you get your crayons out and let me have something in a couple of days.'

'OK, sir, but which of our aircraft should I use?'

'A two-seat Hunter.'

So I saluted smartly and went back to my office to start colouring-in. At least if the Boss caught me I could say it was official duty! A few days later I put a couple of schemes to the wing commander. 'Thanks, Mike, that's better. Leave it with me.'

A few months later Hunter T8 XF 321 went off to be painted and was returned to us looking resplendent in its conformal red, white and blue livery. This was the start of the programme to repaint all the MOD(PE) aircraft in what would quickly become known as the 'raspberry ripple' colour scheme. That summer the International Air Tattoo was held at RAF Greenham Common. The central theme was the Silver Anniversary of the Hawker Hunter and twenty-five Hunters were lined up in the centre of the static display. During the show there was to be a *Concours d'Honneur* with a prize going to the best turned out participant. Vic Lockwood had flown our uniquely painted Hunter there and at the party marking the end of the show he was summoned from the assembled company to go up to receive first prize from no less an aviation personage than Douglas Bader, the legless fighter ace. Fortunately Vic had not imbibed too much and accepted gracefully from the great man a painting of the all-red Hunter WB 188 in which Neville Duke had gained the World Speed Record on 7 September 1953. Actually the prize came in two parts because the artist, Wilf Hardy, was then commissioned to paint a picture of the winning Hunter in flight over its base. Eventually both paintings hung proudly in the corridors of EFS.

Following this triumph, David Bywater then had another arty job for me. He wanted all our bonedomes painted in a matching scheme with the silhouette of a pterodactyl in a white roundel at the back. The pterodactyl was featured on the RAF Farnborough badge. I drew a couple of options, he then chose one and then I had to enter into careful negotiations to get the helmets painted. There was a question over the type of paint, because of the possibility of a reduction of structural integrity, but in the end at least the wing commander's and my helmet were painted. I'm not sure many others were too keen![25]

On even-numbered years Farnborough became the location for an International Air Show organised by the Society of British Aerospace Companies (SBAC). In 1976 everything kicked off about six months before the first week of September, when the show was due to be held. The terraced hill to the south-east of the main runway started to be furnished with blue and white striped tenting; these would become the company hospitality chalets. The main covered exhibition area, under a series of huge marquees, was taking shape at the top of the hill and lorries arrived on a daily basis loaded with metal crowd barriers. We carried on regardless.

But with three weeks to go our trials activities started to wind down so that by the beginning of the week before the show started there was to be no flying, other than the essential ferries from Transport Flight. The week preceding the show was reserved for visiting and participating aircraft to arrive and, for those displaying, to fly their individual routines so that they could gain approval from the Flying Control Committee (FCC). They were a group of experienced test pilots, led by COEF.

So our usual gainful employment as experimental tps was put on hold and we became general dogsbodies for the folks running the show. Mostly this meant driving out to meet and greet the visiting aircrews and get their baggage. Then we had to ensure that they had the required documentation – the most important of which was their insurance policy – guide them to the operations area, and then request those flying in the show submit their display routines to the FCC and agree a date and time for their practice.

It was great to meet all these pilots from other nations and chat to them about their aircraft. Two particularly delightful guys were test pilots from the Italian Aermacchi company: Ricci Durione and Franco Bonazzi. They were flying a pair of brand-new Aermacchi MB-339 trainers. When they arrived it was still only three weeks since the aircraft's first flight, made by Franco. Rich Rhodes and I helped them familiarise themselves with Farnborough, the local area and the display regulations.

During this 'work-up' period I met many famous test pilots: Paul Millet and Dave Eagles flying the Tornado, Duncan Simpson flying the Hawk trainer and John Farley amazing everyone with the Harrier. From the USA there was Pat Henry flying the new F-15 Eagle, the legendary Neil Anderson

25 The helmet colour scheme can be seen on the front cover.

flying the very pretty F-16 Fighting Falcon and Hank Chouteau flying the still experimental YF-17. The American aircraft were presented in eye-catching red, white and blue liveries to celebrate the bicentennial of their nation's independence. Then there was the formidable team from Dassault Aviation in France, led by their CTP Jean-Marie Saget. All of these doyens of aviation put on immaculate shows and, along with the rest, were cleared to fly in front of the trade visitors and the public during the week that followed. The last three days of the show would be the public days when items from a broader spectrum would be included; such as the Red Arrows, and the Battle of Britain Memorial Flight's Lancaster, Spitfire and Hurricane. There was also the RN Historic Flight's Fairey Swordfish and Sea Fury – the latter flown by Lt Cdr Pete Sheppard, whom I had last met when we were displaying our aircraft at Royal Danish Air Force Air Days in 1966.[26]

Of course there were many other lesser-known pilots working hard to show off their wares to the world. One of these was a particularly engaging character. I'm sad that I cannot now recall his name but he was a small, middle-aged Australian flying a small, boxy twin-turboprop transport aircraft with a STOL capability. The aeroplane was called the GAF Nomad and our Aussie test pilot managed a spirited but limited display every day. Each morning the pilots would arrive from their hotels, hopefully in time for the daily briefing, despite having to battle with the crowds making their way to Farnborough for the air show. On his first morning the Nomad pilot arrived and announced to us all: 'The hotel I'm staying at doesn't have coffee-making facilities in the room. I can't get going without caffeine so I had to throw myself down the stairs to bump-start me heart!'

In 1976 I had also managed to fly, under close supervision of course, the DHC Buffalo STOL transporter and the Italian Sia-Marchetti SF 260 trainer. Chalk and cheese!

And it all happened again two years later in 1978 – only some of the aircraft and faces changed. It was during that show that I met a very affable member of the press: Peter Gilchrist. I am usually very wary of those of the journalistic persuasion – it's a matter of trust and credibility – and at first I was cautious with Peter. However, it soon became apparent that he was passionate about two things: aviation and getting his facts right. On top of that he was very good company. Our friendship blossomed and over the next couple of years we produced several articles for *Aircraft Illustrated* aviation magazine based on my assessment of several, usually historic, aircraft types. These included the Blackburn B-2, the Boeing B-17, the North American Harvard

26 See *A Bucket of Sunshine* by this author, published by The History Press, 2012.

and the DHC Dash 8. I wrote the first draft then Peter, having taken the photographs, worked his journalistic magic to make it all a bit more readable!

One fine summer's day a small brown biplane was towed out of A Hangar to an area of grass on the south side of the main runway. I recognised it as an SE5a First World War British fighter; designed and built right here in the 'Factory' sixty years earlier. The story of this genuine article's restoration can wait for another day. But here it was about to be tested after repairs to its undercarriage following a forced landing over a year ago. Our gallant leader, Gp Capt. Reggie Spiers, was there to do that test flight. Before he boarded the diminutive but purposeful-looking flying machine we were allowed to peer into the cockpit. There was an array of antiquated instruments, copper pipes, brass taps and shiny levers. As the group captain strode up we respectfully stood back as he eased his not inconsiderable person into the tiny cockpit. Not long after the ground crew swung the prop and the six-cylinder Wolseley Viper engine burst into life.

After the usual checks of the engine, involving men holding the tail down, Reggie opened the throttle and bumped off across the grass, lifting into the air after a surprisingly short run. We watched as he flew around over the airfield for about twenty minutes then made an immaculate three-point landing in front of us. He taxied back to where he had started from, eased himself out of the cockpit and strode across to the assembled crowd of jealous test pilots with a large smile on his face.

'I'll tell you something, chaps, fly-by-wire and relaxed stability are nothing new,' were his only words to us as he strode by back to his staff car! I wondered how I might get to fly this wonderful flying machine; after all I had well over 1,000 flying hours on 'taildraggers'. I wrote to the wing commander but was gently turned down. What I didn't know then was that ten years later I would fly many hours in SE5a F904.

In the summer of 1978 my 'Desk Officer', of the RAF's Personnel Management organisation, who looked after postings and appointments, called me. A bit like Baldrick he said that he had a cunning plan for my future. By then I had received a 'blue letter', which was not a sad note that started 'Dear John', but an unperfumed missive on pale blue paper with a crest at the top. This contained the brilliant news that I was to be promoted to squadron leader on the next list. 'So what's the plan?' I asked.

'We're going to send you to a Buccaneer squadron in Germany as a squadron QFI,' the man on the other end answered.

'Are they all squadron leaders now?' I asked. In my squadron and CFS Agents days the squadron QFIs were usually senior flight lieutenants.

'It's a new scheme, Mike,' he replied. 'It's called a Hodgkinson Post.'

Well I'd heard of the disease but not the post. 'What does that mean?'

He then filled me in on another cunning plan thought up by a very senior RAF person called Hodgkinson to get a better turnover of squadron leaders through operational executive appointments.

'So you'll do a short course on the OCU, get your instructor's ticket on the Buccaneer and the Hunter and do one year on the squadron as the QFI; then you should move up into one of the flight commander's slots for the rest of your three-year tour.'

'That sounds absolutely great,' I rejoined. 'When? is the only question I have left.'

'End of the year or so, old boy,' was the response.

'Thanks, have a nice day.'

Wow, I thought, at last I'm getting my wish come true. Back to Germany, even possibly to my old outfit – No. 16 Squadron, now flying Buccaneers at Laarbruch. I was a very happy bunny. Bring it on!

PART 3

RESEARCHING RADAR

24 INTO THE BLACK

Meanwhile I was still walking around Farnborough with two stripes on my uniforms and flying suits; I would not be allowed to put the additional narrow stripe between them, indicating my new rank, until I left there. Even then it would be 'acting' rank until the *London Gazette* published the promotion lists on New Year's Day 1978 – five months hence. I carried on with the usual round of trials and check flights, conversion or refresher training and IRTs on the Canberra, on which I had been the Farnborough specialist for most of my tour. It was an added workload and thus I had effectively filled two flying appointments during my time there – experimental test pilot and Canberra QFI/IRE. I didn't mind at all – it meant that I got more flying!

Over the last year of my time at Farnborough there had been changes of personality in our management and leadership chain: Wg Cdr Ian Strachan had taken over from David Bywater as OC Flying and then Gp Capt. 'Chuck' Charles had replaced Reggie Spiers as COEF. Also my replacement had arrived in August, fresh from doing the test pilots' course *en français* at EPNER, the French test pilots' school based at Istres in the south of France. His name was Nigel Wood and he proved to be a sharp-minded man with great natural flying ability, or as we say in the trade – a fine pair of hands. Nigel would go on to fly as a test pilot at Edwards AFB in California's High Desert and be selected to be the UK's first Space Shuttle astronaut. Sadly his mission was scheduled to be the next after the STS-51L Challenger disaster of 28 January 1986. The RAF reckoned that the thirty-two-month hiatus that followed was too long a pause in Nigel's career, so he came home and never did go into space. That must have been the biggest disappointment that any pilot could bear; I know it would have been for me. Nigel finished his time in the RAF as an Air Commodore at Boscombe Down.

In October my Desk Officer's cunning plan of me going to Buccaneers in RAF Germany totally unravelled. His job was complicated enough but, for us RAF officers serving within MOD(PE), there was another layer of personnel management that could interfere with the RAF's plans! This remit was under the wing of an agreeable chap called Bill Sewell who resided at MOD(PE) HQ in St Giles Court, in central London. It transpired in a phone call from him that the present boss of the RRS, based at RAE Bedford, one Alan Holbourne, was about to move on and be promoted to wing commander. Moreover, the present OC Flying at RAE Bedford, Wg Cdr Hugh Rigg (brother of actress Diana), had decided to retire early, so Alan was going to move across the airfield at Bedford and take up residence in the office of OC Flying there.

What this chain of events had to do with me was carefully and gently explained; I think that Bill knew that I would not be best pleased to not to be returning to the front line. I was now going to replace Alan Holbourne as boss of the RRS. The OC was required to be a test pilot who was qualified on the Buccaneer, Canberra and Hunter. I fitted the bill, as did my end-of-tour date – now 26 November. Do not pass GO – do not collect £200 – do not go to Germany – move directly to Bedford/Thurleigh and report for duty on Monday 27 November 1978! By the end of my three-year tour on EFS I had flown over 900 hours on twenty-three types of aircraft, including four marks of Canberra and three marks of Hunter. My final sortie at Farnborough was an air test in the MRF's Canberra PR3, the first time I had flown that mark.

The only thing that I knew about the Radar Research Squadron was that it did what it said on the tin: the squadron flew aircraft fitted with experimental radar equipment on research and development flight trials. The organisation that provided and managed most of the work of RRS was the Royal Radar and Signals Establishment (RSRE) based at Great Malvern. On my first day on the squadron, now wearing my new rank badges, I quickly discovered that RRS occupied a rather secluded area with three hangars and several buildings to house its aircraft, scientists, aircrew and ground crew. Access was via a road from the main gate at the western side of the airfield and the unit was about 2 miles by this perimeter road from the Control Tower, where my boss OC Flying resided, along with ATC, the Operations Staff and the Met Office. It was here where our day would start, with the 8.30 a.m. daily briefing. Our drive to the squadron after that was shortened by kind permission of the ATC staff, who let us cross the runway for a limited time window after receiving a green light from the local controller in the tower.

Once over there I discovered that my office was huge, modern and well-equipped. It was next to the Squadron Operations (Ops) Room, with a small hatch through which communication could take place. There were various individual offices and a large, comfortable crew room in the rest of the building that the squadron occupied, which was about one quarter of the whole complex; the rest being given over to offices for the Trials Officers and their staff, admin and a conference room or two.

My deputy and the Senior Trials/Ops Officer was another squadron leader, a navigator called Dave Broughton. He was a man with the nav's equivalent of the 'tp' qualification – known to all and sundry as the 'Spec N'. Dave was a real asset, especially to a 'new boy' like me trying out his leadership skills on such a mixed bunch of old hands. Dave was an avuncular guy with a ready sense of humour and a wonderful talent for playing the 'old joanna' – especially his renditions of Scott Joplin ragtime tunes. He was also, like many of us were in the 1970s, into making his own wine. I recall going to a party at Broughton Towers and finding that some of the wine bottles did not just have a date on them but a time as well!

There were a total of seventeen aircrew, including Dave and myself, only one of whom was younger than me! Most of them were Specialist Aircrew and they specialised on 'their' aircraft type. There were some real characters among them.

Perhaps the biggest character of them all was a navigator called Jack Cooke. He was a small, wiry individual who was getting a little long in the tooth. However, he was living proof of the saying 'while age is mandatory, maturity is optional'! Jack was always amusing, although he was sometimes a little difficult to understand as he spoke very quickly with a strong south-western burr. His 'party piece' was to stand on his head, with a drink in one hand, and sing – or at least warble – the song 'I like Java, I Like Tea'; this was more often than not performed at Happy Hours or at Dining-In nights and was always amusing. Then there was the moustachioed 'Captain' Geoff Mannings. He was another man heading towards his retirement date, a Specialist Aircrew squadron leader and the RRS heavy aircraft expert – flying the Nimrod and Viscounts – where he reigned supreme over the flight deck. Geoff was also a campanologist in the village church of Sharnbrook, where the RAF 'Married Patch' was. His heavy-aircraft specialist colleague was a man from the far south-west, Flt Lt John Trout, who also acted as a co-pilot on the Puma and Sea King helicopters. Among the other pilots was the helicopter specialist Andy Digby, Canberra leader Dave Watson (a formidable opponent on the squash court who regularly won the RAF veteran's title); Dave had also qualified on the Hunter. There were others who flew the Canberras, such as an outgoing younger guy called Nick Stillwell. Later on Chris White, Stu Waring and Paddy Clarke would arrive to fly the Canberras, as would my old friends from No. 16 Squadron days, pilot John Sadler (who was also a 'tp') and navigator Trevor Carpenter.

Among the other rear crew were a friendly Scot called Jack Stewart, Mo Hammond (who had followed me from Farnborough), Cliff Ware, Geoff Holt and a tall extrovert called Pete Middlebrook; like Mo Hammond he was qualified on the Buccaneer. There was also an Air Engineer called John Pollock. On first encountering him I thought that he was a bit taciturn and tended toward being a bit of a 'barrack room lawyer'. While there was some truth in this impression, as well as being good at his day job, John was a wizard at organising the squadron in-flight rations and extracting the maximum from the system, quite legally. There was always sufficient 'free' food in the crew room to feed everybody. Cheese on toast was a favourite – that was until the toaster broke. When Dave Watson left RRS he presented the unit with a new toaster. However, it was one of the fold-up type. Paddy Clarke observed loudly that it was no good as the cheese would fall off!

When I took over from Alan Holbourne, who as a wing commander I had now to call 'Sir', RRS had a fleet of eighteen aircraft of eight different types on strength; and what a fleet it was:

- One Nimrod (XV 148 – the 2nd prototype)
- Two Vickers Viscounts
- One Hunter T8M
- One Buccaneer S2B (Special build)
- One Canberra T4
- Nine Canberras of various marks, many of which were highly modified for trials work
- Three helicopters – one Puma, one Wessex and one Sea King

Sadly, the squadron's Meteor NF.11/12 had been pensioned off before I had taken over – I had been looking forward to learning to fly that!

I had made up my mind about three things before I had taken command: firstly, I would not change anything within three months (unless it affected flight safety); secondly, I would learn a lot more about radar and how it worked! I had never used radar before and I had a very basic understanding of its magic properties. However, there were lots of technical terms that meant little or nothing to me and I needed rapidly to learn the jargon and banter and what it all meant technically. Dave Broughton gave me several volumes of his notes from his Specialist Navigator's Course and they provided my bedtime reading for several weeks! I soon could keep up with the boffins when they talked about such things as pulse repetition frequency, or the characteristics of wave-guides, magnetrons and travelling wave tubes. The third thing that I had decided was that I would try to lead from the front, particularly in the air. Leadership is like airmanship: you can only become good at it through experience. Fortunately during my seventeen years in the RAF to date I had seen quite a few examples of both good and bad leadership. I hoped to be able to remember the good bits! What I really didn't want was the guys following me solely out of a sense of curiosity!

I also decided that I would get my feet firmly under my large office table and not rush into the air without getting to know the squadron and scientific staff and watching how the well-oiled RRS machine operated. I was greatly aided in the first of these aims by the combination of East Anglian winter weather and very poor aircraft availability. December was drear and grey with lots of low cloud and freezing winds. January proved little better, especially when a good snowfall arrived and put the airfield out of action for three weeks (there was no snow clearing gear at Bedford – 'not cost effective, old boy' I was told).

The other round of visits I made early in my tour was to the air traffic control and operations staff as well as the other test pilots on the airfield, over the other side in Aerodynamics Flight. One of those was George Ellis, who had been on my ETPS course and had won the Patuxent Shield as the runner-up to the top student. But the first port of call on day one was to our hangar to get to know the civilian ground crew, especially the men in charge. From them I discovered that the 'tradition' of the last landing was to be at 5 p.m. unless a very urgent need was satisfactorily demonstrated to 'management'!

As it happened there were only a few trials sorties each day and then only when the weather allowed. The average number of aircraft available each day was but a fraction of the whole fleet. This, I soon realised, was why the aircrew/airframe ratio was so much lower than it would have been on a similarly sized RAF unit; and why a squadron leader was allowed to be the commanding officer. I soon established a regime in which folk did not have to come to work or stay there if there was absolutely no prospect of them appearing on the flying programme. However, all secondary duties, of which there were a good number, had to be bang up to date and excuses for them not being so would not be tolerated.

Some of the guys arranged extracurricular activities, including a memorable visit using the squadron minibus on snowy roads to the Carlsberg brewery in Northampton. Air Engineer John Pollock, altruistically offered to drive. Several roadside stops were made on the way back to Bedford – much to the relief of many! On some days it was possible to call an 'Early Stack' (service speak for a half-day) via a squadron lunch in the Officers' Mess. On one occasion, when the Met Man had poured cold water, gales and all manner of meteorological curses on flying prospects for the whole day, I walked into the Ops Room and drew a red line through the few planned sorties.

'Get all your ground work up to date and we'll take a squadron lunch. Rendezvous in the bar at noon. First round on me,' I announced. I rang the wing commander to let him know that I intended to stand RRS down for the afternoon.

'Don't blame you,' he said.

About one hour into our beer and sandwiches one of my navs, Jack Stewart, said, 'Boss, look out of the window.' I did so to find the sun splitting the paving stones!

Jack continued, 'The wing commander has rung, sends his compliments and wonders whether you will be launching any aircraft this afternoon.' 'Tell him that you can't find anyone to ask,' I replied. At which point the good wing commander walked through the door with a very large grin. I presented him with an equally large gin!

My first flight in 1979 took place on Friday 2 February, when I took to the air back in the familiar confines of the cockpit of a B6 Canberra. But this was a very historic aeroplane. Its military registration was WK 163. Built in 1954 by A.V. Roe at Woodford, Cheshire as a Canberra B2, WK 163 was taken on charge on 28 January 1955 but was immediately transferred to Armstrong Siddeley Motors Ltd at Bitteswell, Leicestershire for Viper engine trials. On 2 December 1955 it was transferred to Napier and Sons at Luton Airport, becoming a test airframe for the new Double Scorpion rocket motor, which was fitted into the aircraft's bomb bay. WK 163 flew again after these modifications on 20 May 1956.

On 28 August 1957 Mike Randrupp, with Walter Shirley acting as flight observer, flew WK 163 to 70,310ft and took the world altitude record for Great Britain. Whilst at Napier the aircraft also tested the air-sampling equipment that was to be used during the Operation Grapple nuclear tests of 1958. The following year the Scorpion programme was cancelled and WK 163 was passed to RAF Pershore in Worcestershire. In April 1966 WK 163 was converted to B6 specification by replacing the wings and engines.

In those first two months I had got to know many of the scientific civil servants and company boffins that we worked with and for. The co-location of everyone involved was a real bonus. At Farnborough it was a 'taxi' ride to see any of our boffins and even to get to some of our aircraft. All that added time and distance to our relationships and schedules. Here in this self-contained and remote location everything was but a short walk away. Security, which was paramount for much of our work, was easy to achieve and retain and there was the opportunity to build good working relationships at all levels.

I had bought a house in the village of Harrold, about 5 miles west of RAE Bedford's main gate, and had moved in during that 'winter of discontent', with significant amounts of snow on the ground and a lorry driver's strike threatened. One oddity of the sale is that it included a motorcycle. When I had looked round the house with the lady owner I had spotted a tarpaulin-covered object in the garage.

'What's that?' I enquired.

'Oh, it's my son's motorbike. He was meant to finish rebuilding it before he went to university. He seems to have lost interest.'

As a motorcycling enthusiast, who hadn't owned one for a good few years, I said, 'Well if you leave it right there I'll dispose of it for you.' She seemed pleased with this offer; how she would square it with No. 1 son I couldn't imagine. But that was not my problem. It didn't take much to finish rebuilding the 650cc Triumph Thunderbird and come the spring I was commuting to work on it every day!

We on RRS were the nearest thing that the UK had to a 'black' outfit and perhaps in a tacit recognition of that our collective radio callsign was Blackbox. Uniquely we did not have personal numbers to identify each pilot but letters. I was to be Blackbox Bravo – B for Brooke, B for Biker and B for Boss!

25 A UNIQUE FLYING MACHINE

There was only one Buccaneer on the strength of RRS. It was the fifth from last to roll off the production line at the BAe factory at Brough, East Yorkshire, which it did in March 1976. Its tail number was XX 897 and, after its first post-production test flight at HOSM, it was delivered to RRS at Pershore on 21 April that year. Then this almost brand new flying machine was put on jacks and underwent an extensive set of modifications so that the Marconi AI.24 Foxhunter radar, destined for the Air Defence Variant (ADV) of the Tornado, could be installed at a later date. The airframe mods included mating the large ADV radome to the nose, which entailed building a special adapter ring and fairings behind the radome on each side of the nose, removing the in-flight refuelling probe, removing the bomb door tank and the wing-fold mechanism.

Then on 9 December 1977 XX 897 was flown to Bedford for the experimental systems to be installed, which included modifications to the front cockpit to allow the pilot to operate and navigate the aircraft autonomously. Civilian FTOs, who would be primarily occupied with trials work on the radar, would occupy the back seat, where the navigator usually sat. A Decca Navigator roller map was installed in front of the pilot, above the flight instrument panel, and the IFF control box was moved from the back cockpit to the front. Finally the A model (pre-production prototype) of the Foxhunter radar was fitted in the nose and all the power, control and test equipment was fitted into the rear cockpit and bomb bay. One important modification was to the fuel system, which was modified so that fuel could circulate through a cooling matrix to absorb the heat from the radar and its systems.

Another eight months went by before 897 broke the surly bonds of earth again, when it went back to BAe at HOSM for post-modification flight clearance, after which it flew back to Bedford, landing back just in time for Happy Hour on Friday 15 September 1978.

I had first set eyes on this sleek version of Mr Blackburn's 'Banana Bomber' on my first day on RRS. She was finished in the two-tone grey and white FAA colour scheme and stood resplendent in the hangar with a few panels open or missing, but no personnel activity anywhere nearby. This would prove to be the case on most days. Once we had got a decent amount of flying activity I went to see the trials folk to find out at what stage the programme was and when I might get my hands on the beast. I then managed to spend some time in the cockpit and received lessons as to how to operate the rather odd navigation system.

I also met the two Marconi FTOs: Messrs Pete Batty and Terry Fletcher. The Marconi Company, along with the other civilian radar manufacturer Ferranti, had offices and laboratories nearby, in a four-storey tower block on the northern edge of the establishment, known as Galsey Wood. The building was notable in that its upper levels had radomes sticking out of the walls pointing east. These were used for research, often in conjunction with our flight trials. The main Marconi Avionics offices were not too far away, in the 'new' town of Milton Keynes, famous for its concrete cows and multiple roundabouts.

I was due to fly my first two sorties in 897 in mid March so I went to the Buccaneer OCU at RAF Honington, along with one of the RRS navigators, Flt Lt Pete Middlebrook, and FTO Terry Fletcher to 'fly' the simulator and go through all the normal and emergency drills and procedures. It was now over three months since I had flown a Buccaneer, so we 'borrowed' one of the Farnborough jets, XW 988, and I flew three training sorties on 1 and 2 March, two with Pete and one with Terry. It was then just a case of waiting for 897 to be made ready for its first flight, which would be a full shakedown and handling assessment as well as tests of all the on-board systems.

On Wednesday 21 March the news filtered through that Marconi were ready to go; the airframe and engines had been ready for ages! But such is the nature of flight trials. On the following day Buccaneer XX 897 got more than just a few inches off the ground for the first time in over five months. When I had signed the aircraft servicing document – Form 700 – I had been intrigued to note that 897 had logged just over eight hours since it had rolled off the production line; it was definitely the 'youngest' aeroplane that I had ever flown! It even smelled new. As expected it was much slicker than the standard Buccaneer; it was lighter and had that longer, more streamlined profile. Indeed, when I did an acceleration at around 36,000ft I had to throttle back at 0.98 Mach – I didn't want to go supersonic over Lincolnshire! The nice thing was that even at that speed there were no adverse handling problems. Pete Middlebrook was equally impressed. At the other end of the speed range I managed to slow down to just 110kt without the aircraft tending to do anything frightening. This was well below the minimum speed at which any future flying would be done. Overall there was nothing untoward and she handled much like any other Buccaneer.

At this stage the aircraft did not have the pre-production model of the Foxhunter radar installed; there was a big weight in the nose instead. The A model was due to get airborne later in the year. The Foxhunter was an advanced radar that was digitally controlled. Marconi had subcontracted the provision of the heart of the radar, its transmitter/receiver, to their rivals Ferranti. This bit was of the Travelling Wave Tube design, which gave all sorts of advantages over the older magnetron and klystron signal generators. The requirement for the production model included an ability to track multiple targets while looking for more (known as Track While Scan or TWS) and an anti-jamming capability. During the trials to come we would be testing all these areas of interest, as well as gleaning general performance data.

After this promising start we flew four trials sorties then 897 was grounded for the installation of the definitive radar and all its associated equipment. This took over six months culminating in several hours spent sitting on the ground with the engines running and Pete Batty or Terry Fletcher playing with the radar. To do this without hazarding anyone with the transmissions we had an area on the airfield to which I could taxi the aircraft and point the nose across open fields with no habitation in sight. The digitisation of the system was such that even the signal to the moveable phased-array antenna in the nose to tell it to leave its parked position and then scan left to right and tilt up or down was all done by noughts and ones. When the FTOs did start the radar scanning I could feel the aircraft react by swaying rhythmically left and right. The radar unit in the nose would spend a lot of its time being taken in and out of the aircraft and moved back and forth to the Galsey Wood lab for tweaking – a technical term I believe!

I was informed that the sleek machine would be ready to fly in December. Because it had been grounded for so long the ground crew and I decided that we should carry out a full engine and airframe test flight. I did two such sorties on 17 and 18 December with an old navigator mate who had moved to Bedford from the Weapons Flight at Farnborough, Flt Lt Mo Hammond.

We were now coming close to getting the whole kit and caboodle airborne – we should have been – it had taken a whole year to get this far! I flew one more sortie in January 1980 and was assured that there were only minor tweaks to do to the radar.

Then something devastating happened. Not so much for us directly, but primarily for one crew, their families and friends and the squadron they served on. A No. 15 Squadron Buccaneer from RAF Laarbruch on a Red Flag exercise in Nevada, USA, had crashed on the Nellis Ranges during a manoeuvre that caused the catastrophic failure of the starboard wing. I learnt later that the pilot, who was killed, was Flt Lt Ken Tait, whom I had known at CFS, although not well. A tragic irony was that he was probably flying one of his last sorties in the RAF. The immediate upshot was a Board of Inquiry.

Subsequent investigation found that a fatigue crack in the front spar caused the wing to fail, as it was unable to withstand the loading experienced during the turn, which turned out to be frighteningly low. I think that it was just the last straw. As a result, the entire Buccaneer fleet was grounded until all had been inspected and a solution to the problem had been found.

One day, a week or so later, I went to look at my personal aeroplane, grounded yet again, and found a man in blue overalls drilling a hole into the lower surface of the wing! Horrified, I enquired as to what he was doing. 'Looking to see if there's any cracks in the same place as on the crashed aircraft,' he replied nonchalantly, with that unsaid question, *and who do you think you are?*

'This jet's still got less than twenty hours in its logbook. If you want to find evidence of fatigue cracks you should examine around the jacking points. It's spent years airborne like that!' I said. He didn't see the irony.

The upshot was that we now had a radar ostensibly ready to start flight trials, but with no aeroplane to take it into the air. My theory was that the RAF had not adapted their use of the Buccaneer from the FAA's modus operandi. I had come to this opinion when I had first flown the aircraft during the Preview exercise at ETPS. There was no need to land on 9,000ft runways as if they were aircraft carrier decks with all the concomitant vertical velocity. With less flap and droop, especially in the unblown configuration (45/10/10), a landing with less impact was achievable. Neither was there any need to taxi for miles with the wings folded, so redistributing the weight and concentrating it on the wing fold line. In fact the only advantage to having the wings folded came when parking in a Hardened Aircraft Shelter, when two aeroplanes could be housed in each one. XX 897 didn't have a wing-fold mechanism and I never used the fully blown configuration (45/25/25) on the 10,000ft runway at Bedford. The selection of 30/20/20, with the blow on, gave the best compromise. The landing speed was only 3kt higher and if an engine failed the aircraft was already in the correct configuration.

It would be a frustrating three months before Terry Fletcher and I would get 897 off the ground again; and that was in very special circumstances. Ken Tait's accident had led to a gross over-reaction at the MOD. There was a fear abroad that all Buccaneers' wings were going to fall off at the first occasion that they produced lift. Admittedly many of the aircraft inspected had the minor manufacturing fault, caused during the milling of the wing panels, which could have been the root source of a fatigue crack. Even 897 had shown that slight defect but, of course, no crack was detected using the usual Non-Destructive Testing (NDT) methods. The engineers at Strike Command and BAe worked on a solution that would involve drilling into the suspect area and blending out the defect. Any cracks detected would have to be either repaired or the wings scrapped. With the whole Buccaneer fleet to inspect it would take some time.

The Buccaneer squadrons in the UK and Germany and the OCU were declared non-effective. To keep the crews current Hunters were reallocated from other units to add to the few already established at each station for training and IRTs. In February 1980 no one knew how long the grounding would last, or even whether the Buccaneer force would ever return to an operational status.

Back at Bedford the inability to proceed with the Foxhunter trials, just when the radar was ready to go, was an enormous source of frustration. The Project Office in London was equally miffed. The days grew into weeks and the weeks into months. I kept pointing out to all and sundry that XX 897 was fine. There were no cracks. The preventative smoothing modification had been done. Moreover the aircraft had been used to test other potential areas of interest and nothing untoward had been discovered. Through contact with Don Headley, the BAe Buccaneer CTP at HOSM, I had discovered that the company were working hand-in-glove with all the essential engineering agencies.

I do not know who forced the issue, but I suspect it was those driving the Tornado ADV project. After all this was an independent move by the UK to develop the Tornado into the MRCA it was always supposed to be, so there was a lot of high-level national kudos riding on its success. An air defence fighter without a radar was as useful as a chocolate teapot!

In early April I was given the news that it might be possible that I would be given clearance to fly 897 ahead of any other announcement about the future of the Buccaneer. This had come from the ivory towers in London to COEF at Farnborough, Gp Capt. Chuck Charles, who had passed the news on to me via Alan Holbourne. The trials folk started making preparations in the second week of April. At the end of that week I was told that authorisation to fly 897 was forthcoming and that I should arrange for simulator training with the Buccaneer OCU at Honington. Terry Fletcher and I flew over there in Canberra B2/6 WK 163 on Monday 21st and 'flew' three hours going through every possible emergency that the staff could dream up. Perhaps with the exception of a wing coming off! I then got hold of Hunter T8C XF 321 from Farnborough and flew three sorties to get myself back up to fast-jet speed. On Thursday afternoon I was informed that 'ministerial approval' had been given for COEF to authorise a flight in 897 the following day – Friday 25 April 1980. I was then briefed on the restrictions for this first flight. They were:

- Indicated airspeed not to exceed 300kt
- G to not exceed 3
- No flying below 3,000ft except to make an approach to land
- Only one landing

Overnight I thought of one variation I wanted to make and put it to OC Flying after the morning briefing.

'Sir, could you ask COEF if I could make an approach, to go around of course, at RAF Honington? I think it would be great for their morale to see that at least one Buccaneer is flying again.'

'OK, I'll see what I can do,' he replied.

The authorisation sheet, signed by Gp Capt. Charles, was to be flown up to Bedford on the lunchtime ferry and I would have to go over to the control tower to initial it. When I did so I got the approval for the approach at Honington, but I was told not to come below 1,000ft. I was also reminded that I was, at least for now, the only current Buccaneer pilot in the world. No pressure then!

Terry and I climbed aboard and I went through the start-up procedures. Then we taxied out and paused on our way to the end of runway 27 for Terry to wind up the radar. When he was satisfied we took smoothly to the air. I think that 897 was as eager as we were to get air under her wings again. I climbed to the east at 300kt and we levelled off at 25,000ft.

'How's the radar doing?' I enquired.

'Well, whatever else we've achieved it's a good ground-mapping radar!' replied my friendly back-seat boffin. I detected more than a little irony in his voice.

'Right, I'm now going to select more power and the fuel cooling system should kick in,' announced Terry.

'OK.'

About thirty seconds later I noticed both HP rpm gauges starting to wind down, rapidly followed by the LP rpms. After they had dropped by about 10 per cent I asked Terry to switch the radar power off. As soon as he did so the engines recovered. My adrenalin level also returned to normal. Having both motors suddenly start winding down is not conducive to the relaxed calm that one always preferred to display during flight tests! There was obviously a problem with the fuel pressure drop caused by the fuel being sent to the cooler; it would have to be investigated further.

So we now set off towards RAF Honington in Suffolk. When we were handed over to the Honington Approach Controller he immediately asked me to confirm that we were a Buccaneer.

'Affirmative,' I replied. 'There'll be a lot of folk out to watch you,' the controller said.

'Well tell them that we're not allowed to come below 1,000ft. Sorry but that's from way on high!' I told him, with intentional sarcasm.

The approach went boringly well and as I flew down the runway at that 1,000ft I could see a host of upturned faces outside the hangars and offices on my right. I thought that they would probably be thinking that it was all a bit sissy. I hoped that it gave them a boost to know that at least one of their favourite aeroplanes was back in the air!

The fuel-cooling problem was fixed, the newer A2 model of the radar started working better and by June we had tracked quite a few targets. Around this time the Marconi trials management decided to have a bit of a 'launch' day. The day before this grand event Pete Batty and I went out in 897 to the ground test area to make sure that all was well. It was and Pete told the team that everything should be fine for the following day. I organised one of our Canberras to be a target and we briefed for the flight. This would include a return to base in formation with the Canberra leading and a flypast over the squadron. Hopefully we would have some good results to show the assembly of the great and the good from MOD and Marconi.

The big day dawned fine and the sortie would take place after a no doubt splendid lunch for our 'audience'. I had my usual sandwich in the crew room! Pete and I climbed aboard on time and the Canberra crew manned their aircraft to await our call to go. As usual we taxied out to test the radar on the ground. After a minute or so Pete told me that he was starting the scanner. Then he told me that it was transmitting.

'Pete,' I said, 'I can't feel the aircraft moving. Are you sure it's scanning?'

'Yes. But I must admit I'm getting a rather odd picture,' he replied.

'Well, there's definitely not the usual swaying motion,' I said.

'OK, we'd better go back in and find out what's going on.'

I told ATC and the Canberra crew to sit tight as we had a problem. When we arrived back in our parking spot, still being watched by the gathered dignitaries, the Marconi Field Trials Manager (FTM) came over in a bit of a panic. I shut down the engines and asked for ground power so that we could keep the kit going. Ladders were affixed to their normal fasteners on the starboard side of the cockpit. A long conversation between Pete and the FTM ensued. Then the nose was opened and the radar antenna exposed. Apparently when Pete selected 'scan' (with the transmitter off) instead of coming out of its parked position and scanning left to right it scanned up and down!

It was decided that nothing could be done. But the FTM, having arranged the event, was desperate to save face. He climbed up my ladder and leaned into the cockpit. He asked in all seriousness, 'Can you fly behind the target on your side so that the antenna then looks as if it is scanning horizontally?'

I disabused him of such an outrageous and impractical course of action. In the end we decided that it would be more expeditious to get the radar fixed than waste time in the air pretending that all was well. Welcome to the world of R&D!

It turned out that after our checks of the previous day someone (FTM perhaps?) had decided to demount the radar unit from the nose and 'tweak' it some more. It was replaced and some bit or other had gone wrong. When will people ever learn that if it's not broke – don't fiddle with it?!

We flew much more regularly during the rest of 1980 and started to work with multiple targets as well as against the ECM Canberras of No. 360 Squadron. Results were variable, as is par for the course. By August I knew that I was moving on at the end of the year and that we would soon need a Buccaneer-qualified pilot to take over the project. As it happened ex-Buccaneer squadron pilot Flt Lt Trevor Brown had arrived as a test pilot on Aero Flight. So, after management had agreed, I flew with him in 897 to refamiliarise him with the Banana Bomber and this rather odd one in particular. He then did a session in the simulator at Honington and some flights in one of the Farnborough Buccaneers.

My last flight in 897 was on 1 November 1980 with Pete Batty. Earlier in the year one of our sorties had included a session of air-to-air photography and on leaving the squadron I was presented with a framed copy. Nimrod pilot Flt Lt John Trout had also procured (I know not whence) a pair of Buccaneer throttles and had them mounted on a wooden plinth. The words 'The RRS Throttle Benders Trophy' were inscribed on a brass plate; probably a reference to the occasional low, fast pass I had made over the squadron in XX 897.

Subsequent development of the Foxhunter radar followed in the stuttering footsteps of 1979 and 1980. Lots of technical problems arose and the Tornado ADV production line and entry to RAF service got way ahead of its radar. The first ADVs had to fly with weights in the nose and pretend to be interceptor fighters. As usual it wasn't my remit to have an official opinion on it all, but I could not help wondering why the procurement system had given the project leadership to a company that had never produced a radar before.

Perhaps Ferranti, who had made Britain's previous Air Interceptor radar for the Lightning, should have been the lead company, not just to produce the heart of the system, but to have driven the development of the rest. However, ours not to reason why!

26 WHIRLYBIRDS ARE GO!

When I had taken over RRS I realised that there were three items on the squadron's fleet about which I knew very little – the helicopters. Not long after I had arrived one of the two professional Rotary Wing pilots and the Puma helicopter were taken off the RRS strength. I now had just one specialist 'rotarian' – Flt Lt Andy Digby – but two helicopters: a Sea King and a Wessex. I discovered that there was no plan to send me a second helicopter pilot. This would mean that the trials involving those two aircraft were going to be subject to more delays due to Andy's leave, sickness and any requirement for both aircraft to fly at the same time. Like Baldrick in the TV series *Blackadder* I came up with a cunning plan, which I put back up the line to HQ. I suggested that if I learnt to fly helicopters and then took over as prime pilot for the Wessex trials we would keep a whole host of boffins happy. Within a few days I received the news that at the end of April 1979 I would go to RAF Shawbury, in Shropshire, to complete a special one-month, high intensity course on the Westland Whirlwind HAR[27] Mk 10.

So on the last Sunday of April I drove from home to Shawbury and took up residence in the Officers' Mess. At 8 a.m. the following morning I reported to the helicopter training squadron and met up with my instructor, a genial young man called Ham Elliott. After joining him in a cup of ambition he took me to the Ground School where I met the redoubtable Flt Lt Lawrence who would give me a rapid, personalised course answering the mystery of how a helicopter got airborne and stayed aloft. My American buddy from the ETPS course, Tom Morgenfeld, had always maintained that helicopters flew only because they were so ugly that the earth rejected them – it wasn't entirely true; although a pretty helicopter is a rare sight!

I rapidly learnt in Ground School that they got up and stayed up because of a big green arrow, always labelled LIFT, which appeared above the helicopter. At least in all the diagrams it did. And that was the easy bit. Then all sorts

27   HAR stands for Helicopter Air Rescue.

of complications came into play. The first being that the natural inclination of the fuselage underneath the whirling blades was to try to rotate in the opposite direction to the blades. This was most undesirable as the poor chap trying to drive would rapidly become dizzy and fall out of his seat! To stop this happening a small rotor was placed at the end of the long tail boom at the back and spun around to produce a small, horizontal green arrow to keep the tail where it belonged.

Then I was introduced to such terms as translational lift, retreating blade stall and lateral cg limits. Finally we moved onto the interesting bits about how the pilot controlled all this whirling machinery above and behind him. The stick was now called the cyclic control and the other lever that was near the pilot's left hand was called the collective. There were also rudder pedals on which to rest one's feet. For a fixed-wing aeroplane driver the stick and rudder pedal bits were reasonably familiar, but the collective was something new. However, the fact that it moved up and down gave a strong clue as to its purpose. It controlled the vertical flight of the helicopter. Next question. Where's the throttle? Well, I was told, there isn't one. The engine automatically adjusts its power output to cope with the pilot's demands. But there was an exception. There always is! If that automatic system broke down there was a twist grip, like a motorbike throttle, on the end of the collective with which the pilot could govern the engine power.

I was given copious notes to read and sent back to the squadron hungry and exhausted. There I found refreshment and Ham Elliott waiting for me. 'Now that you know how it all works, get your flying kit on, we're going aviating in a couple of hours time. I suggest we brief now and then you can spend some time learning your checks on one of the aircraft in the hangar,' he announced. So much for lunch. Grabbing my Whirlwind checklist I headed for the flying clothing room to change and go try on a cockpit for size.

The Westland Whirlwind was a UK-licensed and -built version of an American design from the Sikorsky stable, famous for its helicopters. This model was known as the S-55 Chickasaw (all Sikorsky helicopters being named after Native American tribes) and was originally powered by a fairly large, round Pratt & Whitney piston engine. The Whirlwind was primarily procured for the Royal Navy but then adopted by the RAF for Air Sea Rescue duties. In February 1959 the piston engine was replaced by a de Havilland Gnome free-turbine jet engine, rated at just over 1,000 shaft horsepower (SHP). The rotor diameter was 53ft and the fuselage was just over 44ft long. Like a lot of helicopters of the time it was relatively tall, standing nearly 16ft to the top of the rotor shaft. The really odd thing was that it had four wheels, two large soft main wheels on struts sticking out from under the copious cabin and two small nose wheels mounted under the fuselage immediately below the pilots' cockpit. They were free to castor and looked like something that should have been attached to a large piece of furniture!

It was a bit of a climb up the steps on the side of the nose up to the cockpit where I found myself sitting quite upright with an excellent view of the outside world, except to the left where my instructor was going to be seated. With the checklist on my knee I sat there and worked my way round the cockpit instrument panels, switches and levers and hoped that some of it would sink in.

Eventually Ham came looking for me with the news that our mount was ready and waiting and that I should go and do the checks for real. I had actually been allowed to have a go at flying a helicopter on about five previous occasions, but only the easy bits. Ham now sat patiently while I worked my way through the checks until the engine in the nose was whirring away satisfactorily. Then it was time to engage the rotor and get the blades whirling at a speed sufficient to get us airborne. This was when Ham reminded me that once the blades were rotating then effectively the helicopter was 'flying' so the cyclic stick would need to be restrained in a central position and I was not to move the rudder bar or the collective until we had every intention of getting airborne.

At this point Ham took over and there followed lots of demonstration and 'Follow me through' from he who must now be obeyed. I had a go at flying around and that was no problem. Speed and height were controlled by a combination of the two controls, the engine did its own thing and I just had to keep the tail following the nose with the rudder pedals. As an ex-light aircraft instructor that was second nature.

It was when we came back to the airfield that Ham said, 'Right, let's see if you can hover it,' in a more challenging way than I would have liked. He first put the aircraft into a hover at about 10ft off the ground and talked rapidly about what he was doing, with me following him through by resting my hands and feet lightly on the appropriate controls. I could feel lots of constant tiny movements; it reminded me of the control inputs that happen during formation flying.

'OK, I'm going to give you control of the collective. You just keep us at this height,' he said. That proved to be not too hard.

'Now you have control of the rudder pedals as well, just keep us pointed in this direction.'

The response to any small movement was quite rapid but I tried very hard to be smooth. But now the height had wandered a bit and every time I moved the collective lever up or down the wretched machine turned around its vertical axis so I had to readjust the pedals.

'OK, so far not too bad,' he said, with little praise in his voice. 'You have control of everything.'

He was lying of course. As soon as he let go of the stick everything went to pot. He had been hovering over a point, within seconds I was using a very large, and expanding cube of sky. It was like spinning plates on sticks. Just when you thought you'd got one thing sorted something else went bad!

'Fine, that's enough, sir,' Ham said. Then by way of encouragement, 'Don't worry, sir, you'll soon pick it up.'

I retired early that night with my Whirlwind Pilot's Notes and checklists and tried to get my head round it all. There followed a month's intensive flying with a variety of instructors including the American and French exchange instructors. They were all very helpful but drove me on to make sure that I was soon fit to go off on my own. A memorable bit was the first time I finally nailed the hovering and then was asked to move to another part of the airfield for another exercise. I sat there for a few seconds totally unable to remember what to do next. *If I push the stick forward we'll spear into the ground*, I thought, *and if I pull the collective up I'll climb!* My fixed-wing instincts had kicked in and what I really wanted to do was hold the attitude and push the throttle forward. But there wasn't one. All this happened in at most ten seconds, but the pause was long enough to prompt my man to ask what the problem was. This coincided with me remembering that I had to move the stick forward and stop us going down with a small upwards movement of the collective lever. I did that and sure enough off we went.

'Stop' came the response from the left seat. *What now?*

'You forgot to turn on the spot to look out all around you,' came the admonition. *Oh, yes.*

Over that very busy month I learnt how to land on sloping ground, which can be tricky and if you get it wrong you can end up with the helicopter and all who sail in her being hurled sideways onto the ground. One day we went to Snowdonia in North Wales to learn about flying in mountains, where dangerous, curling down-currents of air present very specific threats and how flying in valleys and bowls with no horizon can trick you into false and dangerous flight attitudes. But the best bit was making approaches and landings on a very narrow ridge with steep, vertiginous drops on either side. On top of all this I had to navigate us successfully to and from RAF Valley where we had stopped to refuel. That sounds easy but it was a long time since I had flown at 90kt and, being much more used to four or five times that speed, I was constantly getting ahead of myself!

Then there were landings in clearings. There were a few holes carved into the Shropshire woodland that the training school used for imparting this skill. They culminated in one that was only just big enough for the Whirlwind's rotor disc to go into and also had the tallest trees. However, once the right procedures had been learnt and applied it turned out to be fun, albeit challenging fun, and a bit tense as the trees came up around you. But, without doubt the most challenging exercises, that never seemed to get easier with practice, were engine-off landings. These were the helicopter pilot's version of glide approaches in single-engined aeroplanes. However, in a fixed-wing aircraft the engine was just throttled back and so was always available should the practice go horribly wrong. But the steely-eyed rotarians did not have that fallback position. Once the descent to land had been started and the helicopter was in what is known as autorotative flight, the engine is pulled back to idle and declutched from the rotors. Thus there was no longer any possibility of re-engaging the power to the rotor blades until the landing had been made and the helicopter was stationary on the ground. That really puts you on your mettle!

I only did one instrument flying trip and no night flying but by the end of May I felt sufficiently well trained to be able to go back and start converting to the Wessex. I had many enduring memories of this new form of flying. But one that abides happened on a solo flight when I was briefed to land in one of the many field sites that Shawbury used by arrangement with the local agricultural community. I navigated my way there successfully and then carried out the approved procedures to establish a safe approach to land. The ground looked firm and I set down. During a pause to take in the fact that I had just intentionally landed in a farmer's field I looked around. Close by and completely undisturbed by this strange machine that had arrived from the sky was a herd of black and white cows, contentedly grazing the lush green grass. Ahead of me was a row of tall poplar trees and, with the wind coming from that direction, I had to take-off over them. There is a specific technique for this eventuality, called a towering take-off, so I applied the power and lifted vertically until I could see over the trees and accelerate forwards into the clear air beyond. There is a lot of truth in the saying that it makes much more sense to stop first and then land rather than using acres of concrete to do it the other way round! Based on my experience at Shawbury helicopter flying was going to be stimulating and enjoyable. I was looking forward to expanding my horizons in this very specific and special from of aviation.

When I returned to Bedford I flew with Andy Digby in the Wessex whenever it was possible. He took me for my first tour of London by air and taught me how to use the Helilanes. These are air routes for helicopters that criss-cross the capital to allow access to various helipads in the city and so fly safely below all the airliners using Heathrow. After about seven hours of flying under his watchful eye, Andy declared me ready for a proper helicopter instructor to check me out. So Lt Thomas RN was wheeled out from Farnborough and he put me through my paces, including quite a few emergency drills and engine-off landings. After two sorties he declared me fit to fly the Wessex on my own – so I did.

Over the next sixteen months I would fly about fifty hours in that old Wessex; I use the term old because it was one of the very early models – a Mark 1, tail number XM 926. The Westland Wessex was a UK-licensed built version of the Sikorsky S-58 'Choctaw'. It was powered by a single Napier Gazelle turboshaft jet engine that developed about 1,600shp and had a payload of about 1 ton. The RRS Wessex had originally been with the Royal Navy in the anti-submarine role, but when the Wessex was upgraded to have two engines – a much safer set-up for hovering over the sea – XM 926 was acquired by MOD(PE). At the time I was flying 926 its role was in the R&D of a radar that had its aerial in one of the rotor blades. The lead company for this was Ferranti who had developed the most difficult part of the system: a very clever waveguide that could transfer the radar signal from the rotating blade down the rotor shaft, then via the signal processor onto the screens, of which there were two. One was in the cabin, for the boffins to watch and control, and another was let into the right side of the pilots' instrument panel.

Getting the Wessex going was much like the Whirlwind, except that the engine was started by an AVPIN-powered starter turbine, just like I had used on the Canberra PR9, Hunter F6 and the Lightning. Once the rotor had been coupled to the engine then all the principles of flying a helicopter came into play. The Wessex had a tailwheel rather than the rather odd four-wheel layout of the Whirlwind, which made smooth landings easier. The extra power was very noticeable and I quickly felt at home.

The Rotor Blade Radar (RBR) trials were very interesting. The detail that can be seen on a radar screen is directly proportional to the length of the aerial. As the aerial was about 4m long then the detail that could be seen on the screen was amazing. For instance when we flew past the grass airfield at Henlow the runways could easily be picked out because the grass on them was several inches shorter. No other airborne radar of the day could have seen that. The scale on the screen could be changed from half a mile across out to over 20 miles. At the lower scale settings fences, power lines and even individual trees could be discerned.

One of the applications being researched was the use of the radar as a piloting aid for bad weather approaches to helipads in cities and on oil rigs. This led to some very interesting and absorbing flights from Bedford, down to the Thames at Greenwich and then up as far as Battersea, where we made approaches to the heliport there. There are rules about flying up and down the Thames in central London. It was to be done at about 1,000ft, or as directed by the Heathrow Radar controller, and always following the right bank. If the engine failed I had to aim to put the aircraft down as close to the right bank as possible. When the tide was out then dry land might be available but it would usually mean landing in the water. We did occasionally get clearance, for our trials purposes, to fly at or below 500ft. This meant that once we had passed Big Ben, going upstream, then I could look into the offices of the top floors of the 400ft-tall Millbank Tower; every now and then there would be pale faces looking out at me! On most of these flights I flew with my head down, using only the radar, and as we got close to Battersea heliport I would have the scale reduced so that I could make an approach right to the edge of the platform that stuck out into the river. I would look up as the radio altimeter indicated 20ft and complete the landing. Of course I always had someone in the right-hand seat to tell me if anything was going awry – it never did. This kit was a great breakthrough for poor weather helicopter flying.

The trials progressed with some amazing results for HT wire avoidance, poor weather field operations and Search and Rescue (SAR) survivor location in rough seas. But the best bit was yet to come. During a lay-up a fixed radar had been installed in the nose of XM 926. This scanned ahead of the helicopter and digital processing of its returns allowed the radar picture to become colour-coded: green for terrain ahead that was below the aircraft's present altitude and red for any terrain above it. After initial shakedown flights we went off to North Wales to fly in the mountains to see whether we could fly through valleys safely without looking out. Indeed we could; interpretation of the picture in the cockpit was instinctive and with close monitoring from the occupant of the right-hand seat, who had the map, we were able to navigate our way successfully, at 100ft above the ground, through a lot of the most mountainous parts of the Snowdonia National Park and surrounding lumpy bits. That is until we were following a road up a hillside to get over a pass into the next valley. I was head-down when Jack Cooke in the right-hand seat warned me that we were about to go into cloud. As we were not supposed to rely on this magic kit to actually keep us out of trouble (a basic principle of experimental flying) I looked up. Sure enough the world was turning light grey as the hillside climbed into the stratus cloud. I slowed right down so that I could hover-taxi, that is fly low and slow, and try to make it over the pass following the road visually. There were no obstacles ahead, only a line of telephone posts and cables off to my left. The radar picture was showing green ahead. The visibility reduced a bit more, Jack said that it was only a few hundred yards to the top and then I noticed a car ahead of me.

Great, I thought, *I'll just follow him.* I then decided to put the landing light on. This was below the nose and could be extended with a switch on the collective, so I moved it to shine at the back of the car. A few seconds later he took off like a scalded rabbit, disappearing rapidly into the mist.

Blast! I'd better turn round and go back. I gently swung round to the right and followed the hillside back into clear air below the cloud. It then struck me that maybe the driver of the car had seen the film *Close Encounters of the*

Third Kind and when he had spotted this bright light above and behind him he wasn't going to hang around for an explanation. So if you were the driver – I apologise!

In early 1980 I received the news that the BBC TV programme *Tomorrow's World* wanted to do a piece on the RBR. This culminated on 18 and 19 March in filming sessions with presenter Michael Rodd at Bedford and then on April Fools' Day flying to and from Battersea. From the heliport there we flew a sortie down the river and back with various cameras taped to an undercarriage leg and around the cockpit. We had three of the programme's staff on board as well as Ferranti FTE Stu Lazenby. I did another head-down approach to Battersea Heliport and landed back on to finish the whole shoot off. Our day and a half's work ended up as a six-minute slot on the programme later that year. That was the last flight of Wessex Mk 1 XM 926; age had overtaken this last example of the earliest of the Wessex line. Sadly the RBR never received further funding for installation in another helicopter.

Despite its huge potential and successful trials the RBR was never adopted by any helicopter operators, civil or military. It was probably too expensive. However, I found that helicopter flying is definitely fun. Whirlybirds ARE go!

27 VARIETY IS THE SPICE OF LIFE

There were a whole host of other trials to keep us busy. The Nimrod was the vehicle for the further development of the Searchwater radar that the operational Nimrods used. The drive was to develop a reliable automatic recognition system using the cross-section of any maritime target. Most of this work had been done on one of the Viscounts – more of them later. Nimrod XV 148 was the second prototype and the first one that flew with the R-R Spey engines; the first Nimrod prototype, XV 147, had retained the original R-R Avons of the Comet airliner, from which the Nimrod had been derived. The crew of the RRS Nimrod was two pilots, one navigator, an engineer and whatever complement of radar operators and FTOs were required for the particular trial.

Still being firmly in the Cold War, one of the items on which we received a classified daily briefing were the positions of any Soviet vessels, particularly the so-called 'trawlers' that bristled with aerials and antennae. A lot of our equipment was at a very early stage of development and we did not want the 'other side' to gain knowledge of their characteristics any sooner than we could help it. On one hand this often restricted where we could fly or in which direction we could transmit. However, for building up the radar image library for the advanced version of Searchwater this intelligence helped the Viscount crew in their hunt for 'Red Funnel' shipping. The aircraft would try to get radar signatures and photographs as clandestinely as possible.

The two Viscounts were an unusual part of the MOD(PE) fleet, but not unique to RRS. ETPS had operated one for many years as had B Squadron at Boscombe Down. The two RRS Viscounts had come on to the books in the mid 1960s. They were both 800 Series aircraft and had interesting histories. The maritime radar research platform, XT 575, was first flown from the Vickers factory at Weybridge in Surrey on Wednesday 17 February 1961, with the maker's construction number of 438. It then spent three years based in Austria as a commercial airliner before joining the RRE's fleet in 1964. The other Viscount, XT 661, had constructor's number 371 and its first flight was on Wednesday 3 September 1961. The aircraft was bought by Ghana Airways and operated in Africa until 1965 when it joined XT 575 at Pershore. By the time I arrived this Viscount was involved in various sensor trials that were highly classified and involved low-level flight by day and by night.

I only flew the Viscounts a few times, always as co-pilot, just to get a feel for the aircraft as well as the trials. It was a unique opportunity to fly this British aviation success story, the first turboprop airliner that sold in its hundreds all over the world. Flying the Viscount at low altitude was a bit of a challenge. The view from the flight deck wasn't great and rolling the aircraft into and out of turns required a good degree of strength.

I flew the Nimrod a few times, again as co-pilot, although I had been checked out and signed up as first pilot on Farnborough's Comet before arriving at Bedford. I had no desire to move either Geoff Manning or John Trout out of the captain's seat. The Nimrod flew very much like the Comet, but it had much more thrust available. I don't mind admitting that I had been quite disappointed with some handling characteristics of the Comet. It had very strong static longitudinal stability, which meant a lot of push and pull force required to change attitude and airspeed, followed by a lot of work on the trim wheel to remove the forces on the control yoke. Levelling off at 1,000ft in the circuit called for quite a lot of anticipation. On the other hand the longitudinal dynamic stability seemed quite low and this mismatch could lead to the aircraft wandering off altitude if the trim wasn't exact. However, once you got used to it and knew what to expect the classic smoothness of Britain's first commercial jet airliner won me over.

I remember two Nimrod events from those days. The first happened in the south-west approaches when we were flying very close to the cloudbase of a large cumulonimbus cloud. I just happened to be looking out of the window straight ahead when I saw a bolt of bright, white lightning come out of the cloud and strike the Nimrod's nose. It is not rare to get hit by lightning, but it's not often that you see it coming!

The second occasion was when we had to take the aeroplane to RAF Kinloss, in northern Scotland, for a second-line servicing. To do this required just four of us. Geoff was once more captain, I was co-pilot, Dickie Doherty was the navigator and John Pollock was the Air Engineer. Geoff generously let me fly the sortie and as we were handed off to Kinloss Approach from Highland Radar Geoff transmitted:

'Kinloss Approach, good afternoon Blackbox Mike a Nimrod inbound to you, four POB (persons on board). Request a TACAN (tactical air navigation system) to ILS approach.'

We got the following response: 'Roger Blackbox Mike, all copied but just repeat your POB.'

'Four, sir.'

There was a long pause then: 'Confirm aircraft type as Nimrod.'

'That's affirmative.'

Slowly and a bit quizzically, 'Roger, Nimrod, four POB.'

We later found out that the No. 18 Group Flying Regulations stated that the minimum crew allowed to be on board one of their Nimrods was six. To add to Kinloss's confusion as we passed overhead at 2,000ft we received the following call:

'Blackbox Mike, there seems to be some discoloration on your aircraft's tail.'

'Yes we know, it's red paint.' It was part of the 'new' MOD(PE) colour scheme; the rest of the 'Ripple' was yet to come!

Being a man with getting on for 2,000 hours experience on the Canberra I flew them regularly during this tour of duty. Not many of the RRS Canberras looked like each other – or any other Canberras. A few were painted in the 'raspberry ripple' colour scheme and many had peculiar shaped and rather bulbous noses for housing the various radars that had come and gone over the years. I was standing beside one such, Canberra B6 XH 953, at an air show when a mother and her toddler stopped to look at it. The little lad was fascinated and said in a piping voice, 'Look, Mummy, it's Mister Nosey.' He was obviously in that phase of reading all Roger Hargreaves' 'Mr Men' books.

Other of our Canberras were finished in all-over silver-grey and looked fairly conventional. There was a whole host of trials of radars and other sensors going on throughout my time at RRS for which the Canberra was an ideal platform. It could fly high or low quite economically, so had good range and endurance. With one exception it had two seats in the back, so that a civilian FTO could be carried to do all the scientific work and a navigator to keep us on track. There was also lots of space in the bomb bay or the tail-cone for extra equipment and aerials.

It would be tedious to list all the work that I was involved in on the Canberras, but a few of the trials provided some interesting flying. For instance, we were involved in flying trials for two anti-shipping missile systems: Sea Skua and Sub-Harpoon. The BAC Sea Skua was being developed with Marconi Defence Systems as an air-launched, sea-skimming missile and the McDonnell Douglas Harpoon had been procured for the Royal Navy to use, primarily from attack submarines as well as some surface vessels. A Sea Skua radar receiver, normally resident in the missile's nose, was mounted in the large nose radome of Canberra B6 XH 568 and we spent a lot of time flying over the sea at very low heights pretending to be a missile. Naval ships were arranged for us to 'attack' and the Marconi man in the back played with the kit to analyse how well it was doing. As the system was coming to maturity in 1979 a trial was arranged in the Cardigan Bay danger area to finally prove the system before trial firings of the real thing from a Sea King helicopter. The brief was that we were to fly under the Sea King, which would be hovering at 500ft and illuminating a ship target with its 'Seaspray' radar. I would then fly as directed by the FTO who was watching the radar return as seen by the missile receiver. Well, it was good in theory but as we did our first pass under the helicopter, simulating the launch of the Sea Skua, there was an almighty thump and momentary downward movement as we flew through the considerable downwash. As we were at 100ft this gave me a bit of a start. I had considered the downwash but thought that with us flying at 350kt it would not have any meaningful effect. Suffice to say that, for the subsequent passes, we asked the helicopter to go up a bit and we passed beneath at 250ft, then descended to 100ft after a hundred yards or so.

The Harpoon was an American weapon, but its performance against ship targets in rough seas had proved to be unsatisfactory for RN operations. Hence a UK avionics company had been subcontracted to improve the radar's performance. This naturally led to us having to arrange naval ship targets in rough seas. One day I was dispatched in Canberra B6 WT 333 to an area midway between northern Scotland and Norway where we were to rendezvous with a Dutch frigate. The weather there was forecast to be such that the winds would have raised the waves enough to give a high Sea State (SS). Like the Beaufort Scale for winds the World Meteorological Organisation gives a numerical rating for SS. We needed SS 4–6; which is rough or very rough, with wave heights between 2.5 and 6m.

We flew out at high level to a point about 25 miles short of the RV and I let down into some very thick cloud, hail, snow and rain with a lot of turbulence. We broke cloud at about 1,000ft above a steel grey sea, heavily streaked with white breakers and spume. I was in radio contact with the ship and my navigator, Geoff Holt, gave me a steer towards it. Mr Pope, sitting next to Geoff, in the cabin behind me was working the radar. It really was rough as I descended towards 100ft to simulate the missile's final attack height. The trouble was that the waves and the underlying swell were moving the sea surface up and down so much that a truly constant height above the sea was impossible. I did my best as I searched ahead for anything that looked like a frigate.

'About 5 miles to go,' announced Geoff.

I could see nothing but sea! Then the top of the farthest wave looked like it had a square lump superimposed on it. No sooner had I seen this weird apparition than it disappeared. Ten seconds later it was back: a large, grey, rectangular block on top of a wave! Gone again. When it came back into view once more we were much closer, after all we were travelling at 300kt. Now I could see something whirling around at the bottom edge of the square. Then it clicked. I was looking at the underside of the stern of the frigate with its prop coming out of the water momentarily as it slid down the next wave!

I called the ship to tell them that we had them in sight and flew past their starboard side. I think that they were very surprised to see us! But we went on to make attack runs from various angles as they ploughed their way through the mountainous seas. Despite all the bucketing around the guys in the back were on the ball and I think that Mr Pope was quite pleased with what he was seeing.

Later another rendezvous was arranged with a 'Grey Funnel Line' vessel in Arctic waters off the Norwegian coast. As it was now May the Met folks had said that we would have to go north of the Arctic Circle to get rough enough seas. We arranged a short detachment to the Royal Norwegian Air Force Base at Bodø and set off on Tuesday 20 May. During the transit the Norwegian radar controller told us that a Russian Tupolev 95 'Bear' was headed our way at about our altitude. I asked the controller to give us an intercept heading, promising not to get too close to it. He did so and a few minutes later there was the huge four-engined bomber in all its stately splendour heading south-west, 1,000ft above us, laying thick condensation trails to mark its progress. It was truly a stirring sight. My suggestion that we gave it a squirt of our missile radar fell on deaf ears! As it turned out the weather was beautiful for the next three days, the ship was late and the seas too calm, so we did very little of any use, except a lot of sightseeing around Bodø, including a visit to a very impressive maelstrom (that's Norwegian for a lot of fast, very turbulent water flowing through a small gap!).

Sometimes it was amazing the type of work that came our way. Once I was asked to provide a target for a weapon trial at Larkhill Range, in Wiltshire. The target aircraft was required to fly across Salisbury Plain at 100ft and 300kt, following the contours of the ground. This was one of the few times when I pulled rank. If I was going to get this authorised by my lords and masters I was going to fly it! I prepared by first flying the required tracks across the Plain in the Wessex at a sedate 90kt to make sure there were no hidden obstructions. There weren't and, although demanding a lot of attention, the actual trial flight went well and I received a very nice thank-you letter from the trials manager.

After another Canberra test flight, this time assessing something called Infrared Linescan, which was day and night airborne reconnaissance equipment, I ended up being interviewed by the RAF's Special Investigation Branch (SIB). They were the folk who, inter alia, investigated low flying complaints by the public; especially any that had escalated up to Parliamentary level. On the day in question the trial protocol had required us to try to capture images of moving vehicles when we were flying at various speeds and heights. The way that the Linescan kit worked meant that it could be limited to a maximum speed/minimum height combination, known as the V/H ratio, and work was ongoing to maximise this value.

To give ourselves a consistent ground image that included moving vehicles we used a stretch of the M1 motorway between the Watford Gap services and Junction 16, north-west of Northampton. As the Linescan looked through an arc of about 60° each side of the vertical we could avoid flying directly overhead the motorway by flying about 100 yards to one side. The final run was done at a high V/H factor: 360kt and 250ft. Post-flight analysis would prove whether this was a limiting case. At the end of the final, southerly run, just before Junction 16, I turned left and started to climb for our return at 2,000ft to Bedford, just a few minutes away.

The trial was a success but three days later I had the aforementioned SIB visitor. This followed an earlier telephone call when I had told the investigating officer that I was indeed flying the aircraft reported as being 'dangerously low' near the M1 on the afternoon of the day in question. Since that call I had asked the boffins to give me a copy of the altitude readout for each run at 250ft. So when my interrogator asked what height I was flying at I told him that the lowest height had been 250ft above ground level.

'Yes, I know that was the lowest height you were authorised to fly at but the statement from the complainant estimates that you were at 100ft or even less,' said the SIB man. 'Here's a copy of the letter he wrote to his MP.'

Now was the time to produce my evidence. 'Here's a readout of the altitude on the lowest of our runs. As you can see there are occasional records of just less than 250ft but the lowest of those is 245ft, so I'm afraid that the visual impression that the complainant got was an error.'

'Well, I can't argue with that, sir,' was the very agreeable response. With that he went on his way to wherever the SIB have their home.

The most exciting of our Canberras to fly was a modified PR9, tail number XH 132; officially it was called the SC9. I believe the letters stood for 'Short's Conversion' because the large and rather unbecoming nose job, and other internal changes for the aircraft's trials role, had been carried out by Short Brothers Aviation in Belfast.

Because of its peculiarities only three of us flew the SC9: Dave Watson, Chris White and myself. Essentially the machine was a PR9, which had 50 per cent more thrust available than the other RRS Canberras, hydraulically powered flying controls, an autopilot and lots of fuel. But it also had a Ferranti Air Intercept (AI) 23 radar in the nose, which was operated by the pilot. In addition to all this, the normal Canberra tip-tanks had been modified to carry other sensors. As neither Chris White nor I had previously operated the AI 23 radar I arranged for us to go to RAF Binbrook, home of the AI 23 equipped Lightning fighter, to learn how to use it. After a couple of sessions in the Lightning simulator and some classroom instruction, we both felt able to use the radar to intercept the targets we would be using in the forthcoming trials. These were related to the on-going UK development of the US Sparrow air-to-air missile, known in the UK as the Skyflash. BAe were the prime contractor, but we were working with Marconi Space and Defence Systems who were developing a completely new seeker for the missile. This was semi-active, so it homed onto the radar reflection of the target illuminated by the fighter's radar. As Skyflash was being developed for the ADV Tornado then it worked in the frequency band of the AI 24 Foxhunter. As the SC9's AI 23 did not operate in that frequency band it directed a transmitter of the correct frequency housed in the port wingtip pod onto the target. The Skyflash seeker was housed in the starboard wingtip pod so that the FTO, in the front seat of the SC9, could assess and record what it was 'seeing' and how it was performing. Between us we flew sufficient trials sorties to give the Marconi folk enough to work on. Using the AI 23 was very interesting, especially in some of the more advanced interceptions, at low level or with manoeuvring targets.

One day the ATC Briefing in the morning had included a plea for anyone airborne with some time to spare to 'call in' at RAF Cottesmore. The reason was that the base was gearing-up to receive its new aeroplanes and become the Tri-National Tornado Training Establishment. The air traffic controllers there were trying to get up to speed and qualified. That day I flew the SC9 out over the North Sea to work with two targets but the second one did not turn up, so we could go home early. I then remembered the plea from Cottesmore and asked if they would like us to go there to do some approaches. They were delighted to accept our offer and we spent over half an hour doing a couple of instrument, radar-guided, approaches followed by a few visual circuits. When I felt that the fuel had reached the level where it would be prudent to return to Bedford I told the local controller that the next circuit would be the last and we would like to depart to Bedford.

'Roger, Blackbox Bravo, request your heading and height en-route,' he enquired.

'Blackbox Bravo requests heading 170 and Flight Level 155,' I replied.

'Roger, I'll pass that on.'

I then flew downwind for a touch-and-go landing. I chose not to use the flaps so that I could lift off and climb quite rapidly. I knew I would have to increase the power in stages because I was not allowed to use 100 per cent until we had achieved 190kt. When I made my downwind call, opposite the upwind end of the 9,000ft long, south-westerly runway, I told the controller that I would like clearance to climb to my cruising height immediately after lift-off.

'Roger, Bravo, that will be OK.'

I touched down and then applied 90 per cent power, lifted off, accelerated to 190kt, pulling the nose up and applying full power as I did so. The climb angle was very impressive and I changed frequency to the radar controller. As we passed 5,000ft I turned left, heading towards base. As I did so I noticed that we were still over the airfield. Homesick angels weren't in it; this was amazing! I rolled out on heading 170° and almost immediately had to start to level off at 15,500ft.

'Blackbox Bravo is steady and level,' I announced, perhaps a bit smugly. I noticed that the TACAN navigation system was showing that we were less than 5 miles from Cottesmore.

The controller indicated his surprise at the aircraft's performance. 'Yes, not bad for an old girl, eh?' I replied. 'Can your new jets do that?' Silence.

As well as flying all the Canberras I had arrived already qualified on the Hunter – so that was also within my remit. Dave Watson shared the flying of this particular type with me. Like all RRS aircraft this was a very special aeroplane. Being one of only three produced this mark of Hunter wasn't unique, but it was a very different version of the original two-seat, dual-controlled Hunter T7. It was designated T (for trainer) 8 (indicating a naval version with an arrestor hook) M (this letter simply indicated that it was fitted with the Ferranti Blue Vixen radar that was destined to equip the Sea Harrier for the FAA). Of the three built ours, XL 603, was the last. The nose had been fitted with a Sea Harrier profile radome and the appropriate electronics stashed neatly inside. As the Foxhunter had for our Buccaneer, the Blue Vixen made the profile of the already good-looking Hunter even sleeker; it also had the grey and white naval paint job. The cockpit had been modified to incorporate the radar screen and the opportunity had been taken by the manufacturer to update the instrument panels and centralise the Hunter's previously scattered and haphazard warning system.

Although it looked modern and svelte the T8M flew just like any other two-seat Hunter! The Blue Vixen trials were well advanced when I took over the unit and subsequent progress was steady. Some very good results were being achieved for such a small radar and its ability to operate under jamming conditions was steadily improving. To aid that, the transmitter was what is known as 'frequency agile' so allowing the signal to get around some of the less sophisticated ECM. This trial provided a contrast to the Foxhunter in its thoroughly good management and the overall high experience levels of the Ferranti team.

In order for me to ensure that all our pilots remained well practised (what the RAF calls 'current on type') some periodic training was necessary. Understandably, the trials management folk did not want lots of precious flying hours on their research machines absorbed with pilot continuation training sorties; they also wanted us to keep the risk levels as low as possible. So we had to manage our training requirements another way. The RAF had simulators for the Nimrod and the Buccaneer, which we used on a mandatory six-month cycle, but for the rest we had to use trainers. For the Canberra that was T4 WJ 992 and for the Buccaneer and Hunter we had to share a common resource with Farnborough and Aero Flight; that was Hunter T8 XF 321. The boss of Aero Flight and I had been pushing for some time to get a two-seat Hunter established at Bedford for our sole use. Eventually this was agreed. However, not long after it had finally arrived it was detached to Farnborough where someone there landed it with its wheels still up and it was written off. No names – no pack drill! Back to square one.

The RAE's Air Fleet Management organisation, often much maligned, came up with a wizard wheeze. The RAF was replacing its Folland Gnat trainers with the BAe Hawk and there was one, XP 513, which still had over 400 flying hours to go before its next major servicing. Effectively that would give us at Bedford at least a couple of years grace for 'fast-jet' training. Being a disposal the deal was essentially a free one and, as Aero Flight already operated a Gnat for esoteric aerodynamic research, the servicing requirements were already well known. However, the Aero Flight Gnat had only one seat because all the scientific equipment filled up the rear cockpit, and it was a valuable research tool.

The 'new' Gnat arrived in late October and I first flew it with my old ETPS course mate George Ellis sitting bravely in the back, dispensing eloquent words of wisdom. We flew together twice while I learnt all about the tiny jet and its foibles. When George was satisfied that I was not going to get into trouble I was sent off 'solo'. That was on Wednesday 7 November 1979. There was a special irony in this first solo on type for me. In May 1963 I had been posted to the first ever Gnat course at RAF Valley. However, delays to the aircraft's introduction to service had changed all that and I flew the Vampire T11[28] instead. It was only after this first solo Gnat flight that I realised that far from being one of the first to fly the Gnat I was probably the very last RAF pilot to convert to it! After all, it wasn't even in service any more! It was a great little jet and, as long as you were fully aware of the possible complications of a hydraulic or engine failure it was enormous fun to fly and certainly kept me 'sharp'. I never flew it alone. Whenever I told my guys that I was going to fly the Gnat there was a chorus of cries, 'Got room for a small one, Boss?' or 'Isn't it my turn now?' When I left Bedford the little red-and-white jet was still there.

Being a test pilot also got me some interesting flights with my compatriots from the more refined climes of Aero Flight. I flew quite a lot of sorties in a simulator that aimed at giving airlines an economical way to land safely in very poor visibility using contemporary airport ILSs. The prime tool for achieving these landings was a small HUD in which a flight path demand symbol was generated by a computer that received signals from a variety of sources, including a radar altimeter. All the pilot had to do was to follow the demand using the flying controls and, even without seeing the ground, safe and reasonably smooth touchdowns could be achieved. The laws that drove the demand symbol could be varied and it was our job, as test pilots, to feedback what we thought. Much use was made of the good old Cooper–Harper rating scale. It was good to be doing real test pilot things again. The system was installed in the flight's Avro 748 twin-turboprop airliner – but, sadly, I didn't get to fly that. The Aero Flight guys used to go off to the foggiest airports they could find and shoot approaches when no one else could get in! It struck me as odd that Amsterdam Airport Schiphol was a frequent overnight destination – was it really always that foggy in Holland?!

I also got to fly and assess the first colour cockpit displays in the flight's BAC-111, a very interesting flat panel LCD display in their Wessex helicopter and I made various types of approaches using a system called MADGE (Microwave Aircraft Digital Guidance Equipment) – nothing to do with the singer Madonna!

Aero Flight had the use of a two-seater Harrier. It was used for many things over the years but when I was at Bedford it was used to quantify the optimum angle for the then still experimental 'Ski Jump' to be built onto the front of the RN's new 'Harrier Carriers'. The Ski Jump ramp had been erected on a strip of concrete to the north of the main runway. So, at infrequent intervals the Harrier-qualified guys would taxi out towards the ramp prior to launching themselves skywards. Lots of data was recorded and no doubt

28 See *A Bucket of Sunshine* by this author published by The History Press, 2012.

worked on elsewhere to ascertain the best solution for the use of Harrier designer, John Fozard's, great idea for increasing the Harrier's payload on take-off. The balance to be achieved was the maximum upwards velocity that could be given the aircraft as against the loads that would be put on the undercarriage as the slope increased. The ultimate angle to be tried was 22°.

One day several of us were driving past the ramp in the squadron minibus when the Harrier was out being lined up for a take-off using the ramp. What we didn't know at the time was that this was the end-point of the trial.

'Let's stop and watch this,' I suggested. Everyone agreed. We didn't have to wait long. The Harrier crew went through their final engine acceleration checks and then taxied forward to face the ramp. Having walked out there one day I knew that they were looking at what seemed to be a very intimidating, apparently vertical grey wall. The engine ran up, nozzles fully aft, brakes off and the jet shot forward and was pushed firmly upwards as it rose rapidly up the ramp. Then we all saw sparks and flames coming from under the nose. *They're using rocket-assistance now*, I thought. Then I saw something streaming from the underside as the Harrier flew away with the nozzles producing half of the lift. The noise was phenomenal. The aircraft then flew back and we noticed that the main wheels were still down but that the nose wheel appeared to have not retracted fully. We continued to watch as the Harrier flew around overhead for a good ten minutes. It then set up for an approach to land, but not onto the runway. Just to the south of the main runway there was a pit, about 10 yards square, with a steel grid over the top of it. This facility had been built and first used for the very early vertical take-off and landing trials in the early 1960s using a very peculiar aeroplane, the Shorts SC.1. Now the Harrier, with its nose wheel still not down, made an approach to overhead the pit and then descended slowly to land on it. By using what is known as the braking stop position of the four nozzles the Harrier was in exactly the right, slightly nose down attitude to land smoothly on the grid. It was a great piece of flying.

I later found out that the captain was none other than George Ellis and in the other seat was a recently arrived Aero Flight test pilot, Mike Bell, on his first trip in the Aero Flight Harrier. Mike had been a student at Glasgow and Strathclyde University Air Squadron when I had been an instructor there. What a way to be introduced to Harrier trials flying!

George later told me what had happened. The normal procedure was that all the variables, such as the aircraft's weight, the ambient temperature, headwind and ramp angle were put into a calculation that came up with a distance. This distance was measured back from the top of the ramp and marked on the ground. This gave the Harrier pilots their start point. On this occasion a new young scientific civil servant had been given this job. When the distance was calculated he proceeded to mark it out from the bottom of the ramp. Hence the jet was now a good 25 yards further away than it should have been. So when George gave it maximum forward thrust the Harrier arrived at the 22° upsweep doing a lot of knots more than it should have been doing. The resultant G-force from the up-thrust of the ramp was just too much for the nose wheel leg, which gave way. Then the nose hit the deck and the ensuing sparks gave me the impression of rockets! Trials and errors, eh?

28 FIASCO

In the mid 1960s the British government began looking around for a radar system that could be used to provide Airborne Early Warning (AEW) for the UK Air Defence Region. At the time, the only recognised AEW aircraft in British service inventory was the FAA's Fairey Gannet AEW.3, operated from RN aircraft carriers. These aircraft were fitted with the AN/APS-20 Radar, which had been developed during the Second World War and was rapidly becoming obsolete. In the early 1960s work had been started on an AEW platform to replace the Gannet, which would have a new type of radar system mounted on a new aircraft, the Hawker Siddeley P.139B. This proposal would use two radar scanners at the front and back of P.139's rather tubby fuselage; this arrangement was known as the Fore-Aft Scanner System (FASS). While the defence cuts of the mid 1960s led to the cancellation of the P.139B, work continued on a wholly British-designed radar system. Strategic thinking led to a decision that the RAF also needed an AEW aircraft to operate as part of the national air defence strategy.

The type of radar that had been proposed for the jet-powered P.139B was deemed by the experts at RSRE, Malvern, to be the best for the job; it was known by the horrendously complex, descriptive title of Frequency Modulated, Interrupted Continuous Wave. I will make no attempt to explain what that really means or how it works! However, the scanner size required was big and thus a large, turbojet-powered airframe would be needed. Designers at Hawker Siddeley came up with a proposal that would see the new radar system installed in their Nimrod aircraft. This proposal was initially rejected by the MOD as being too expensive. In the interim, to provide a land-based AEW aircraft, radar systems from withdrawn Royal Navy Gannets were installed in similarly surplus Avro Shackleton maritime patrol aircraft and, in 1972, commissioned into RAF service. At around the same time, it was decided not to proceed with proposed FMICW radar technology as the basis of a UK AEW system, as American research had shown that a different type of radar, known as Pulse-Doppler (PD), was superior. As a consequence, the idea of a new land-based AEW aircraft for the RAF was re-examined, and this time it was decided that the Nimrod met the requirements. There were a range of options:

- Purchase the US PD radar system and all its associated avionics and fit them into the Nimrod.
- Purchase the US PD radar and combine it with a British avionics package.
- Purchase the US Navy's Hawkeye radar system and combine it with a British radar transmitter, receiver and avionics package.
- Go back to square one and develop a wholly British radar system and avionics package using a twin scanner FASS.

While the fourth option would create and sustain many thousands of British jobs, it was also far riskier than purchasing an off-the-shelf product or spreading the risk across multiple partners. A politico-industrial conundrum.

Meanwhile, the US had made an offer to NATO to purchase several of the new Boeing E-3 Sentry AEW aircraft, which were then being delivered to the USAF; this option was intended to provide AEW cover for Europe's NATO nations without them having to rely on the United States. In 1980 that procurement matured as the NATO E-3A Component manned by personnel from around NATO. However, the complex multilateral negotiations were obviously too much for the UK government and eventually led them to pursue the all-British development route.

In 1977 an RAF Comet 4, XW 626, was modified for flight testing with the nose only radar and conducted a series of trials, the results of which proved promising enough for an order of three prototype AEW Nimrods to be built, using redundant MR1 airframes. The first of these was rolled out in March 1980, flew for the first time in July and was intended to test the flight characteristics. The second airframe planned to carry out trials on the Mission Systems Avionics, based around a GEC 4000M computer, which processed data from the two radar scanners and all the other mission-related equipment.

As far as I recall, until mid June 1980 the Comet XW 626 was flown and operated by a joint BAe/GEC/Marconi trials team based at Woodford airfield, just south of Manchester. Our aircrew became involved as time went by. Whenever I heard about these trials it never seemed to be good news. Progress was very slow, the aircraft often being offered for flight far too late in the day to maximise its long endurance. Various faults recurred, not least of which involved the Auxiliary Power Unit (APU), which was a small jet engine specially installed in the tail of the Comet. The APU's electric generator was needed because the Comet's four R-R Avon engines could not produce sufficient electrical power for both the aircraft and the radar systems, which was only half the full system as no rear scanner was fitted. As the first of the three AEW Nimrod airframes were being prepared for trials at Woodford, it was agreed that the Comet would be taken over by RRS and operated from Bedford. Complementary radar trails would continue in parallel with the early Nimrod trials. On Thursday 12 June there was a handover ceremony and party at a hotel near Woodford, hosted by the BAe Woodford Director of Flight Operations, Charles Masefield, and his team. The following day the RRS 'Heavy Mob' flew the Comet back, with a selection of boffins down the back. I flew the Canberra I had taken up there, via another flight trial, back to Bedford in formation with the Comet.

Now it was our responsibility. The trials progressed but only spasmodically. On 24 July, just over a month since its arrival at Bedford, I flew XW 626 as co-pilot to 'Captain' Geoff Mannings. We flew out over the North Sea and when settled 'on condition' we started the APU and then, when we were sure that it was producing the volts and amps required, told the seven guys down the back that they could start squirting the radar beams out over the ether. It wasn't long before the big red light that told us that the APU had shut down came on. All the radar stuff was turned off and that was the end of the trial for today. The only recourse was to jettison a lot of fuel, about 8 tonnes of the stuff, into the North Sea and go home.

This was not a rare occurrence. The APU was a unique installation and it had been given, quite rightly, rigorous safety protection systems. The trouble was that these various limiters were totally automatic so any small excursion outside the speed, sideslip or air temperature limits shut the thing down, and there seemed to be no method of restarting it in flight. In my experience it wasn't the first time, and wouldn't be the last, where the special trials equipment, that was not the item under test, caused the failure of the prime test mission.

We soldiered on with the AEW Comet programme but, after I had moved on, it was pensioned off. The AEW Nimrod prototypes' problems with mission systems control and integration, radar cooling and synchronisation of the forward and aft scanners all became too vast to be cured. On top of that, by late 1980 the US solution, in the shape of the Boeing E-3 Sentry, was already up and running. During an earlier visit to RSRE Malvern for a briefing on the UK's AEW programme I had been taken aside by the RAF's liaison officer into another room. He had flown in both the E-3 and the AEW Nimrod and told me, in somewhat hushed tones, that based on his observation of the two systems' performance, he thought that the latter would never come to fruition. He opined then that the RAF would be better off if the Nimrod programme was cancelled and the Sentry was procured instead.

In the end that is what happened. The integration of all of the AEW Nimrod's systems into a single package proved too difficult for the underpowered computer, which had an ultimate data storage capacity of only 2.4MB. Additionally, when operating at full power, the radar scanners and on-board electronic systems generated a significant amount of heat. A system was developed to channel this via the fuel system, from where it could then dissipate, but it only worked satisfactorily when the fuel tanks were at least half full.

Many of the developmental problems were not purely technical but revolved around who was the prime and who was the secondary or subcontractor. Who had overall control and fiduciary responsibility? Millions, if not billions, of pounds were wasted. The AEW Nimrod airframes were flown to RAF Abingdon, where they languished for many years before being 'recycled' with cutting tools. After the TSR-2 debacle it was unforgiveable that the UK government and its aerospace industry had repeated the same sort of expensive fiasco! Then, many years later, it all happened again with the Nimrod MR4, so proving the adage that all we learn from history is that we learn nothing from history!

29 MOVING ON AGAIN

This tour as OC RRS was supposed to be my one flying tour as a squadron leader and last for about three years. It should have been followed by a staff tour; that is 'flying a desk' somewhere. However, in the middle of 1980 I encountered Wg Cdr Jim Watts-Phillips at a Farnborough social event; he was the CO of ETPS. He asked me if I would be happy to return to the school as a tutor. I told him that I would be delighted.

I later received a phone call from one of the ETPS tutors who had mentored my course in 1975 – that favourite son of the Falkland Islands – Peter Sedgwick. He had left the RAF and was now in the employ of BAe/HSA at what had been de Havilland's airfield at Hatfield in Hertfordshire. There the CTP, Mike Goodfellow, was building up a team for the flight test programme of the company's new regional airliner – the HS 146. Peter told me that he had recommended to Mr Goodfellow that I be invited for an interview. After Pete had called me, I said that I would need to talk over the options with my wife and look into the implications of leaving the RAF only two years before my pensionable option date, at my 38th birthday. In the end I thought that there was nothing to lose by travelling down the A1 to Hatfield to see what was on offer. I spent a very interesting couple of hours there, talking it all over with Mike Goodfellow and getting a guided tour of the production area. We then discussed all the working arrangements and he told me who else would be on the team, many of whom I knew. We also talked about remuneration and that sort of thing. I promised to give him an answer within a week. Next I looked into the likelihood of receiving approval to retire prematurely. I discovered from the ivory tower that dealt with such things that, because I was actually replacing someone who had unavoidably been unable to take up the post at ETPS, it was 'going to be difficult'! The other factor was that instead of a pretty good gratuity and, in time, a graduated pension, I would receive a grant of just £2,400. After talking it over, my wife and I were not too keen to lose out financially and I personally felt that, in terms of the sort of flying that I enjoyed, the ETPS job was a better offer. I rang Mr Goodfellow to give him the news.

Then it all happened again. Dave Eagles CTP at BAe Warton rang me and said that they had a job that might suit me. I arranged to go to Warton and see Dave. He and the Director of Flight Operations, Paul Millet, interviewed me; however, it soon transpired that not being qualified on the Jaguar would probably be a big hindrance, as the company could not afford to pay for the conversion course. Moreover the same problems about leaving the RAF so near my gratuity and pension date applied, so that job went by the board too! In the meantime I had received full and official notice of my move back to Boscombe Down.

Then there was a nice irony. Since I had done the ETPS course in 1975 the school had acquired two Jaguar trainers and I was to attend the Jaguar OCU starting in early November. I made a mental note to ring Dave Eagles again after that! So it was off to Bonnie Scotland and RAF Lossiemouth in the far north; and it was winter. I had received all the usual joining instructions for the course, which was called a Senior Officers' Short Conversion Course; as I was a short senior officer I thought that quite appropriate. I would be allowed only twenty flying hours to get a thorough working knowledge of the Jaguar and its somewhat complex navigation and weapon-aiming system – standby for another acronym – NAVWASS! This was particularly important because I had been told that when I arrived at ETPS I would be the aerosystems specialist among the tutors and the Jaguar was central to that part of the syllabus. The NAVWASS depended on gyroscopes and accelerometers to work out where it had gone from its starting point, which the pilot had to enter accurately.

The Jaguar programme began in the early 1960s, in response to a British requirement for an advanced, supersonic, jet trainer to replace the Gnat and the Hunter T7. This coincided with a French Air Force requirement for a cheap, subsonic, dual-role trainer and light attack aircraft to replace three older combat aircraft. In both countries several companies tendered designs: BAC, Hunting, Hawker Siddeley and Folland in Britain; Breguet, Potez, Sud-Aviation, Nord, and Dassault in France. A Memorandum of Understanding was signed in May 1965 for the two countries to develop two aircraft, a trainer and a strike/attack aircraft.

This joint Anglo-French venture was launched in 1966 to produce an aircraft that would suit both air forces' needs. As in all international collaborative ventures, all sorts of other factors went into the mixing pot: industrial, political and national status being the main ingredients. The final outcome was that the RAF decided that their need for a new trainer could be met from another source and that the Jaguar would become a fighter-bomber and reconnaissance replacement for the McDonnell F-4 Phantom, so freeing that aircraft to move into the air defence role. So the number of two-seat aircraft was scaled down to 35 and the single-seat order increased to 165. In the end the Jaguar entered RAF service in 1974, six years after the flight of the first protoype.

On 9 November 1980 I travelled north by train to Elgin, where RAF transport took me to my final destination – the Officers' Mess at RAF Lossiemouth. It was an all-day expedition but, until darkness descended, with much fascinating scenery. The next morning I started the inevitable series of lectures uncovering the mysteries of all the Jaguar's inner workings, with many hours spent on the NAVWASS. The cockpit of the Jaguar was the most modern that I had thus far sat in. It was a mix of the familiar and the foreign: those were the French bits. For instance the fuel gauges for the three main tanks were cleverly combined on two dials with a display that helped monitor that the CG stayed within its limits. They were also in litres, which was new to me. Dominating the lower part of the instrument panel was the circular Fresnel lens of the coloured moving map display. I supposed that this would make up for not having a navigator with me and, what's more, it couldn't talk back. Mostly the cockpit was well-arranged and felt a comfortable place to work.

After three weeks of ground training it was time to climb into the Jaguar flight simulator to practise starting everything, including the inertial navigation system, then 'flying' around using the HUD and learning how the weapon aiming system worked. Inevitably the simulator instructors would throw emergencies at us at the most inconvenient moments. The visual system for the Jaguar simulator, like the aircraft's role, majored on low flying. Hence there was a very large, detailed, three-dimensional model over which 'flew' a small fibre-optic head and tiny lens feeding the TV signal onto screens ahead of the cockpit windscreen. In those days, when computer-generated imagery was still some way off, it was as good as you could get and gave a pretty realistic view of the outside world. That was until you flew down certain valleys (or should I say glens?) where the staff had planted very small toy monsters, which appeared 100ft high! As they say, age is mandatory but maturity is optional.

Eventually we had to give up the fairground ride practice and go do the real thing. When I arrived in the OCU crew room I was told that my instructor would be one Flt Lt Whitney Griffiths. I soon picked up from sniggers and whispered asides that Whitney was the 'hard man' on the staff. I met up with him later that day and he briefed me for our first sortie. He certainly came over as abrupt and unsmiling so I promised myself that I would try my best not to upset him.

So much for the plans of mice and men! The next morning we walked out to Jaguar T2 XX 146 and I climbed up the ladder to start the pre-flight checks, which included getting the inertial navigation system out of its inertia. After the external inspection I started strapping in. It was much harder than in the simulator because now I was wearing the bulky and rather unyielding immersion suit, lifejacket and anti-G suit for the first time. Then disaster struck. I had just finished connecting everything and was about to start the internal checks when I realised that the rudder pedals were too far forward; my little legs couldn't reach them! The adjustment was done by a handle at the very base of the centre pedestal, behind the stick and almost on the floor. As we were now in communication I had picked up already that Mr Griffiths was getting a little impatient with my tardiness. Then all he could hear were my grunts and sharp intakes of breath as I struggled to reach that wretched handle. I turned my microphone off and continued the struggle in silence, well as far as Whitney was concerned. But no matter how hard I tried, I could not reach it!

'What the hell is going on up there?' came ringing in my ears.

'Sorry, Whitney, but I can't adjust the rudder pedals; I can't reach the handle now that I'm strapped in,' I explained. 'I'll have to unstrap and then sort it out. Sorry.'

Expletive deleted!

Eventually I was back, somewhat sweaty and a bit more nervous, and I got on with the checks. A cold silence was all that emanated from the back seat. Eventually we were ready to go. I put the power up, released the brakes and the attractive, sharp-pointed jet moved forward. After a quick check that the brakes were working, I turned left to follow the yellow line, passing in front of a row of Jaguars all neatly lined up awaiting their crews. There didn't seem to be a lot of room for me to get through. I said as much, but got no reply. Then I remembered that the Jaguar was not overendowed with wingspan. *I'll try a bit of humour*, I thought.

'It's OK, I'll just pretend that I'm in a Buccaneer with the wings folded. Mind you, I hope that this little jet doesn't fly like a Buccaneer with the wings folded!'

Silence still reigned.

Once we were up and away I soon felt at home in the Jaguar. It handled very nicely and the more I did, under Whitney's watchful eye, the more I enjoyed it. When we got back to Lossiemouth I felt even more at home – it was quite like the Lightning in the visual circuit: very similar speeds and lots of buffeting. Landing was easy and on the final one I streamed the brake parachute, which was very effective.

In the debrief Whitney was not too rude about me, and he said that we would fly again after lunch. I made a mental note to wind the rudder pedals fully towards me before I even started strapping in. The second sortie went well and after briefly going supersonic, doing a loop that took up a lot of sky and then flying around on one engine, including in the circuit, Mr Griffiths seemed a lot happier.

'You can go off on your own tomorrow,' he said, almost enthusiastically.

The single-seat version flew much like the trainer and the course literally flew by; by 17 December, just two weeks since I had started flying the Jaguar, I had finished. The twenty hours had included instrument and formation flying, low-level navigation and three bombing sorties on Tain Range, across the Moray Firth from Lossiemouth.

Two memories have stayed with me. The first was on my first low-level navigation trip, during which I had to fly from the Great Glen and Loch Ness across the mountains to the west coast. The weather was generally good but as I travelled up the valley to pass over the hills I could see that the head of the valley was in cloud. I would have to turn around. I was travelling at 420kt and so I crossed to the right side of the now rather narrow valley before starting a hard left turn to go back the way I had come. As I turned I noticed that the speed had dropped quite a lot. I was used to aircraft like the Buccaneer and Canberra with lots of lift available. But the Jaguar's small, highly loaded wing wasn't able to generate lift without also producing lots of drag. I put the throttles fully forward. The speed was now down to about 300kt and, after 90° of turn, the opposite side of the valley seemed to be getting ever closer. There was nothing left for it but for me to engage the reheat on the engines. This was usually not allowed at low level overland because it might frighten the horses (and the natives). But I thought that the extra push to help me round the corner was much better than getting close to hitting the hillside, which would frighten me as well as the locals! It worked and I found my way back to the Great Glen and rejoined my planned route further south.

The second memory illustrates the hypnotic effect that new 'magic kit' can have on pilots not used to it. The first navigation exercise for the long course guys was to be flown at around 15,000ft. This was so that they could get used to handling the NAVWASS switchery without worrying about being near the ground. The route was a triangular one to two distinct landmarks. One of the course members was a wing commander who had no previous experience with advanced avionic equipment. After his return we were sitting in the crew room chatting about the moving map display and operating 'the kit'.

'It was marvellous,' he enthused. 'When I got to the second turning point it was spot on, right in the middle of the circle on the map.'

'Could you see the ground?' I enquired.

'No, there was full cloud cover below me,' he replied.

'So how do you know that the navigation system was "spot on"?'

'Well, as I said, the point on the map was right in the centre where it should have been,' he answered.

'Yes, but …' Then I gave up. He would find out eventually!

Because of the relatively short notice of the change to my tour length, and the need to find my replacement, I was given an in-post date at ETPS of 1 March 1981. However, I was then detached from Bedford to Boscombe Down with effect from 5 January so that I would be able to convert to all the school's aircraft, and generally get 'bedded in' before the students started flying in early March. So off to Boscombe it was!

PART 4

BACK TO SCHOOL

30 BACK ON THE LEARNING CURVE

I knew that returning to ETPS as a staff member would, at least initially, demand almost as much from me as doing the course had. I knew my own limitations, especially academically, and that there were many areas of the syllabus that I had not practised much in the five years I had spent as an experimental test pilot. As I was not officially posted to ETPS during the first two months I would not be put on the waiting list for a married quarter until at least March; so I had to live in the Officers' Mess single accommodation. This was located in an old single-storey block behind the main mess building. At least I was allocated a 'suite' that had a study and bedroom, albeit of bijou proportions! This was actually a benefit as I would be able to spend some time in the evenings catching up with the academic syllabus, preparing briefings, marking reports and generally trying to keep myself at least one step ahead of the students! As things turned out a married quarter did not become available until towards the end of my first year at ETPS, in November 1981, so the Mess became my home for eleven months, to where I commuted weekly to and from Harrold.

I arrived at ETPS on the first working day of the year. I had to settle in during the rather quiet period, the 'Phoney War', before the students arrived in February and started flying in March. That gave me two months to get 'up to speed'. I needed to requalify on some of the school's aircraft and I started with the Jet Provost and the Hunter, neither of which were strangers to me. However, after about a week of this I was told to get my bags packed to fly to the USA. We were making a staff visit to our sister Test Pilots' Schools in the USA. More on that later.

The personalities at the school had, of course, changed in the five years since I had departed east at the end of 1975. The OC was Wg Cdr Robin Hargreaves, an ex-fighter pilot who had been the first RAF test pilot to fly the Jaguar. Robin had done his test pilots' course in France and was a bit of a Francophile. I soon noticed that he could hear the clang of the teapot lid going down from anywhere within the ETPS building. Robin had recently arrived and was a jovial character, but he soon got a firm hand on the tiller. The other Fixed Wing tutors were Sqn Ldr John Thorpe, Sqn Ldr Jock Reid and Lt Cdr Keith Crawford, USN. The man I was replacing, Sqn Ldr John Blake, was still there, waiting for his departure on retirement in March.

There were some familiar faces around the place, in particular Mrs Linda Wood, the PA to the CO, and the Ops Officer, Mr Ted Steer. But there were other folk new to me. In an office up the corridor was Sqn Ldr Ron Rhodes, who had taken over from the indefatigable Mike Vickers as the unit's QFI and IRE. Then over in the hallowed halls of the Ground School, which had moved from its previous location about a mile away to just around the corner from the ETPS Hangar and offices, there were the 'new' Ground School instructors: Sqn Ldr Alan Mattick and Sqn Ldr Andy Debuse. These guys had the usual qualifications of having brains the size of planets and more post-nominal letters than were in their names. The rotary element of the school was still collocated with the helicopter test outfit, D Squadron, on the other side of the vast airfield. I made a promise to myself to not get involved with them – despite my helicopter experience I would have enough on my plate!

By the time that the 1981 courses had started I was current on half the Fixed Wing fleet and by the time the students were allowed out of Ground School, at the end of February, I was fully up to speed on all of them. This included the twin turboprop Andover, which had replaced the Argosy. I had also got fully at home in the Jaguar, especially with sitting in the rear seat from where I would dispense my instruction and guidance to the students. The mysteries of operating the Variable Stability System in Bassett XS 743 were also demonstrated and I had practised those with some of the other tutors. Finally, and best of all, I had 'converted' to the T5 version of the Lightning; the T4 that I had flown during my course, XL 629, was now resplendent on a pole, like a giant Airfix kit, outside the main gate. It's still there!

The first three students that I was allocated were a good representative selection of international ETPS students. From the USA was Capt. Blaine Hammond, from the Netherlands Flt Lt Ed Van Kleef and from 'Down Under' Flt Lt Greg Rulfs. These guys all had fast-jet backgrounds and were, initially at least, eager to get back in the air and learn new things. The conversion sorties continued apace and then they soon became immersed in the first-term test flying exercises, bringing with them the usual workload of producing sensible test plans, test cards, programming their flights, analysing data, and writing their reports. The first time I had to assess a report and return it to the student with the shortest possible delay brought my workload into sharp focus.

My initial thought that the first year of 'tutoring' would be about as much work as being a student again was not far off the mark. However, it was even more fun. I was flying seven or eight vastly different types of aircraft every month, gaining 25–30 hours in the process, and interfacing on a meaningful level with some of the world's best aviators. I was glad that I had not joined an aerospace company – this was a much better number!

The wide range of experiences and knowledge that these guys exchanged in the crew room enhanced much of the work that we tutors did; I remembered that it was a major factor on my own course. These were men who would be leading aerospace development in their various nations. Helping them to acquire the skills and knowledge to do so was going to be both a privilege and a pleasure.

31 TUTORING AND OTHER FLYING STORIES

Over the next three years I took personal oversight of the training of over two dozen of the world's future test pilots; I flew occasionally with many more. It was always rewarding, sometimes frustrating, occasionally exciting and rarely frightening. Some of 'my guys' went on to greater and higher things. For instance, USAF pilot Blaine Hammond became a Space Shuttle pilot and flew two missions. Wolf Haverstein would become involved with and fly the Eurofighter/Typhoon. Two French exchange students, Jean-Pierre Hagneré and Michel Tognini, became cosmonauts and flew on Soyuz missions; Michel flew a Shuttle Flight as well and ended up as the head of the European Space Agency's Astronaut Branch. But they all had to start from the same place and that was where we tutors came in. To help, teach, coach and train.

Many incidents come to mind from those three busy but exciting years. Like the day that I was sitting in the back of a Jaguar with someone up front who had flown it only three times before. But he was making a good fist of it and we carried out a few circuits before our time was up. Just after turning onto the final approach to land I heard Jock Reid's voice call that he was at 3 miles on his final approach to land. I knew that Jock was in the Lightning and that he would be down to the minimum fuel level. So when my man had finally touched down and streamed the brake parachute I told him to turn off the runway at the first exit so that Jock could land behind us; he would have been very short of 'go-juice' if he had been made to do another circuit. But my student test pilot, a USAF fighter pilot, did not use the brakes anywhere near their maximum capability and we sailed passed the turn-off. However, I knew something that he didn't.

'I have control!' I said and turned right onto the grass, applied power to get clear of the runway and jettisoned the 'chute when I knew that it wouldn't blow back onto the runway.

'What are you doing?' came an amazed voice from the front seat.

'Well, the Jaguar is allowed to be taxied on prepared grass surfaces and this bit of the airfield is our grass runway,' I replied.

'Gee! Wait till I tell the guys back home about this!'

That student was the aforementioned Blaine Hammond and we had another bit of excitement together. From the first part of this book you may recall that the Hunter can go into an inverted spin if aileron is applied during one of the many hesitations that occur during the normal spin. One of the demonstrations we had to give the students was how to avoid that and they had to practise applying the aileron so that the aircraft did not go inverted. On this occasion I had done my bit and handed back control to Blaine for him to try. We climbed back up to 40,000ft and, after carrying out all the usual radio procedures and looking out all around and below, Blaine applied full left rudder and full back stick. After about a turn and a half I told him to apply full right aileron not at a hesitation. By the time that he had decided which way to move the stick another hesitation was upon us. *Wait*, I thought. But no, the stick went rapidly to its full travel to the right. *Oh-oh!* I thought. There was a brief pause and then the aircraft suddenly and quite violently went upside down and started spinning again.

'OK, recover,' I said. He did so successfully. I looked at the accelerometer on the instrument panel. It showed −4.5G – well over the negative G-limit.

'We'd better go home,' I said, 'and get the old girl checked over.' Blaine readily agreed. The ground crews gave the aeroplane a thorough check but nothing was bent or broken.

The other incident that I recall was when I was asked to take one of the ground crew flying on a Hunter spinning sortie. He had asked to experience an inverted spin. This had been approved because it was during the time when we staff members had to get ourselves up to speed for that phase of the course. I had a good long chat with him to make sure that he knew what he was getting into; at the end of which he was still as keen as mustard! The flight would take place in the afternoon so I told him to have a light lunch and make sure that he had a readily accessible sick bag about his person. He was waiting eagerly when I arrived to sign for the aircraft wearing all the correct flying kit. As we lifted off the ground half an hour later, he was visibly excited and we chatted and I pointed out landmarks during the fifteen minutes it took us to reach 40,000ft. After a couple of upright spins, during which he had seemed relatively unperturbed, I made sure that he still really wanted to experience the upside down version.

'Yes, please,' he replied eagerly.

'OK, here we go.' I used the rolling inertia-coupled entry and she went in as smooth as silk. After three turns I applied recovery action. The stick went forward and as it passed the place where the spin usually stopped we continued rotating. *Oh-oh!* I thought. I kept the stick moving forward and rechecked that I had used the correct direction of rudder application with my feet. As the stick reached its full forward travel the spin stopped. *Phew!* I thought.

'How about that then?' I asked my passenger, trying my best to appear unconcerned.

His reply was to offload his lunch into his sick bag! All the way home all I could smell was strawberries. I haven't been able to enjoy strawberry yoghurt from that day to this!

The Lightning sorties always provided that added spice to the variety of our lives. The most demanding of which could use all the fuel down to the minimum allowed in twenty minutes. Due to its complexities the Lightning was the only aircraft that we did not allow our students to fly as captain. A member of staff always occupied the right-hand seat but we tried not to interfere at all and let the students fly their test profiles without comment. We were only there to keep an eye on things and take over if a serious emergency should develop.

This philosophy was amply demonstrated on the return from one of those flights. Everything had gone to plan and I was talking the student through the procedure to set up an ILS approach using the autopilot. I told him not to lower the undercarriage until we reached the final descent point where we intercepted the glidepath. Sure enough that soon arrived and he punched his undercarriage button. Instead of getting three green lights the left main wheel indicator stayed on red – showing us that it was down but not locked. I took over control, told the approach controller that I was going around and changed to the tower frequency. What I knew was that the Pilot's Notes said that in this situation it was not safe to land the Lightning and that the only option, if one main wheel red light stayed on, was to eject. I didn't mention this to my companion yet. One of the other ETPS tutors was flying in the visual circuit so I asked him to fly as close behind and below us to see if the left leg looked as if it was fully down. He did so and said that it was.

As usual in the Lightning I was keeping an eye on the fuel gauge, because if what I was going to do next didn't work we needed enough fuel to fly down to Portland Bay and relieve ourselves of this broken flying machine via

Mr Martin Baker's excellent ejection seats. What I did next was to fly a circuit and do something we didn't usually do in the Lightning – a touch-and-go landing. So I flew a normal circuit and crept up on the runway using all available cover on a shallow approach angle. As we came over the touchdown area I flew level with the ground and used a small reduction in power just to kiss the tarmac with the main wheels. As we did so the left undercarriage indicator light went green. It was just a maladjusted electrical micro-switch. I applied power, heaved a big sigh of relief and went round for the final circuit, which I let the student fly. I never did tell him that we might have had to eject.

I was flying one test exercise in the Lightning and the student coped very well with the very challenging flight profile, which was measuring roll-rates while flying supersonic at 20,000ft. Apart from a reminder for him to climb immediately, without using reheat, at the end of the run and turn back towards Boscombe he did very well. As we taxied in I noticed a condensation trail hanging in the south-western sky. I pointed it out to him.

'We made that eighteen minutes ago,' I said. He was amazed. Actually, so was I!

Sometimes, as with the ground crew air experience trips, we were asked to fly visitors who had convinced senior management that their reason for flying with us was acceptable. The fact that I was always keen to drop anything to fly the Hunter or the Lightning meant that I used to get quite a few of these. One day a Royal Navy Surgeon Commander, who was also a pilot, arrived with the appropriate piece of paper clutched in his hand that indicated that he was medically fit to fly in a fast jet. The Lightning was free and, for once, serviceable, and so was I.

'Brookie!' went out the call. I appeared from my office to the glad tidings that, should I have the time, would I care to take the good naval officer for a trip in the Lightning. The mouths of gift horses came to mind.

'Yes, I'd be delighted. Follow me, sir,' I replied.

I took my visitor to the safety equipment section where the good Tony Gee, still there after all these years, kitted him out. I then gave him a briefing on the ejection seat and the usual banter about the fact that, if the worst should happen, I would shout 'Eject, eject,' and if he didn't go quickly enough a third call would be an echo. Then we walked out to our silver steed and I supervised him strapping into the right-hand seat.

As it happened there was a howling wind from the north-east so we were using runway 05, which meant an extended journey to the end of the runway. But it wasn't too long before I was calling ATC for clearance to depart, climb overhead the airfield and depart to the south-west. I received approval coupled with the news that the wind was now blowing at a steady 25 knots, with gusts to 30. As I lined up a naughty thought crossed my mind but refused to exit on the other side: *I wonder how fast this jet will be going when we get to the other end of this 10,000ft long runway?* If I could hold it down after lift-off, and get the nose wheel up successfully before we reached 240kt (where the air pressure would overcome the hydraulic pressure trying to retract it), it would be interesting to see. So I lined up on the centreline, moved the throttles to match the two engines at 85 per cent of maximum rpm, checked everything looked good, released the brakes, applied full power and off we went.

'Wow,' said my passenger.

'You ain't seen nothing yet,' was my riposte.

At that point the afterburners lit and we really were off. Scalded rabbits came to mind. I managed to successfully retract all three undercarriage legs while holding the aircraft at about 20ft off the ground. Once that had happened I just aimed at the far end of the runway moving the stick forward as the speed increased to keep us at 20–30ft. As we passed over the arrestor barrier the speed was 365kt. There was only one thing to do with all that speed so I pulled up vertically, not too tightly until we were on our backs over the airfield at about 12,000ft. I then rolled out on the south-westerly heading and changed to Boscombe Down's radar controller. The rest of the trip was the usual rapid climb to 40,000ft, a bit of handling up there, then a descent to 10,000ft for a loop and a roll or two, followed by flight at 650kt at 2,000ft before a return to Boscombe for a couple of circuits. I never came across anyone who did not enjoy their flights in the Lightning, or any of our aircraft – not that we did a lot of this sort of flying!

Much of the flying we did was on similar exercises to those when I had attended the course in 1975. However, some of the aircraft were different. The Argosy had been replaced by the Andover military transport, but it wasn't in the same class for size and weight, and our single-seat Hunter F6As were pensioned off at the end of my first year: 1981. During that year three sparkling, brand-new Hawk trainers arrived all decked out in the by now standard 'Raspberry Ripple' colour scheme with 'Empire Test Pilots' School' emblazoned on each side of the fuselage. The three had consecutive military registration numbers: XX 341, 342 and 343. During the second half of the year they would be individually taken out of service for the fitment of all the special instrumentation that we required for the test exercises. That meant that we could use the other two for staff training, especially for Keith Crawford and myself, who had not flown the Hawk before. John Thorpe had been one of the first two RAF test pilots to fly the Hawk and had carried the original Preview. Jock Reid had also flown it and it was he that showed me round the Hawk's flight envelope before I went off on my own.

The Hawk was yet another good-looking aeroplane from the old Hawker aircraft stable. Of course, being built from the start as a trainer didn't give it that warplane edge that the Hunter always had. Its R–R Ardour turbofan engine didn't have the raw power of the Hunter's Avon but it was much more economical on fuel. The way that the rear seat was raised above the front gave the instructor almost as good a view forward as the student; a huge improvement over its predecessor the Folland Gnat.

The cockpits were much more modern too and very comfortable. The Hawk had a totally independent internal starting system via a small jet engine in the spine, above the engine, the APU. There was also a ram-air turbine in the spine, just ahead of the tailfin. This would pop out into the airflow and would whiz round to provide hydraulic power to the flight controls in the event of an engine or hydraulic system failure.

Flying the Hawk was an enjoyable experience every time. It handled well, with very few vices and for me with a very short back length, it was virtually the first aircraft I had flown in which I didn't have the seat at its fully raised position. In fact I had a lot of trouble at first in keeping the aircraft level because I just couldn't believe how high the horizon was above the nose!

During the summer of 1981 John and Jock worked on the spinning exercise for the Hawk. There were two problems to be solved: in the more advanced spins that we and the students would be doing it was relatively easy to put the engine into what was called a locked-in surge condition. That meant that it would not produce thrust when you needed it and would overheat as well. Most undesirable. The other was that BAe, who designed and built the Hawk, had banned deliberate inverted spinning for structural reasons. The former problem was overcome by transmitting the engine temperature to the ground pilot's station and the latter by retaining the two-seat Hunters for inverted spinning.

Our students of 1982 and 1983 missed out on the excitement of flying the single-seat Hunter but they all praised the virtues of the Hawk, which we used throughout the syllabus. But there were occasional 'gotchas'. For instance it was possible to synchronise the compass 180° off the correct heading (a fault later removed by a modification to the gyro systems). I was flying with a very experienced and capable pilot one day when he did that very thing after a session of aerobatics. He had earlier tuned the TACAN navigation system to the beacon at Yeovilton, which was about 40 miles west of Boscombe Down. When he was told to turn east by the Boscombe Down radar controller he complied, but he was actually heading west. After a few moments the controller asked him for our range – that is, how far we were from Boscombe Down. He looked at the TACAN and told the man '15 miles'.

'Tester 52, I don't have you on my radar at 15 miles,' was the reply.

'12 miles now,' said my companion. Meanwhile I sat there very quietly wondering how long it would be before he noticed that the sun was ahead of us and not behind us and remembered that the TACAN was not tuned to Boscombe.

'Tester 52, Squawk Ident,' said the controller. That gave an extra boost to our particular blip on his radar screen.

'Ah, there you are! Your range is 30 miles and you appear to be heading west,' said our radar-equipped guardian. Cue huge think bubble over the bonedome of the front-seat occupant! I told him what had gone wrong, he reset his compass and turned around then, very quietly, went home.

One day a Royal Australian Air Force flying instructor came our way. He had approval from both his and our ivory towers to fly a sortie in the Hawk. The Australians were at the time considering the Hawk as a replacement for their aging Italian Aermacchi MB-326 trainers. I got the job of flying with him.

'I'd prefer to fly in the back seat,' he told me, 'then I'll get an instructor's viewpoint.'

That actually made life a bit easier as I could get the jet started for him and then let him do the rest. We briefed for a mixed flight profile with a climb to high altitude, a couple of spins, some aerobatics at around 10,000ft and then a descent into the south-western low flying areas for about fifteen minutes at 250ft. After that I would show him and let him have a go at a few visual circuits, with touch-and-go landings.

The trip went as briefed and if he enthused about the view from the back seat once he must have done it a dozen times. He liked the handling very much and actually made a good fist of flying and landing the Hawk. But it turned out that the thing that seemed to most make an impact on him came as we taxied back in. We had flown for one hour and fifteen minutes on a very varied flight profile, which had already impressed him, but then I pointed out how much fuel we still had left.

'Wow! That's real bonzer!' he enthused. 'When I get back I'll tell the folks to get their order in real quick!'

Another new aircraft on the Fleet was the Andover. I had flown it occasionally as a co-pilot at Farnborough, but only for about twenty-five flying hours. Here I had to become a captain and instructor. Thankfully the air engineers that were previously employed as operators and 'minders' on the Argosy had been retained for the Andover. There were three of them – the jovial Brian Jones ('BJ'), the worldly-wise 'Mr Fixit' Ed Jacotine and the urbane and cool Brian Hemming. These guys and their collective expertise and knowledge kept us amateur 'truckies' out of trouble on many occasions.

Once one got used to handling the R-R Dart turboprops the Andover was a fun aeroplane to fly and operate. It challenged the fighter pilots among our students and had enough quirky characteristics to keep them on their toes. We used it mainly for the asymmetric power and take-off and landing exercises, although it did feature in some of the others. It was also the 'school bus' for our various visits around the UK and Europe.

One of the things that did require some practice before we demonstrated it to the students was the short take-off and landing. The Andover was equipped with a system to boost its engine power for short periods of time. So this was used for the short or heavyweight take-offs. It was an injection of a mixture of water and methanol into the engines – known as water-meth. Vic Lockwood, who joined us in 1982, called it 'reheat for truckies'! The system was armed before the take-off run was started and as the power reached its maximum the system was activated and you really could feel the surge in power. When combined with the correct flap setting a very short take-off run was achievable. In fact, it was easy to be caught out. However, once airborne the aircraft was flying at a speed below its safety speed if an engine should fail, so you had to have your wits about you. With all my years flying the Canberra I was used to that!

For the short landings we used the grass strip alongside the main runway. This was a novelty for almost everyone. Hurling a 15 tonne aeroplane at green ground and not tarmac was a bit alien. And then to get the shortest possible run the throttles had to be closed and the reverse pitch lever pulled up and back as soon as possible after what was often a shambolic arrival. Then all you had to do was keep the thing going straight and apply as much brake as you dared. It was easy to get it wrong! But the old Andover had seen it all before and put up with our brutal treatment very well. A really odd thing about all Andovers was their smell. As soon as you boarded via the passenger door at the back there was always a strong scent of horses; it was just like walking into a flying horsebox!

At the end of each year we tutors were allocated a team of two or three to lead for their final exercise: the Preview. I covered the Phantom once and the Buccaneer twice; the second of these was not done in the November cold and East Anglian gloom of RAF Honington but the sparkling skies of RAF Akrotiri in Cyprus. That was some compensation for me not picking up the Tornado team! The Preview was quite a workload for the students but we had to mark their vast tomes in just a few days, and evenings!

My final recollection returns to the Lightning – always a source of great stories! I was flying with one of the RAF students, Martin Pitt, and we were recovering to Boscombe with, as usual, not a lot of fuel. At about 3 miles from touchdown we received a rather urgent sounding radio message telling us not to land as the runway was blocked.

'How long will it be blocked for?' I asked.

'Tester 52, don't yet know,' came the not very helpful reply.

I looked at the fuel gauges, something you do often in the Lightning, and saw that we were down to our minimum to carry out a diversion to Lyneham.

'Boscombe, Tester 52, I'm afraid I can't hang around to find out – diverting to Lyneham.' I put out an emergency call to ensure that we got priority handling. Meanwhile Martin, who was a big aeroplane man, was sitting there wondering what was coming next. I reached down and opened the cross-feed fuel cock, which would allow one engine to feed from both fuel tanks, and then asked him to shut down the number one engine. We then flew towards Lyneham at 250kt at 2,000ft. In the end we landed safely with absolute minimum fuel. I had got Martin to relight the number one engine, but leave it idling, because its hydraulic pump provided the shove to push out the brake parachute, which I wanted to have available on Lyneham's 7,000ft runway.

We landed safely and taxied to the Visiting Aircraft Flight's hard standing. Then came the very embarrassing bit. First they had to find a set of stepladders tall enough to allow us to get out and down to the ground safely. We then went to VAF to ask for some fuel and, eventually, a huge bowser turned up and one of the ground crew came to fetch me from the crew room.

'The bowser driver wants to know how he refuels your jet, sir,' he said.

Good question, I thought. *I've no idea!*

Anyway, I strolled out as nonchalantly as I could while trying to remember whether I'd ever seen the guys at Boscombe refuelling the Lightning. A vague memory of it being under the wing came to mind, but which side I could not recall. As I came up my embarrassment was saved by the man having found the refuelling panel all on his own.

''Ere we are, sir,' he said cheerily as he applied his screwdriver to open the panel's little door. Inside were the hole into which he would push his hose and a few switches and lights. I looked in and saw that they were clearly marked so put them to ON. With the usual thump the fuel started going in under pressure. I left the scene as nonchalantly as I'd arrived. Just as I arrived at the door of the crew room there was a loud shout from behind me. I turned around and saw that the Lightning was behaving like a horse with a weak bladder, a stream of fuel was pouring out of the ventral tank underneath the fuselage. Thankfully the tanker driver had turned everything off as soon as he had spotted the overflow, disconnected the hose and we put all the switches back to where they had started from and closed the panel door.

'How much has gone in?' I enquired. When he told me I knew that would be enough to get home with. But I'd no idea why we had made such a mess all over the pan. At which point a big red fire engine turned up and started hosing all the fuel away. Meanwhile I had climbed up to the cockpit and turned the battery switch on to find out how much fuel there was in the main tanks; they were both full. I returned to the VAF and called station operations to book our departure.

'Can you arrange for me to climb directly after take-off to flight level 360 (36,000ft) with a hand-off to London Military Radar, please.'

'OK, sir, we'll ask for that and the controller will confirm it when you taxi out,' came the helpful reply.

Sure enough we were cleared to do that so Martin got another practice at the reheat climb. As we pierced the altocumulus cloud layer at about 15,000ft, lying on our backs doing nine-tenths of the speed of sound, I couldn't help thinking how much I was going to miss all of this when I was moved on to whatever would come next!

32 AMERICAN VISITS – USAFTPS

There were two categories of visits to and from ETPS. The first were the staff visits made to the two American test pilots' schools at Edwards AFB, in the high desert of California, and at Naval Air Station Patuxent River, on the shore of Chesapeake Bay in Maryland. They also made reciprocal visits to Boscombe Down. The others were the visits that the staff and students made to aerospace industrial and R&D sites. The latter visits, as they were in my day as a student test pilot, were part of the syllabus. However, there had been a great improvement in that there was also a European Tour, which took in aerospace companies and test and evaluation sites in Italy, France and Germany.

In January 1981, when I had been on the staff only a few days, I joined the party that was setting off westbound across the Atlantic. On this occasion we were only going to visit the USAF Test Pilot School (USAFTPS) at Edwards AFB so when we boarded the Friday VC10 out of Brize Norton bound for Washington Dulles International Airport it was going to be the first leg of a long journey. We spent the night in Bachelor Officer Quarters at Andrews AFB, near Washington DC, from where we were to pick up our transcontinental flight the next day. This turned out to be an Air National Guard Boeing 737, which was fitted out as a navigational trainer. It was sitting on the concrete awaiting us parked not far from the huge Boeing 747 'Air Force One', resplendent in its blue and white livery and liberally applied stars and stripes.

I managed to get a window seat and I spent much of the following six hours watching the USA passing by 6 miles below. It was fascinating to see the different types of landscape, but I wished that I had brought a map to follow our progress. After what seemed an age I spotted a dark, sinuous line ahead. As we got nearer I realised that it must be the mighty Mississippi River.

There was a large conurbation to the left and as I peered intently I could pick out a silver arch and its darker shadow. *That must be St Louis*, I thought. The Gateway Arch, which commemorates the pioneers of the westward expansion of the USA, is over 600ft high and its silver finish made it clearly visible, even from 36,000ft.

We continued across the plains and prairies where huge multi-coloured circles had me totally puzzled and the grid pattern street layout was repeated in virtually every town or city. It was long after that I learnt that the circles were made by vast, rotating irrigation machines. Eventually the country became more sparsely populated, vast fields with a farmstead in one corner and dead straight roads criss-crossing the panorama. After I had finished the contents of the cardboard box given to each of us by the way of victuals, had drunk yet another cup of mild American coffee and visited the flight deck, I went back to my observation post. We were now passing over sand, stone and scrub. I picked out buttes of Monument Valley, spidery tracks that seemed to lead nowhere and I thought of those families trudging west seeking a better life. 'Just over the next ridge, honey. Then we'll be there.' I wondered how many times that had been said by those brave pioneers.

Now there were jagged mountains, snowfields and conifers – the Rocky Mountains. I felt a real thrill at seeing something that I had read about and heard of since childhood. Then I heard the engines being throttled back by the captain, who, like his co-pilot today, was an ex-USAF pilot now flying the Boeing 737 for an airline. We descended into thick cloud, the first significant cover I had seen since we left Washington. We were stopping at Luke AFB in Arizona on the way to our final destination, Los Angeles International Airport (LAX). When we landed, there was a solid overcast and it was raining. Of course we thought nothing of it. However, as we sat in a large aircrew room, we were the butt of such banter as, 'No wonder it's raining guys, the limeys are here.'

After our onward flight to LAX and a long ride in the American equivalent of the RAF springless coach we finally arrived at the gates of Edwards AFB. There was desert all around us, with one large, flat, white dry lakebed alongside the road. Until then I thought that Boscombe Down covered a large area – but here it was about 10 miles from the main guard post to the base complex, where we were delivered to the Bachelor Officers' Quarters (BOQ). We were finally at our destination having travelled over 6,000 miles in about thirty hours. No wonder we were tired – we had been doing an average of 200mph since we left Brize Norton and had crossed eight timezones!

During this visit we would be hosted and entertained right royally by the staff of the USAFTPS – barbecues, beer calls and dinners were all on the schedule. At the first of these I found that I had to take part in a bizarre, inter-school competition of which I had received no warning. It was apparently a tradition of questionable status that the two most recently arrived staff members would attempt to eat a slice of Key lime pie without using their hands; Key lime pie is a green variation on lemon meringue pie and this event would take the form of a race. So my opposite number and I were each supplied with a plate of the said dessert. We were allowed to support it with one hand, the other remaining firmly behind our backs. On the word 'GO' I went face down into the pie. The initial effect was that much of the soft meringue went up my nose hampering my breathing. However, I ploughed on. It was not a race against the USAF; it was one between the nasal ingestion of meringue and the gathering and swallowing of the delicious pie. I had no idea how well I was doing, there was lots of vocal support for us both, but when the pie had all gone I put the plate on my head and discovered that my opponent was still face down in green and white pudding. I had won! Much applause! Was this a good start to my ETPS tour, I wondered?

There were also staff interchanges, briefings and even some flying on offer. On our second day I was slated to fly in the front seat of one of the school's F-4 Phantoms. I met my pilot-in-command, Major Dave Spencer, the previous evening and he said that we were due to take off at 7.30 a.m. and would meet at the base canteen at 5.30 a.m.! So that night I set the radio-alarm in my room for 5 a.m. Waking was not too difficult because my body clock was still way ahead of local time, but when I stepped out of the door it was both dark and foggy – a real 'pea-souper'!

'Good morning, Dave,' I said. 'How long will this take to clear?'

'I have no idea,' he replied.

'Well, how long does it normally take at this time of year?' I pressed.

'I dunno – in the two years I've been here it's never happened before.'

In the end it had not cleared by 7.30 a.m. and we were stood down.

'We'll try again tomorrow,' said Dave. The fog had happened because of the rainstorms that had passed over the area the previous day; the same rain that we had experienced at Luke AFB. The huge Rogers Dry Lake bed, usually very dry, was now a few inches underwater and the moisture had caused the fog to form. The weather folks said that it should clear in the early afternoon.

However, the alternative activity arranged for us did not disappoint. We were taken to Palmdale airfield, the home of the USAF Plant 42, a part of Lockheed's Skunk Works Facility, and Rockwell's Space Shuttle construction and refurbishing works. It was amazing to walk into the vast Rockwell hangar where three of these unique and very special air vehicles were being built. We were shown how they glued the black heat-absorbing tiles underneath the wings and fuselage. We climbed onto elevated walkways and looked down into the cavernous payload bay. We were briefed on the Space Transporter

System or STS (the official name of the Space Shuttle) programme and told that the first launch was due only three months later.

After that we were allowed to look over and get inside one of two B-1 supersonic bombers that were sitting outside. They were large, impressive aeroplanes and the cockpits for the four-man crew were state of the art. But, as someone had said – for the price of one B-1 bomber you could have 200 cruise missiles. President Jimmy Carter cancelled the B-1 programme in 1977, but testing of two of the four prototypes had continued. In fact the B-1 programme was resurrected a year after our visit, in January 1982, under President Ronald Reagan and the B-1B Lancer is still in USAF service today.

I did get to fly the Phantom the next day. When we had walked out to the big jet I climbed in the front cockpit so that Dave could give me a quick tour of the real estate. It was very spacious, with ample room for even the biggest Texan fighter pilot! In fact the seat was set at its lowest position and, with the hydraulic power off, the stick was resting at its fully forward position, away from me. The two throttles were large and topped with rather fetching, turned wooden handles. I couldn't help but ask, 'Can I have a smaller size, please? This one's too big!'

Dave had asked me what I would like to do and I told him that a low-level navigation exercise would be my choice. He bravely agreed (he was a fighter pilot by trade and not a 'mud-mover') and drew up a route, which he loaded into the inertial navigation system. There was no moving map display in the F-4 like that in the Jaguar – I just had to follow a steering command on the compass. I got the mean machine started under Dave's tutorage and he offered to make all the radio calls. An offer that I gladly accepted; US radio terminology can be quite different to what I was used to.

We taxied for what seemed like miles to use the 15,000ft long runway, and then we stopped at the place short of the runway itself that they called 'Number One'. There a man with ear defenders on his head walked around and under our jet for what seemed like hours, looking for anything untoward. Eventually he gave us a thumbs-up, Dave called for departure, we lined up and I wound up the engines to maximum dry power, let the brakes off and applied full afterburner. The acceleration was similar to that of the Lightning. The big jet unstuck very cleanly and I got the gear up and away. Dave gave me instructions as to heights and headings until we reached the area where we could go low level. Now I was in my element and started to follow the valleys as we climbed further up into the mountains. Dave became very quiet in the back – I was enjoying myself and now feeling very much at home in this large cockpit. Holding 420kt was easy, there was plenty of power to spare from the J79 engines and the controls felt just right for the job. I could see the top of a mountain peak up ahead. We were now above the snowline.

'That's the top of Mount Whitney, let's go over the right-hand side of it,' said my 'navigator'.

'OK,' I replied.

As I got near the top of the ridge I swung right so that I could over-bank to the left and minimise our time above the skyline, a standard low-level flying technique. So we crested the ridge with the snow, ice and rocks above our heads. Dave had obviously never seen this before, as there were a series of unintelligible grunts from the back seat! Once on the eastern side of the Sierras the ground dropped away rapidly towards the Owens Valley and its dry lakebed. I could fly this section of the route with the engines throttled well back and still maintain my height and speed. It was fascinating to see the altimeter unwinding from around 14,000ft as we passed the peak of Mount Whitney, the highest mountain in the contiguous United States, back to less than 2,000ft as the ground rushed by about 300ft below us. By the time we reached the dry lake Dave had obviously had enough of all this bomber pilot stuff.

'OK, let's head west again and climb to 20,000ft,' he instructed. I complied as he dealt with contacting 'Eddie Radar' for our return to base. On the way he suggested I try a roll or two and then slow down until the AOA reached the maximum allowed. At that angle and speed he said that I should not use aileron to keep the wings level but use the rudder instead. It was an interesting characteristic that certainly worked. After not very much longer we were descending over Edwards AFB and joined the visual pattern (USAF-speak for circuit!). The Phantom was less responsive now and needed a bit of a firmer hand. However, there was really not that much difference between flying it and the Buccaneer around the circuit and down the final approach. Landings, of which I did four, were easy. The big, low-mounted wing cushioned the arrival so the 'naval' style of the Buccaneer wasn't on the menu! It was a great experience to fly such a legendary jet and I felt very privileged. I would fly the UK version of the Phantom twice more later that year while leading the ETPS Preview Team at RAF Coningsby in Lincolnshire.

During this visit I also flew a very special old jet trainer – a T-33. A company called the Calspan Corporation, which had originated from the New York state based Cornell University's Aeronautical Laboratory, operated it. The Calspan pilot was one Mr Rogers Smith, whom I would get to know well over the coming years. The T-33 was equipped with a selectable fly-by-wire control system, a side-stick and an HUD. It was used for giving the test pilot students an insight into modern flight control systems and their problems and some potential solutions. I had a really fascinating flight being shown and experiencing many aspects of this technology.

My third flight was in a Blanik sailplane from an airfield in the hills west of Edwards with the delightful name of Tehachapi, no doubt of Native American origin. A day later we were on another flight – back to Blighty. In fact it was a series of flights; the first in the back end of the USAFTPS's Boeing KC-135, a modified Boeing 707. This took us to Alameda AFB in San Francisco Bay, where we boarded an old Air National Guard C-130A Hercules for a ten-hour transcontinental voyage to Patuxent River. Then ground transportation to Washington for the following day's VC10 back to Brize Norton and home.

The following January we repeated our visit to Edwards AFB and added a few days at the USNTPS on the way back. Our sponsors had made similar transcontinental flight arrangements and this visit to Edwards was memorable for me on three particular counts. The first being two flights and the third one of those almost surreal events when you continually want to pinch yourself to make sure that you are not dreaming.

The latter was an evening get-together in the Officers' Club at which several distinguished and famous test pilots were present. Among them were men such as X-15 test pilots Pete Knight and Bill Dana, Col Jimmy Doolittle III and the legendary and apparently evergreen Chuck Yeager. I had actually met the latter the previous day – more on that later. We were first shown a gallery of photographs in a room in which the walls had been covered with grey wooden planks. This was a tribute to the collection of similar photographs of past test pilots made by the formidable aviatrix who had owned an airstrip and stables on the edge of the base area – Pancho Barnes. In the film *The Right Stuff* the future Mercury astronaut Gordon Cooper (played by Dennis Quaid), who has just arrived as a new test pilot at Edwards, boasts that he will soon have his photograph up there with all the others. His considerable ego is instantly deflated when Pancho tells him, in her usual direct manner; 'Sure you will, sonny. All those guys are dead.'

This guided tour of the gallery was followed by a convivial dinner at which many pilots of all ages sat around shooting down their wristwatches as they told their flying stories. However, eventually Chuck Yeager announced that Pete Knight had agreed to tell one to top them all; something, Yeager said, that he rarely does. So Pete stood and started a story that was so amazing that had anyone else told it you would have had difficulty believing it. It was about one of his many flights in the X-15 hypersonic research aircraft that NASA flew in the early 1960s. Pete Knight would later set a world speed record of 4,520mph (6.7 Mach) that would last for nearly twenty years, until the Space Shuttle started flying.

On this occasion he had been dropped from the NASA B-52 that air-launched all the X-15s and had carried out the first part of his acceleration and climb profile. At the apogee the aircraft's electrical system failed. Up at the edge of space in a complex flying machine this was not a desirable situation. Pete told us how he used those instruments that were not electrically driven to fly the re-entry manoeuvre and then looked around for somewhere to put his sick, supersonic steed down safely. He spotted the white acres of what he recognised to be Mud Lake and set himself up for the curving descent onto the dry lake bed. Using his considerable skill and experience he landed successfully. However, he told us that the deceleration felt stronger than usual. He was down safely, he was alive, but his troubles were not over. Raising the heavy canopy took considerable effort; he then jumped down to the lakebed and found himself standing in several inches of water! That's why the X-15 had slowed down so quickly. Meanwhile, back at base nobody was sure just what had happened. The electrical failure had affected the device that helped the radar track the X-15 and radio contact had been lost. The fear was that Pete had lost control during re-entry. So it was now a case of finding the wreckage. NASA's DC-3 was fired up and dispatched back along Pete's last known track. Eventually they spotted an apparently intact black delta shape sitting in the middle of the white expanse of Mud Lake. Pete had now been there for some hours and was relieved to see the DC-3. However, when he saw that it had lowered its wheels he realised that they were going to land. Not a good idea with the water on the lakebed. He started waving to discourage the crew of their intent. Of course, they took this as signals of delight and relief! The DC-3 landed and just avoided nosing over. Pete closed his story with the line: 'So NASA now had two airplanes stuck in the mud at Mud Lake!'

The following day, 7 January 1982, I met up with Capt. Jay Jabour, a man who would later go on to higher rank within the USAF, so that he could brief me and then take me flying in a Northrop T-38 Talon. The T-38 was the USAF's standard advanced flight training aircraft and at Edwards it was used by the school for some of its exercises and by Test Operations Wing for continuation training and chase sorties. The latter stemmed from the long-standing USAF philosophy of 'chasing' virtually all test flights; this practice often paid off, especially if something went wrong. We Brits did not use chase aircraft habitually, but reserved the practice for photographically recording certain types of flight test profiles. Not only was it expensive but also it meant that if the chase aircraft went unserviceable then the test could not go ahead. This practice became a real headache for the tests that Edwards AFB was undertaking with cruise missiles. The count of aircraft required soon mounted: a B-52 launch aircraft, a spare B-52, one or two chase aircraft for the launch, a KC-135 tanker to refuel the chase aircraft and two specially equipped F-4s to chase and monitor the missile on its long flight from a launch position out in the Pacific to its target on a local bombing range. A minimum of seven airframes were to be available, ready and manned and co-ordinated for the launch day. Only the Americans could do programmes like that!

My flight in the T-38 was very interesting mainly because this one had modifications to its airbrake that allowed it to make glide approaches to the lakebed runways at Edwards that followed the landing flight profile to be used by the Space Shuttle. Jay briefed me on the pattern, which was to climb to 30,000ft and set up at right angles to the final approach. The throttles would be closed, the speed reduced, the landing gear lowered and the extra large airbrake extended. Then one had to hold 230kt and at 23,000ft turn on to the final approach, holding 230kt and a glide angle of 23°. The airbrake could be modulated to bring everything right. Having absorbed all that we walked out to our pretty, white-painted jet, strapped in and got the two little engines going.

Jay called the tower and we taxied out. After the usual pre-flight inspection at 'Number One', he talked me through the take-off, I retracted the wheels and we set off on our climb to 30,000ft. Jay directed me into the ideal position; he then took over and closed the throttles to demonstrate the approach. The first thing that happened was that my ears popped, the cabin pressurisation felt like it had failed! He said that it always did that. With everything hanging down we set off earthwards. It was just like a very big version of the glide approach in the Hunter. The Shuttle runway was marked out with black lines and the touchdown area was clearly visible. We continued rapidly earthwards and at 1,500ft Jay raised the nose to point at the ground just before the touchdown markers; the speed reduced and at 150kt we continued our descent until we were a few feet above the ground. Jay had said that we were not allowed to land on the lakebed so he pushed the throttles fully forward and we went back up for me to have a go.

After I had set us up I did what I always did in the Hunter and aimed for a point a few hundred metres short of where I wanted to land. Holding the speed at 230kt was not difficult and I just held the little jet pointed at the white expanse of salty mud. The gradual flare towards a low go around was no problem and I was encouraged to go back up to 30,000ft for a second and final approach. That went well although my eardrums were beginning to suffer from all the changes in pressure.

Jay then threw in a bit of tourism and we flew down the length of Death Valley, at the minimum allowed altitude of 2,000ft. But even from that height the place was impressively awesome. It was easy to sense the desolation that gave it its name. There were old buildings and tracks, leftovers from the late nineteenth century when the men who extracted the mineral borax shipped it out using mule trains. Back at Edwards Jay let me fly a few visual patterns and I found that handling the T-38 was a bit like the Jaguar, although it could fly at speeds about 20kt lower.

That evening Dave Spencer, with whom I had flown the F-4 the previous year and who was still serving on the school, invited me round to his home for an evening meal. When I got there another couple had already arrived. He was another of the USAFTPS staff and while we were chatting his tall, blonde wife got up and went into the adjoining room. It soon became obvious that there was a fairly new baby in there. Over the meal I asked about opportunities for spouses to work and the new mother said that she worked on the base.

'Oh, what do you do?' I asked.

'Well, I'm still on maternity leave but otherwise I head-up T-38 operations here,' she replied. I assumed that this would be in some sort of civil service administrative role.

'I flew a T-38 today; I really liked it – it's a great jet for the job here,' I said.

'Yes, I like flying it too,' came the response.

Well, this was well before the first women entered the RAF as pilots so I was a bit surprised; I tried not to show it. But I was intrigued by the small person in the next room.

'How long before you had the baby did you have to stop?' I asked.

'Well, once I was sure that I was pregnant they restricted me to a maximum of 3G and then I stopped at six months.'

'When will you be able to start again?'

'In a couple of months now,' she said coolly.

We then talked about all sorts of other flying related topics – as pilots do when they get together!

The following day started with a hugely pleasant surprise.

'Brookie,' John Thorpe announced, 'you and Jock are going to fly the F-15.'

'Wow!' I replied. 'I suppose that you don't mean together?'

'No, you silly boy. You go today and Jock has a trip tomorrow.'

I was told to get transport to the F-15 Joint Test Force (JTF) on what was known as 'Constructors' Alley'. The JTF was the final stage of test and evaluation in which both the manufacturer of a new aircraft type and the service user carried out all the tests that would culminate in the aircraft being acceptable for service and operationally effective.

When I arrived I was introduced to Major Steve Cherry who was going to sit in the back seat of one of the prototype F-15 Strike Eagles while I flew it. Heroic medals came to mind! The Strike Eagle was a modification to the basic F-15 interceptor fighter to enable it to fly attack missions carrying a wide variety of ordinance. There were also modifications to the landing gear to allow the Eagle to operate at higher weights and the carriage of extra fuel tanks fitted to the outside of the fuselage. These were known as conformal (zero-drag) tanks and McDonnell Douglas, the F-15's manufacturer, claimed this as a world's first. I didn't have the heart to tell them that the conformal (zero-drag) bomb-door fuel tank on the Buccaneer had been flying for about fifteen years by then! The other major modifications were to give the F-15 a new high-definition radar for accurate ground mapping and target acquisition and multi-mode electronic cockpit displays.

However, Steve explained, the airframe that we were going to fly (tail no. 77-0166) was an F-15B two-seat trainer that had yet to receive all of those modifications. He said that we would fly with an all-up-weight at take-off of 48,000lb, whereas the Strike Eagle would routinely operate at weights up to 68,000lb. To prepare me for this momentous event Steve first gave me a run-down on all the essential items I would need to know, especially on how to start the engines, as he could not do that from the back seat. Illustrations of the HUD, instrument panels, actions in the event of engine failure or fire and the ejection drills were all covered.

I was then given a checklist and Steve took me to the big grey bird sitting on the ramp, alongside two other single-seat Eagles. He showed me how I was going to strap in and the location of all the really important knobs and levers.

'OK, you stay there and work your way through the checklist,' he said. 'I'll order us a burger for lunch, so come back to the crew room at midday.'

So, being a good little Brit pilot I did what I was told. By noon I felt sufficiently confident that I could fly this big beast well enough for Steve not to have to grab his stick and throttles too often and I dismounted via the ladder. The cockpit was about 8ft from the ground, much like that of the Lightning. As I reached terra firma I saw that the person that had been sitting in the single-seat F-15C alongside my steed had also climbed down. I looked at him and recognised immediately the crinkly features of no less a personage than Chuck Yeager! He looked across at me and nodded so I went up to him and introduced myself. He was intrigued as to what a 'limey' was doing here. I told him. As if in reply to my unasked question as to what he was doing he explained that he was going to ferry the F-15C back to the manufacturer's plant near St Louis. I asked him how much time he had on the F-15.

'Enough,' was the laconic reply.

Chuck Yeager was a Brigadier General in the USAF Reserves and so he was allowed to fly occasionally for Edwards. It was uncanny to be walking alongside and chatting to this legendary man. He had gunsights for eyeballs!

After consuming my burger and wishing General Yeager fair winds and a safe arrival at St Louis, Steve and I kitted up for our flight. Before the flight I had been taken aside by OC ETPS, Robin Hargreaves, and asked to concentrate on assessing the Eagle as a ground attack machine; I was also asked to write a post-flight report, but not to disclose this to anyone else yet. Much later I learnt that the RAF was considering the acquisition of the Strike Eagle to replace the Tornado in the 1990s. This intention was highly confidential; hence I was not told at the time. Accordingly I asked Steve Cherry for some low-level flying, air-to-ground attack profiles as well as any self-defence manoeuvres using the radar.

We walked out to the jet and I climbed aboard and strapped in while Steve checked the exterior of our steed was all that it should be. The first event was to start the small jet engine in the back of the F-15, which would then be used to start the engines; it was known as the Jet-Fuelled Starter (JFS). This was a very similar system to that in the Hawk. However, a rather strange American practice was not to have batteries in their fighters, so to start the JFS I had to give it the impetus via a pull-cord on the inside of the right foot well. It was just like starting my motor mower back at home! I pulled the cord and, unlike my motor mower, it started first time. I could hear the whine of the little jet engine behind us and an indicator light came on to prove that it was up and running and ready to do its job. I then had to select the start switch to the left to start the port engine. Beforehand Steve had told me that the checklist for this bit was misleading. It told me to open the high-pressure fuel cock, by moving the throttle forward through a detent, when the engine had reached 12 per cent rpm. However, the rpm gauge was electrically operated and the aircraft's generators would not come on-line until 18 per cent. So I had to count five seconds and then open the port throttle. I did so and there was a satisfying, deep rumble as the engine started winding up. Sure enough at 18 per cent the whole cockpit came to life with lights and captions suddenly illuminating.

After we had got both engines going and all the captions on the rather large warning panel at the lower right of the instrument panel had gone out I carried out the post-start checks and before too long we were on our way to the end of Edwards' westerly runway. The field of view from the cockpit was terrific; the sills were down at elbow level and I could easily see over the down-swept nose. The nose wheel steering operated via the rudder pedals but, even at idling power, the engines produced enough thrust to accelerate the jet so I had to keep braking using the large foot brakes. When we reached the holding area the procedure I had by now got used to of a man looking round the exterior of our mount started. It was then that I noticed another USAF idiosyncrasy: there was no parking brake. I had to push hard on the pedals to stop us creeping forward, especially as 'Joe' was out of sight below us. He seemed to take forever and, by the time that he reappeared and gave us a cheery thumbs-up, my calves were on fire! We then moved onto the runway.

But I still had to hold the brakes on once again as I ran the pair of Pratt & Whitney F100 engines up to full power. When I had made sure that there were no warnings showing and that the engine indications were all satisfactory I could relax my legs and off we went. I immediately selected full afterburners and within seconds we were at 125kt, which Steve had told me was the speed that I should pull back on the stick to get us off the ground. As soon as we were up I retracted the undercarriage with the chunky lever on my left and kept the nose coming up to hold 250kt, using the HUD to monitor everything.

Before our flight Steve had said that we would do this 'Gee-whiz' departure – 'just for the fun of it'. Hence we were lying on our backs holding 250kt in a near vertical climb. This was even more impressive than the Lightning! We were on our way up to 36,000ft. At 15,000ft Steve asked me to turn right, using 45° of bank, and to hold 0.9 Mach. As I turned I could easily pick out the far end of the 15,000ft runway still well ahead of us, we were still over the middle of the airfield and climbing like a homesick angel!

We were headed for the local supersonic corridor over the desert to the north-east of Edwards and as I approached 33,000ft I overbanked to help us level off at 36,000ft. Steve told me to keep the 'burners on and accelerate to 1.5 Mach. That took virtually no time at all and I then throttled back to hold that speed. It was less than two minutes since we had lined up on the runway and we had not made the most energy-efficient climb profile. It just showed that a 20-ton aeroplane propelled by 24 tonnes of thrust is a real fighter pilot's flying machine!

I was then encouraged to handle the Eagle at this supersonic speed, pulling up to 6G, rolling through 360° in both directions and simulating a gun or missile tracking task; the aircraft handled immaculately. Now it was time to slow down and descend for some manoeuvring at around 10,000ft, which was equally impressive. Using up to 30° AOA and 7G the fighting agility was well demonstrated. Then we did a deceleration in level flight to around 45° AOA: the speed was now less than 100kt and the aircraft felt to be right on the edge of controllability. Steve had said that I should use the ailerons to keep the wings level – 'but gently!' he added. He also told me to watch the rudders in the rear-view mirrors as I did so. I could see that, as we hung there, when I moved the stick left or right the rudders moved appropriately and, watching over my shoulder, there was no movement out on the wing. McDonnell Douglas had learnt from the F-4 Phantom and had mechanised the Eagle's flight control system to use the rudders for lateral stability and control at high AOAs – so relieving the pilot of the need to remember to change over during his high agility combat manoeuvring.

We then did some loops from 250kt using full afterburner and up to 30° AOA. The G level was not high and the aircraft went round smoothly and easily within a height band of less than 2,500ft. This led into a couple of interceptions with a T-38 flown by no other personage than Sqn Ldr Nigel Wood, who had taken over from me at Farnborough and was now on an exchange tour at Edwards. Nigel was down at a couple of thousand feet and we headed towards him at 5,000ft. Steve talked me through the manipulation of the radar using controls on the throttles. Once we had a radar lock on the T-38 a small box appeared in the HUD, in the centre of which was the still invisible target. As we closed on it the box tracked down the HUD and Steve told me that when it reached the bottom of the display I was to roll inverted, pull to 30° AOA and try to level off with the box in the centre of the display. It was only out of total trust in Steve and his wonderful jet that I rolled until the desert was over our heads and pulled. There was no need to worry, she came round beautifully and in less than thirty seconds we were right behind our target at the ideal range for an infrared missile shot. After that we did a couple of manoeuvring 'dogfights' – Nigel didn't stand a chance – and it was an ex-mud-mover beating an ex-fighter pilot. Like in Formula One it's the mount that counts!

We then moved off to fly at low level for a while, heading towards Mount Whitney, into the forest-covered valleys to check out how the Eagle flew at 250ft. The ease of manoeuvrability was not an issue, however; as we gained altitude up the side of the Sierras the surface winds were obviously increasing because we started to be thrown about a lot more. After a while it was as uncomfortable as it used to be in my Canberra in the hills and valleys of southern Germany or the highlands of Scotland on a windy day. In fact after one particularly bad episode of severe turbulence I pulled up as I no longer felt totally safe at 250ft and 420kt. After that very interesting episode I told Steve that I wanted to try some simulated air-ground gunnery. I selected the correct mode in the HUD, found a prominent target out in the desert and flew a low-level pattern, pulling up to around 1,000ft before taking sight and descending. I noticed straight away that as I held the aiming mark on the target I had to push to keep it there, so the angle of descent was increasing as we closed on the target: not ideal! I tried several variations of the attack with the same result.

How time flies when you're having fun. We had to return to base. I flew back and joined the circuit. The F-15 again showed its pedigree here too. The circuits were easy to fly; in fact I don't think that I have found an easier aircraft to fly round the visual pattern, before or since. When the undercarriage went down the HUD recalibrated itself to give more easily read values and it was straightforward to keep speed, height and AOA correct. The final approach was equally easy to fly and it didn't seem to matter whether the flaps were up or down, or the huge dorsal airbrake was in or out. Touchdown accuracy was also no problem. There was plenty of tailplane control to hold the nose high for aerodynamic braking effect and in the brisk headwind we could have stopped in less than 2,000ft. But we had to make the turn-off taxiway further down the runway so I let the big jet coast until we got there.

As I taxied this amazing fighter/bomber back to the 'Eagles' Nest' in the bright blue desert day I reflected on what I had experienced. This machine was like a Lightning on steroids but with a lot more fuel! However, were there any concerns about its operational utility as a low-level strike/attack in a European scenario? I had to write some sort of assessment so I had to get my thoughts in order. I would later write that report and describe what I had done, what I had found and what it might mean.

Overall, of course, there was no getting away from the fact that the F-15 was an impressive and formidable aeroplane. It was breathtakingly simple for what it could do. The flight control system was not totally digital but it was heavily stabilised and had some clever 'fixes', such as the rudder-aileron interconnect controlled by AOA. There was also an auto-trimming system for the longitudinal control; this I found was a mixed blessing as the clue as to speed given by stick position and the need to trim was removed. This reduced slightly the overall situational awareness for the pilot and I found it actually off-putting in the air-ground gunnery attacks. It was also not operationally useful to have to push during those attacks to keep the aiming point on the target. This was due to the fact that, as standard on an air-to-air fighter, the gun had been installed in the right wing root at an angle of 2° above the longitudinal fuselage datum. That was a normal practice for fighters where a bit of built-in lead angle was helpful. But for a ground attack aircraft the gun is usually depressed by 2 or 3°, just to avoid the unsafe situation of the attack dive steepening, as the ground got closer. The fact that the gun was built into the structure of the wing might be a fundamental problem. I would also like to have more than one gun for the attack role. I had suffered many 'stoppages' on one gun during my operational tour of 'mud-moving' and having at least one 'spare' was a good idea.

Another rather negative factor was the response of the F-15 to low-level turbulence; this is known as 'gust response'. Because of its low wing loading, that is the wing area divided by the weight, and the design of the wing's cross-section to give a rapid increase of lift with increases of AOA, the F-15 became uncomfortable and less easy to fly accurately when contour-following at low level in high winds; I thought that this was undesirable. It would get better at higher weights but not by much. Some sort of gust alleviation system might have to be built in.

Then there was the size of the jet. It was well known that in mixed fighter combat exercises the radio call of 'Where are you in relation to the F-15?' was often used because it was so big and easily picked out in a busy sky. Some pilots even called it the 'Flying Strafe Panel'! Size does matter, whether for visual or radar acquisition. It was, I wrote, sobering to note that this fighter is only a few inches shorter than a Lancaster bomber, has similar empty and maximum operating weights and just less than half the wing area. Not a showstopper but something else to be taken into account. Of course, it wasn't down to me to make any sort of decision – that was for the masters.

During my final visit to the USAFTPS, in January 1983, I was temporarily unfit to fly in ejection seats but I did spend an hour and a half sitting in the left-hand seat of the school's Boeing KC-135 under the watchful eye of Major Dan Vanderhorst. The main aim of the sortie was to introduce me to an experimental visualisation of the ILS on an HUD. Before we flew a few of those approaches Dan let me fly the big, four-engined jet 'up and away'. One very interesting feature was when he showed me what is called a lateral stick rap. This is a test to discover something about the lateral control system or, at high speeds, to see whether there is any tendency for the control to oscillate and, perhaps, go into a dangerous state called flutter. When Dan did give the control yoke a sharp input in roll the aircraft responded with a shudder and a couple of seconds later the cockpit rose and fell sharply as if we had just flown through some turbulence. Interesting!

It was fascinating to fly a big, four-engined jet – I had done it before in the Comet and Nimrod – but the Boeing 707, which is what the basic airframe of the KC-135 was, felt like a bigger aeroplane and had that slow response and relatively heavy control forces of the passenger/freighter/tanker. I was still pretty sure that it wasn't something I would want to do for a living!

The mention of the Comet and 707 reminds me of a favourite flying story. In the early days of jet airliners crossing the Atlantic a BOAC Comet was flying westbound at 40,000ft and its usual cruising speed of 0.76 Mach. Coming the other way was a Pan Am 707 at 33,000ft. As they crossed in mid Atlantic the BOAC captain said on the radio:

'I say, old boy, what are you doing down there?'

'Mach point 8 and makin' a profit,' came the reply.

In early 1983 I would be once more winging my way across the Atlantic at 0.8 Mach in the back of a Varig Airlines Boeing on the way to Rio de Janeiro. I was accompanying the A&AEE Commandant, Air Cdr Reggie Spiers, ETPS CO, Wg Cdr Robin Hargreaves and the Principal Tutor (Rotary Wing), Sqn Ldr Dave Reid on a visit to Brazil at the invitation of the CEO of the Embraer Aircraft Company and the Head of the Brazilian Flight Test Centre, located at the airfield of São José dos Campos. After a very pleasant stopover in Rio we were flown up country in an Embraer aircraft to make our visit. There I got to fly one of the Tucano YT-27 trainer prototypes. One of the other prototypes had been lost during testing in August of the previous year and Señor Gabral, who had jumped out of that one, was the man I was due to fly with. The Embraer Tucano was powered by a Pratt & Whitney PT6A free-turbine turboprop. The cockpit was very well designed and I particularly liked the fully glazed, curving canopy with no arch in my field of view; it was the first time I had ever flown a powered aircraft with a completely unobstructed view of the outside world.

The Tucano handled very nicely with a good balance between power and controllability. We climbed to carry out stalls, spins (including two inverted) and a full range of aerobatics. I had very little to criticise about the aircraft; it was truly delightful to fly. Then came the best trick of all. Once back over the airfield Senor Gabral asked me to pull the throttle back through a gate at the rear end of its travel. This caused the prop to feather, but the engine continued to idle. We then carried out a practice forced landing. Once I had touched down I moved the throttle out of its gate and progressively forward. The power response was almost instantaneous. During the couple of circuits that we flew after that I found the Tucano very easy to fly accurately, the only tricky bit was in keeping straight with the rudder when power was increased for touch-and-go landings on the runway. The final trick was the ability to use reverse pitch to help slow down. I had been asked to make an assessment of the Tucano as a replacement for the Harvards at Boscombe Down, which were used to chase parachute trials. Accordingly I had tried flying the low-speed, steep turns that were needed. Unfortunately they could not be done safely at the speeds we flew in the venerable Harvard. However, I was very impressed with the machine as a trainer and particularly liked the ability to make PFLs under near-real conditions with the prop feathered. In other types of turboprops, where the turbine is not free, it can be a bit of a distraction trying to maintain zero-thrust while carrying out an already challenging exercise.

Although, as far as I am aware, my report did not circulate outside Boscombe Down I thought that the MOD's decision to re-engine and part-redesign the Tucano under a contract with Short Brothers was a retrograde and no doubt politically driven step.

33 AMERICAN VISITS – USNTPS

In January 1982 the ETPS staff made a visit to the US Naval Test Pilot School (USNTPS) at Naval Air Station Patuxent River, situated on the shore of Chesapeake Bay in Maryland. We had arrived to find the weather very cold and frosty with, initially at least, clear blue skies. After a day of orientation and interchanges with the USNTPS staff there was some flying in their aircraft on offer. On Tuesday 12 January I was slated to fly the Douglas TA-4F Skyhawk in the morning and the Rockwell T-2 Buckeye in the afternoon. A busy day was ahead!

Ed Heinemann of the Douglas Aircraft Company originally designed the Skyhawk in the 1950s as a light attack aircraft for the US Navy, to replace the piston-engined A-1 Skyraider. The Skyhawk has a low-mounted delta wing small enough not to require the usual wing-folding mechanism common on naval, carrier-borne aircraft. The two-seat T model was used for operational conversion and the USNTPS had at least two of them in their fleet. I was to fly with Lt Cdr Bob Vessely and we walked out to our diminutive white and red jet sitting rather prettily on the tarmac. Bob helped me strap into the aircraft and gave me a whistle-stop tour of the tiny cockpit. The Martin Baker ejection seat and cosy cockpit made me feel at home; it was not dissimilar to the single-seat Hunter. I had sole control for starting the engine and that turned out to be a bit of a trick. As the engine wound up, under the influence of the external electrical power, I had to open the throttle a bit to allow the fuel in and then push it outboard to initiate the electrical igniters (like spark plugs) in the engine combustion chambers to get the fire going. At the first attempt I couldn't make it work, but one of the ground crew climbed up and showed me how!

Once we had checked everything we moved out towards the runway. The Skyhawk was easy to manoeuvre with its sensitive nose wheel steering and, when we had done all the pre-take-off checks, I lined up on the runway. I wound the J65 engine up to full power against the brakes, made sure there were no adverse indications and released the brakes. The acceleration was good but not startling and we lifted off at about 130kt. Holding a shallow climb I retracted the landing gear and accelerated to the climbing speed. We soared up over Chesapeake Bay, with the Atlantic seaboard soon in view beyond the Delaware Peninsula. Bob told me to stay over the bay and gave me a free hand to throw the Skyhawk around as I wished. The roll rate was quick and it was easy to stop it where I wanted to. A loop from 360kt used up about 3,500ft of sky and the little bird turned well at that sort of speed using full power at 5–6G. One slightly bizarre thing that I noted was that if there was any sideslip at all when G was applied a wing went down quite rapidly. This was due to the slats on the leading edge of the wings being operated by increased AOA and/or gravity. If one dropped before the other the lift on that wing would, temporarily at least, increase more than on the other: hence the undemanded roll.

But that was the only problem I came across. It was no wonder that the Skyhawk, which had sparkling performance for its size and could carry its own weight in ordinance, was such a success. It had been in USN service since 1956 and sold widely around the world. It was equally pleasant to fly around the visual pattern, although being a delta the nose was quite high at the lower speeds. There was a dummy deck with the appropriate lights to guide the pilot, simulating an aircraft carrier approach, so Bob showed me one and I had a couple of goes. There was one at Boscombe Down so it wasn't totally new to me. I think that my back-seater was reasonably happy with my attempts!

After an American aircrew lunch – coffee and doughnuts – I met up with Commander John Watkins, the CO of the school and a 1974 ETPS graduate, for my flight in the T-2B Buckeye. This was another 1950s USN airplane that was still doing sterling service as the service's intermediate jet trainer. It was powered by two Pratt & Whitney J60 turbojets, each delivering 3,000lb of thrust at maximum power. That gave the aircraft a power-to-weight ratio of 1:2. The main aim of the trip was to let me experience the various spin modes of the Buckeye, including the inverted spin. John briefed me on the actions required to get the T-2 into the latter; it was rather complicated so I paid attention.

When we took off I was pleasantly surprised by the Buckeye's performance with an initial climb rate of over 5,000ft per minute. It was not one of those aircraft that looked good: it was rather short and 'stubby' with the profile of a rather overweight porpoise! However, it handled well enough for its role. Once we were up and away, high over Chesapeake Bay, John took control to demonstrate an erect spin. It was relatively unremarkable for a straight-winged jet, fairly smooth with a steady spin rate. I then climbed back up for a couple of my own. After that John said it was time to go inverted. He took control once more to demonstrate the entry and recovery.

He started by accelerating and then pulling up to a vertical climb. The throttles were closed and as the speed dropped the stick went fully forward then fully left, after which full right rudder was applied and the stick came fully and centrally back. The timing of each of these inputs was completed to the chant, 'One potato, two potato, three potato – four'!

The result was a wildly gyrating tumble that quickly settled into a fairly fast upside-down rotation with at least −1G, possibly a bit more. After four or five turns (I had lost count by then) John recovered the gyrating Buckeye back to normal flight.

'OK, Mike – your turn.'

I took control and tried my best to emulate what John had done. The result was satisfyingly similar but this time I noticed just how much noise the airframe made as if in protest to this abuse. I recovered on John's call and asked if we could do one more. He agreed so I put the poor old Buckeye through it all one more time. That was enough. Then I was allowed to try some aerobatics, with John prompting me as to the best speeds. It reminded me of the Vampire, except that I could see out better!

Back in the visual pattern John coached me round the circuit and we did some landings, including a couple to the dummy deck that I had used that morning in the Skyhawk. The Buckeye 'came aboard' about 20kt slower than the TA-4 and a fairly smooth landing was not difficult to accomplish. However, I supposed that 'greasers'[29] were not much taught by the Navy! The following day was very cold, with snow, icy roads and no flying. We had been given the use of a minibus and, for reasons I can no longer remember, I was the designated driver. After spending some time at the school we were invited to look around the hangars of the primary test squadron at Pax River –VX-1. As we entered the huge, thankfully heated, space we were greeted by the sight of several brand-new F-18 Hornets, the US Navy's latest fighter. The aircraft's full test and development programme had been flown from Pax River since the late 1970s and it was due to go into US Navy and Marine Corps service the year after our visit. I had heard about various problems encountered by the Hornet in its early testing, including an inability to match the required rates of roll. As it used ailerons as well as other devices on the back of a 'plastic' wing I had wondered whether the problem was caused by some adverse twisting of the wing, due to the aerodynamic force on the deflected aileron, so reducing the rate of roll. I sneaked up to one of the shiny jets and reached up to grab the missile guide rail on the wingtip. Sure enough it took little effort to move it up and down by several inches! While flexibility is a key to the use of air power it can have its limitations!

As development progressed the flight control folks had to work hard to achieve what the USN and USMC wanted. It was rumoured that, in the end, when the pilot moved the stick to the left at high speed no fewer than seven aerodynamic surfaces moved. Notwithstanding all that, the Hornet soon became a formidable fighter and, later, strike/attack aeroplane.

When we had received some more briefings and chatted with a few of the resident test pilots it was time to return to our rooms in the BOQ. We walked out to the minibus, very carefully because of the ice on the ground. The vehicle was totally glazed over in thick ice. Rain was falling and freezing on contact with everything it landed on. I had to crack the ice to get the key in the door lock, meanwhile the guys were all banging the sides of the bus to get their doors to open. We finally got aboard, started up and I drove us back to our quarters at about 5mph.

When I got to my room, I turned the heating up and switched the TV on. There seemed to be some sort of disaster movie on. A helicopter was flying above water with chunks of ice in it. Then a woman, hanging desperately onto a rope lowered from the chopper, was being towed to the bank of what was clearly a river. The rope slipped from her grasp. I continued watching wondering what film it was. Then a man dived into the icy water, fully clothed and managed to drag the woman to the other people gathered on the bank. This was very exciting and realistic stuff! Then the picture switched to a bridge and the camera was carried along towards some cars that had obviously been crushed by something. I saw a bloody hand. Then the camera

29 'Greaser' is aircrew-speak for a very smooth landing.

panned out to the river where a blue painted aircraft fin and rudder was sticking up out of the water.

Then the realisation came. This was no Hollywood disaster movie – it was real and live. Then a pair of news anchors came on and brought new viewers up to date. An Air Florida Boeing 737 had taken off from National Airport in Washington DC but had descended after take-off onto the 14th Street Bridge and crashed into the Potomac River. Then we were taken back to the helicopter, a Bell JetRanger, doing its extraordinary work of trying to get the few people that were still alive and floating in the river to the shore.

After our experience only 60 miles away I was surprised that any aircraft had tried to take off that afternoon. The icing on the wings and tail surfaces must have made them less than aerodynamically efficient. We learnt much later that icing, not just of the wings but also of very important probes that gave the pilots wrong information as to the thrust of their engines, was the cause. It was a great tragedy that should never have happened. Seventy-eight people perished that grey, glacial afternoon, including four in the cars on the bridge. It was horrific to watch the aftermath.

The next day we visited the NASA establishment at Langley, Virginia – also home to the National Security Agency – but we were not allowed anywhere near that. Our journey from Pax to Langley was by Boeing Vertol CH-46 Sea Knight twin-rotor helicopter; it would take about an hour. The previous night the heating in my room had failed and I had passed the night in very cold and fitful sleep with all my heavy-duty clothing on or over my bed. This one hour ride in the back of an unheated Mini Chinook was not helping! Some of the guys were quite worried about me and they weren't alone. Hypothermia was setting in. I just huddled down in my RAF greatcoat (officers for the use of) and waited for it all to be over.

We eventually reached our destination and were welcomed by the nice NASA folks with large mugs of steaming coffee and yet more doughnuts. By the time we went in to the welcoming talk I was warming up and soon back on form. After some lectures we were taken on a guided tour during which we were shown a series of wind tunnels, one of which was enormous, and the Light Aircraft Crash Rig. This was used to drop real light aircraft from a large gantry onto concrete at varying angles and rates of descent; all aimed at helping the industry build more survivability into them. We had been shown lots of films of the work there and there was a test specimen in the rig. Sadly it had already been dropped so we didn't get to see an impact for real. The dummies inside the crumpled 'spam-can' certainly didn't look too happy!

A lunch and more lectures followed and we mounted the still serviceable Sea Knight for our return journey in the late afternoon. As was the custom a social event followed, an evening out at Evans' seafood restaurant, where the tablecloths were either brown wrapping paper or non-existent, but the food was terrific. There I discovered that I don't like oysters unless they are cooked. However, my prowess as a one-handed Key lime pie eater had preceded me and I had to take on their newest instructor. Thankfully I won again!

Visits to the US Navy at Patuxent River were always congenial, educational and a very useful interchange of ideas. They made return visits each year, once memorably delayed because their own transport, a rather aged Lockheed P-3 Orion, gave up on the way. If I recall correctly they spent a couple of days north of the Arctic Circle while it was fixed! However, that did not inhibit their enthusiasm while they were with us – for sampling the flying on offer nor the beer and skittles in a local pub.

34 EUROPEAN TOURS

During every course, visits were made to centres of aerospace excellence in the UK and on continental Europe. The UK visits were much as I have described them earlier and the students seemed always to enjoy them as much as we had – especially the lunches and dinners! However, I have some memories that stand out. During a visit to Westland Helicopters at Yeovil, after a good lunch, we were sat down in a softly lit room for a series of lectures on Westland's vision for their future. One of our number, who shall be nameless to protect his reputation, and who was in the seat closest to the lecturer, quite quickly nodded off! His head then progressively sank towards the table. The presenter bravely carried on by dint of never looking at the recumbent figure in front of him, but addressing all his remarks to the back wall! Embarrassing or what?

Visits were usually flown in our Andover, XS 606, and I can recall several amusing happenings involving such passenger flights. The first was when John Thorpe and Keith Crawford were flying us to Rochester airfield in Kent for our visit to the avionics company of Marconi-Elliott. The airfield at Rochester was all grass; normally no problem for our Andover, but on this day we arrived just after it had been mowed. This became very apparent after landing when John selected reverse pitch on the propellers and we disappeared in a green cloud. The engineers were picking bits of grass out of all sorts of places on the aeroplane for days afterwards!

On another occasion we were on our return leg from a visit to Singer Link-Miles at Lancing in Sussex; this time it was my turn to be co-pilot to John Thorpe. We had left Shoreham Airport a little later than planned and so we were cruising at the best speed to make it back before the airfield at Boscombe closed. I was, as is usual duty for the 'co', doing all the radio chat. As we got closer to Boscombe Down I was instructed by Farnborough radar that the Boscombe approach controller had us on his radar and that I should now call him. So I did: 'Boscombe, this is Tester 54, we are an Andover, over Andover, on a radar handover, over.' Bless him, his reply was, 'Say again?' So I got to say it twice. Opportunities in life like that come along so rarely!

When I flew the Andover, especially as captain, I liked to use the on-board Public Address (PA) system. I would welcome everyone on board this 'Sunshine Airways' flight to wherever we were going, with all the 'Captain Speaking' bits about heights and speeds, time of arrival and weather. Such fun!

Somewhere along the route I liked to ask the folks down the back to look out for a major landmark and, if they spotted it, to please let the navigator know. I usually closed in-flight messages with: '... and there is nothing wrong with the starboard engine.'

However, on one return to base the port engine had a problem that required it to be shut down. Once we had feathered the prop successfully I put out the following message on the PA system: 'Those of you sitting on the port side and are still awake may be aware that the port propeller is not doing its usual thing. Please do not be alarmed. We are continuing our journey back to Boscombe Down – and be assured there is nothing wrong with the starboard engine.' We landed safely off a single-engine approach.

On another occasion Boscombe greeted us with the news that some sort of mishap had blocked the main runway and that the second runway was, as we already knew, being resurfaced. We were told that we were diverted to RAF Lyneham.

'Boscombe, Tester 52, is the grass runway available?' I asked.

'Affirmative,' came the reply.

'OK, we'll use that.'

I then got on the PA system and told the talking ballast that we could not use the runway and that we were being diverted; however, I purposely omitted to say to where. It was Friday afternoon and Happy Hour was due to start in thirty minutes. There was an audible collective groan from the back. It was time to let them off the hook.

'Oh yes, I'm sorry I didn't tell you. We are diverted to the grass strip. You'll still make it to happy hour!' I announced on the PA system. Cheers all round.

Another thing that we did with the Andover was to renew the procedural element of our instrument ratings by flying on the airways system and carrying out an ILS approach and landing at our destination. Occasionally we used to fly these sorties to and from Guernsey in the Channel Islands. This gave us an opportunity to re-qualify two of us and show our collective thanks to all those folk around Boscombe Down that helped the school in its work: such as typists, technicians, mechanics, photographers, secretaries, scientists and painters.

The flights would be arranged and the word put around that places were available on a first-come, first-served basis. We rarely had trouble filling the forty or so seats and the excursion, aft of the cockpit door at least, would quickly take on the atmosphere of a school trip or works outing! After landing at Guernsey Airport at about 11 a.m. there would be about three hours' free time for people to take a bus or taxi into the island's capital, St Peter Port, for duty free shopping at Bucktrouts drinks emporium or sightseeing and a pub lunch; or any combination of the three!

One time I was doing my test and so sitting in the left-hand seat. I had settled the aeroplane down on the airway and the autopilot was tracking us towards the next radio beacon. We had received a request for some of the ladies from the typing pool to come and look at the flight deck, which had been approved by Ron Rhodes, my examiner and captain. It was time for a 'wizard wheeze'!

I pulled the oxygen hose out of its box on the left-hand side and fitted one of my gloves over the end of it, securing it with an elastic band supplied by our navigator, Cliff Ware. I turned on the oxygen supply and the glove inflated, then I wedged it onto the left-hand end of the control yoke and dropped my right hand onto the autopilot control panel alongside my right thigh. The women arrived. The usual question, 'how do you look at all those instruments?' was answered with the usual answer: 'One at a time.'

Then one of the women noticed the thin green 'arm' and its podgy 'hand' on the controls. 'What's that?' she shrilly enquired.

'Oh, that's the autopilot – we call him George,' I enlightened her. Nervous giggles ensued. 'Do you want to see it work?' I asked.

Curiosity got the better of them, 'Oooh, yes please.'

'Turn right please, George,' I intoned politely. With my right hand, resting casually on the autopilot control panel and well out of the ladies' field of view I turned the bank controller to the right. The control yoke moved and, of course, 'the hand' went with it.

After a few seconds I said, 'OK, George, please now turn left back onto our heading.'

I hit the required button and the aeroplane did exactly what it was programmed to do. More nervous giggles followed.

'Would you like to tell George what to do?' I asked. Eventually one of the women said she would.

'OK, go ahead,' I said.

Rather timidly she said, 'Turn left, George.' Nothing happened.

'It doesn't work – I don't believe you!' she said, now less timid.

'It does,' I replied, 'but you forgot to say "please".'

'Oh. Turn left *please*, George.'

I did my fiddling with the autopilot controls, still unnoticed, and there were squeals of delight. It was all getting a bit too much for dear old Ron so we asked the women to leave and I got on with the rest of the test! I passed.

Then there was the time when we nearly didn't get home from Paris. On 2 June 1983, the Boss, Wg Cdr Robin Hargreaves and I, as co-pilot, flew the school staff and students to Paris Le Bourget for a day at the Paris Air Show. It was great to be able to deliver our chattering cargo right into the heart of the show. After we had parked, lowered the rear ramp and the whole aircraft through the unique 'kneeling system', all were warned to be back at 5 p.m. at the latest. We had a departure slot at 5.40 and if we missed that we would probably not get out of Paris until well into the evening.

With that caution ringing in their ears the hordes departed for their day out and individual invitations to various aerospace companies' hospitality chalets. When our engineer, Flt Lt Brian Hemming, had secured the aircraft, we crew set off for our individual dates with destiny; however, unlike the rest, we would not be partaking of the *rouge* or the *blanc* with our lunch.

We reconvened by the Andover well ahead of time, opened up and I got on the radio to confirm our departure slot. 'Tester 50, eeet eez still at 17.40 hours,' was the reply. 'Please call when you start your engines.'

As our watches (aircrew for the use of) approached 5 p.m. the noise in the cabin had increased markedly as everyone related their stories of the day, in voices no doubt amplified by their consumption of good food and wine. Brian Hemming went to do a head-count.

'We're two down,' he announced when he re-entered the cockpit.

'Who?' asked the Boss.

'The two Aussies,' came the almost predictable answer.

'Well we can't wait much longer. We'll start the engines but I'll leave the ramp open. Keep the ladder handy in case they turn up,' the Boss instructed. 'Mike, call the tower for permission to start.'

I did so and they replied with yet another confirmation of our departure slot. By the time we had got the engines going and carried out the after-start checks we were still two short. I called for permission to taxi, which was instantly approved. We had to reverse out of our parking slot, so Brian stationed himself on the ramp and plugged into the intercom, so he could warn us if anything got in our way. Or even if any Aussies suddenly appeared.

'Feet on the floor!' stressed the Boss. He and I had to keep our feet well clear of the toe-operated brakes so that we did not instinctively try to stop or slow our rearward motion with the brakes and so endanger the aircraft by tipping it tail-down. He then selected reverse pitch on the props and the aircraft slowly started its rearwards journey. Once we had moved a few metres the Boss used the nose wheel steering to turn us onto the taxiway that had been behind us. Now we had to stop, so reverse pitch was cancelled and a modicum of forward thrust was selected. After a few seconds we stopped and then started moving forward. We followed the taxiway towards the centre of the airfield and as we passed the end of the crowd barriers we heard, 'There they are!' from Brian at the back. He had seen two figures vaulting the crowd barrier, being chased by a small group of Gendarmes. The Boss stopped and Brian lowered the ladder. The escapees ran directly towards us, gradually outstripping the long arm of the law.

'Tester 50, why 'ave you stopped?' enquired the tower controller, 'Do you 'ave a problem?'

'Only a minor one,' I replied, 'We will be on the move soon.'

'Well you only 'ave three minutes to make your take-off. Eef you miss zat, you will not be able to go before 19.45.'

I looked at the Le Bourget airfield plan I had in front of me and noticed that there was an access taxiway to the runway well before the far end.

'Are you happy to take off with 5,000ft of runway available?' I asked the Boss.

'Of course,' he replied. 'Are those reprobates aboard now?' he asked Brian.

'Yes, Boss, you can raise the ramp now,' came the reply. I selected the appropriate switch as the Boss set off at a merry pace.

'We are OK now and we request departure from taxiway Charlie,' I transmitted. We had one minute to go. The Boss went through the pre-take-off checks with Brian, who was now back up front with us, and completed them just as we arrived at the runway.

'Tester 50, you are cleared for departure. Follow ze standard Le Bourget departure procedure and call Paris Control on 123.55 after you pass 1,000ft. Bon voyage!' We arrived home before the airfield closed and drinks were on the Aussies that night!

The other visits to the Continent included the French Test Pilots' School and Dassault Aviation, both based at Istres in Provence; the Italian Flight Test Centre at the airfield of Pratica di Mare outside Rome; and the German Air Force Flight Test Centre at Manching near Munich. All these locations made for a motivating, educational and entertaining time for us all, especially the students. There was usually some flying on offer and plenty of interaction with test pilots and engineers involved in some of the latest aerospace R&D. Of course, as was usual when industry has the opportunity to influence possible international future movers and shakers, they tend to entertain royally. The high spot each year was the Dassault lunch, which included ample quantities of their own wines; the short straw of each tour was to be nominated as crew for the leg from France to Germany! Perhaps the low spot, for me at least, was the *Schweinshaxe* to which we were treated in Bavaria. Lots of people seemed to rave about it, but I was with Andy Mechling, one of our US Navy students, when he spotted a Bavarian branch of McDonald's on our way to the hotel. 'Great! There's a McDonald's – real food!'

In Rome the Italians always gave an introductory lecture that included the history of Italian aviation, which started surprisingly early and was very innovative. While visiting Pratica we always stayed in hotels in Rome, about 20km north-east of the airbase. The coach journeys to and from Rome were invariably full of incident and entertainment. Once we collided with a lorry, on another occasion our driver took a shortcut down some narrow Roman backstreets and eventually became firmly wedged between parked cars; the Carabinieri were not amused, nor were the owners of the several Fiat 500s involved, which had to be lifted out of the way!

However, evenings out in the Eternal City were a wonderful experience, although the highly inflated Italian currency, lire, made the bills seem inordinately expensive. Strangely the international four-letter code for the air base at Pratica di Mare was Lire! During my sojourns in Rome I took in most of the sights: the Colosseum, Vatican City with St Peter's Square and Basilica, the Spanish Steps, eating al fresco in the Piazza Navona, the Trevi Fountain (with the obligatory coin chucked in) and much more. However, the historical site that made the biggest impression on me was the Roman Forum; it just oozed times gone by. But in Rome's present the fearsome pace of the traffic and the habitual triple parking by the natives made me resolve to never bring a car into Rome! In speaking of this to one of the Italian test pilots, Luca Evangelisti, he explained that Roman traffic lights had more than three colours. There were not only red, amber and green, but also red-red and red-green as well as green-green and green-red! He tried to explain it but soon lost me; it was all to do with the adjacent pedestrian crossing lights! No wonder there are so many road traffic accidents in Rome!

While at Pratica I flew an Aermacchi MB-339 jet trainer, an Aeritalia G.222 transport and an Agusta-Bell 204 (Huey) helicopter. All the pilots I flew with were very trusting and accommodating in letting me fly for most of the sorties. The MB-339's performance was not as good as the Hawk, but it had an HUD and an on-board navigation system that needed some management. In lacking these the Hawk fell short, at least in my opinion, as a trainer for the likes of the Harrier, Jaguar and Tornado. The G.222 handled very nicely and had an amazing trick up its sleeve: reverse pitch could be selected in flight so allowing astoundingly steep dives and approaches to be made. I thought that there might be some safety loopholes with this. The trip in the 'Huey' was brilliant. In typical Italian fashion the captain, the Boss of the test centre Col Anzani, seemed to assume that I knew how to fly helicopters without asking me. Fortunately, of course, I did. All I needed were a few numbers to aim at. The AB 204 was as rugged and basic as it appeared and we 'wokka-wokka'ed' our way around looking at the scenery. The good colonel did all the navigating and got me to fly over the Pope's summer residence at Castel Gandolfo and the adjacent Lake Albano. It was a pretty impressive holiday home sitting on the ridge of the hills overlooking the glassy waters of the lake. I wondered if the Pope ever took a bit of time out to go fishing! Back at base I asked if I could try an engine-off landing but was politely but firmly told that such things were not done unless absolutely essential!

During our visits to Istres I only flew once. There was some more exciting stuff on offer, such as Mirage and Alpha-jet, but all I got was a flight in the left-hand seat of a pocket-sized twin-turboprop transport aircraft called a Nord 262 Frégate. It was a sort of high-winged, two-thirds scale Andover with about two-thirds of the latter's performance. Commandant Thomas and I took the aircraft out over the Camargue at around 8,000ft and I stalled it, flew around on one engine, tried to establish its critical speeds and looked at the 262's handling and stability. It was all fairly unremarkable and we then returned to Istres where we used a very small portion of the 4,000m runway for a few circuits and landings.

But the most memorable flight of all our European trips was to happen at Manching on 16 October 1981. On the second day there I was told to go meet with Herr Horst Philipp. Horst had been a civilian test pilot with the German Air Force Flight Test Centre for almost twenty years and already was a bit of a legend in his own lifetime. He had flown many experimental types including the Harrier-like VFW VAK 191, and its 'Flying Bedstead' predecessor the SG 1262, both of which were VTOL research machines. Horst had also flown many operational types from around the world, including the American F-15, F-16, F-18 and F-20 as well as French types such as the Mirage 3 and Mirage 2000. But he probably had most time on the Lockheed F-104, which the Luftwaffe had procured in the mid 1960s. And it was the dual-controlled version of that very sharp-pointed flying machine that I was going to fly, with Horst sitting in the back. What a brave chap!

We walked out to the shiny, low slung, almost wingless fighter and Horst showed me round. It didn't take long! There were red flexible guards on the wing leading edges because they are so sharp that they could cut and be easily damaged. The wingspan was only just over 20ft! The high T-tail at the back of the tube-like fuselage looked too big – but at Mach 2 the directional stability would need all the help it could get.

I climbed into the front cockpit and Horst gave me the guided tour. Like most American cockpits there was sufficient room for comfort, if not for swinging felines, and the instrument panel was very typical of the era. Horst talked me through the engine start sequence and very soon the Pratt & Whitney J-79 was rumbling satisfyingly behind us and it was time to go. But then the trip almost came to a stop before it had started. Horst had showed me the button on the stick for selecting nose wheel steering and I had my middle finger poised over that as I waved the chocks away and added a modicum of power before releasing the brakes. After rolling forward a couple of metres I stabbed the toe-brakes to check that they were working. They were. We were parked outside a hangar and the doors ahead of us were partly open. It was then that I noticed that a crowd of ETPS folk were standing there watching. Ignoring them I pressed the required button to select nose wheel steering on. There didn't seem to be a light or a caption to tell me that it was, nevertheless I put on full left rudder to turn us away from the hangar doors. Nothing happened.

'Have you pushed the button, Mike?'

'Yes.' By now I was stabbing at the left brake to try to initiate a turn, but the little machine was reluctant to go where I wanted it to. Then we stopped – Horst had applied his brakes.

'You have to push the button and *hold it in.*'

'Oh – sorry I didn't realise that!'

'OK – try again,' said Horst with a chuckle in his voice. Sadly he wasn't the only one chuckling; all the students and staff watching were falling about in mirth at my struggle with the jet. Banana skins came to mind! Once that had been sorted out, I could steer the F-104 easily; I had assumed that it was a one-press activation, like the Jaguar.

When we arrived safely at the end of the runway Horst went through the pre-take-off checklist with me, called for departure and asked for entry into the supersonic corridor.

We lined up, I applied full power, let the brakes off and rocked the throttle outboard and further forward (just like the Lightning) to get the afterburner lit. When the thrust from that kicked in we were motoring well and at 150kt I eased the stick back and she unstuck at about 180kt. Gear and flaps up, accelerate to 450kt and then point at the sky. It wasn't quite as sensational as the Lightning but the F-104 was no slouch. Horst was doing the radio and at 20,000ft he asked me to turn from our westerly heading onto a south-easterly one. I initially put on 60° of bank and held 0.9 Mach. The jet virtually stopped climbing, which was a bit of a surprise. *Ah, its those tiny wings*, I thought. *They don't work so well at subsonic speeds.* So I backed off the bank and G and we started up again, but not so fast.

Eventually we got onto our heading, levelled at about 36,000ft, left the 'burner' in and swept through the 'sound barrier' with barely a murmur. At 1.4 Mach I cancelled the extra power and, under instruction, carried out a couple of 3G turns. Now the little wings were working well! After that bit of handling we descended to 12,000ft and Horst was brave enough to invite me to do some aerobatics. Rolls, both rapid and slow, were relatively easy, the handling was good, but the stick forces for pulling manoeuvres like loops and barrel rolls were a bit heavier than I was used to. But that was generally normal for US aircraft, especially of the 1950s. Moreover, a loop took up almost 12,000ft of vertical airspace!

After cavorting in the southern German skies we descended to low level so that I could experience the F-104 in the role it was procured for: low-level fighter-bomber. With those small wings it rode the air turbulence very well, steady as a rock. The ease and precision with which I could roll the aircraft made it easy to turn down valleys and minimise our exposure. We were doing 450kt and I noticed that the fuel-flow gauge was showing 4,000lb per hour. That was about the same as my old Canberra B(I)8, but at 150kt faster. But it was a bit more than the twin-engined Buccaneer at the same speed.

Thankfully, Horst was on top of the navigation and after fifteen minutes or so cruising round very attractive parts of Bavaria we climbed to a couple of thousand feet and made our way back to Manching. We still had enough fuel to do a few circuits so Horst demonstrated one and then let me have a go. Like the Buccaneer the Starfighter used air from the engine compressor blown out through thin slots at the rear of the wings to give them more lift when the flaps were down. The speeds I had to fly around the pattern were similar to those of the Lightning or the Jaguar, so were not too unfamiliar. However, I noted a definite need to use rudder with roll once the blow was operating, otherwise the jet seemed to want to carry straight on instead of turning. I had also noted that Horst had used a shallow approach angle. This helped him to keep the power up so that the blow pressure stayed high enough to make the magic work. I therefore followed his example, although on the first attempt I probably overdid it, creeping up on the airfield using all available cover. The only forward view that Horst had for this bit was through an extendible periscope and he was coaxing me not to go any further below the glidepath! Like all the modern jets that I had flown, it was desirable not to throttle back until the wheels were on the ground – so I didn't. Touchdown speeds were about 160kt so the braking parachute was streamed once I had the nose wheel firmly on the ground.

What an experience it all had been. What a brilliant aircraft designer Kelly Johnson of Lockheed was. To go against the grain and not use swept wings for his supersonic fighter typified his genius and willingness to push the envelope. He invented the concept of the ultra-secret Skunk Works, from which came the U-2 (which was a Starfighter with very long wings), the SR-71 Blackbird and the F-117 Nighthawk stealth bomber. My friend Tom Morgenfeld would end his career as a test pilot by flying for Lockheed's Skunk Works for about twenty years – lucky man! For me the future would be quite different but similar, in that I would spend another ten years as a test pilot bringing my total in the flight testing world to twenty. But that was for the as yet unknown future. Now it was on with the ETPS motley!

35 OPERATION CORPORATE

On Friday 2 April 1982 Argentina invaded and occupied the self-governing British Overseas Territory of the Falkland Islands. This action was the culmination of seventeen years of diplomatic interchanges between the British and Argentine governments, overseen much of the time by the United Nations. The Argentines had, throughout, maintained that the territory, known to them as Las Malvinas, rightly and historically belonged to them.

During the weekend that followed the surrender of the small force of Royal Marines on the islands, the UK Cabinet, headed by Prime Minister Margaret Thatcher, authorised the dispatch of a naval task force to the islands. The UN also passed Resolution 502, which demanded the immediate withdrawal of Argentine forces. In an amazing show of effort, ingenuity and sheer persistence the initial component of the task force was assembled and sailed south only three days later. The operation was given the codename 'Corporate'.

Over the following three weeks more elements of the task force sailed south, initially to Ascension Island off the west of Africa, while frantic diplomacy involving the two belligerent governments and the USA continued, with the UN playing referee. When it was clear that there was to be no solution without conflict, the UK Government approved military action to retake the Falkland Islands; the task force and all its logistical support headed into the South Atlantic.

During the war the only offensive air assets available to the British operational commanders were twenty-eight Sea Harriers and fourteen Harrier GR.3s on board the aircraft carriers HMS *Invincible* and HMS *Hermes*. There were also Wessex, Sea King, Lynx and Gazelle helicopters embarked with various seaborne elements. Additional helicopter support, vital for the operation, was to come from five Chinooks, which were being carried aboard the Cunard container ship *Atlantic Conveyor*. The ship was hit by two air-launched Exocet missiles and sank with four of the Chinooks still on the deck.

As the war developed, long-range bombing missions using Vulcan bombers were conceived; these missions were to be air-to-air refuelled on the way to and from the Falklands by Victor tankers based on Ascension Island. More thought was then given to extending the range of other aircraft, such as the Nimrod maritime patrol aircraft, by installing a flight refuelling probe, and modifying some Hercules and Vulcans to become tankers. Then there were operational modifications required for the Harriers, even including the use of a jettisonable pod for dropping mail to the troops on the ground.

At Boscombe Down the work quickly ramped up for the test squadrons as the urgent operational requirements flowed in. The usual timescales were cut, so much so that the Nimrod in-flight refuelling system was designed, installed and tested in five days, and that included pilot training time. Of course we on ETPS were aware of the increased work going on, especially as the airfield working hours were extended, even to some flying taking place over the weekends. We did not avail ourselves of the latter, but we were able to catch up with the syllabus deadlines by flying into the early evenings.

Then we were brought into Operation Corporate. Initially by making our Andover and a crew available for special and short-notice transport tasks that were within the remit of the R&D business. After a couple of these rather ad hoc sorties, taking people and equipment from one place to another and then often others to a third destination, we named ourselves 'Ruskin Airways'. This was in homage to a TV series called *Airline* that had been screened in January and February of 1982. The programme starred Roy Marsden as Jack Ruskin, a post-war ex-RAF pilot, using surplus DC-3s to start an airline. However, the Boss wouldn't let us get the paint shop to put the Ruskin Airways logo on the nose of the Andover!

I flew one of these trips on 4 and 5 May. The brief was to fly to Southend Airport, pick up some civilian personnel and some 'special' kit and fly them all to RAF Kinloss in northern Scotland, one of the two UK Nimrod bases. We were to stop there overnight and then check in with base the following morning for the next task. After arriving at Kinloss I met up with a pilot from my CFS course in 1967, Ernie Banfield, who had been training to do in-flight refuelling with the Nimrod's new air-to-air refuelling probe. While there we first heard the news that an RN submarine had sunk an Argentine cruiser called the *Belgrano*.

The following day we were told to take something from Kinloss to RAF Odiham and then come home. It was all fairly routine stuff as far as the transit flying was concerned; but it was a bit odd not being told who and what we were carrying!

Another task for the Andover was to fly to the South of France, pick up a 'special' classified cargo and take it to Gibraltar. The crew included Lt Cdr Keith Crawford, US Navy, as co-pilot. Not long after they had disappeared over the southern horizon someone said to the Boss:

'Do you realise that you've just dispatched an American citizen, whose country is neutral in this conflict, on a British operational sortie?'

The Boss, as was his wont, smiled broadly and said, 'Oh yes – what a shame – will you tell?'

We also flew photo-chase sorties in our Hawks, often in the evenings. I chased a Nimrod over Salisbury Plain as it dropped 1,000lb dummy retarded bombs – a new role for the Mighty Hunter. We also chased a lot of refuelling sorties using a plethora of tankers and receivers. On one occasion the modified Vulcan tanker had refuelled a Hercules tanker, which then gave some fuel

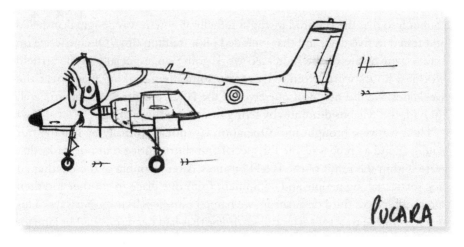

The author's cartoon of a Pucará done at the Farnborough International Air Show of 1978. (Author's collection)

to another Herc tanker. Then a Harrier appeared, flown by Tim Allen of A Squadron, to take fuel from the second Hercules. As he closed up on it a voice came over the air, 'I wouldn't touch that fuel if I were you, Tim, you don't know where it's been!'

Operational sorties should be entered in one's logbook in green ink. It was a little bizarre to be doing that while I was on a training tour, 8,000 miles from the arena of war!

A footnote to Operation Corporate was that two Argentinean FMA Pucará twin-turboprop, attack aircraft were captured pretty much intact and were shipped back to Boscombe Down. From these two airframes an airworthy one was assembled and flown by A Squadron test pilots on a variety of assessment and evaluation sorties. This aircraft was officially taken on charge with a military registration of ZD 485. There was discussion as to its possible use as an ETPS aircraft to broaden the experience of the test pilot students on a variety of exercises. I was to have been the ETPS Project Officer for the introduction of the Pucará and actually did fly it once with the A Squadron project pilot, Sqn Ldr Russ Peart. I was very pleasantly surprised with the Pucará's handling and performance, the only drawback being increasingly high forces when rolling the aircraft at much over 200kt; these became distractingly objectionable at 250kt. But it flew well enough on one engine and had a good STOL capability and I did all the landings on the grass strip.

Despite the fact that the 1960s conventional airframe construction and instrumentation were simple, the Astazou engines were almost identical to that in the Gazelle helicopter and so the Pucará was very economical to operate. However, the engineers argued, succesfully, that too little was known about the two airframes' histories, hence the fatigue life could not be calculated. Pucará ZD 485's last flight was from Boscombe Down to RAF Cosford where it went on display in the RAF Museum there.

Another knock-on effect of Operation Corporate was that the C-130 Hercules that had been earmarked for joint B Squadron and ETPS use was returned to operational duties at RAF Lyneham just as it was ready for us to take it over. Again I was the project tutor and I had, along with Ron Rhodes and our air engineers, spent many happy hours in the C-130 simulator at Lyneham. And this time I didn't even get to fly the real thing!

The search for a new 'heavy' aircraft then continued and I went to Hatfield to fly in the prototype BAe 146 four-jet regional airliner. I only got to watch my erstwhile ETPS tutor, Graham Bridges, as he flew it around. This machine was now surplus to requirements at Hatfield and it was on offer 'as is'. This meant that it would come with the water tanks for varying the CG and all the usual suite of flight test instrumentation. It seemed ideal to me but the appropriate ivory towers were not impressed with the asking price. Eventually a BAC-111 was purchased for the job. The real irony, however, is that as I write this in 2014, ETPS now operates a BAe 146 – just thirty-one years later!!

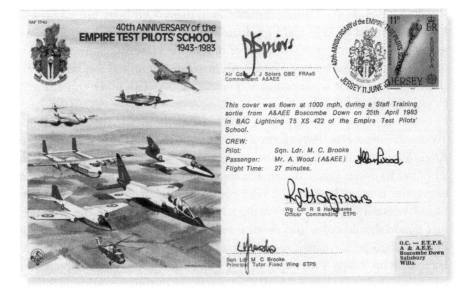

The ETPS 40th Anniversary First Day Cover flown at 1,000mph by the author and Allan Wood in Lightning T5 XS 422 on 25 April 1983. (Author's collection)

36 ANNIVERSARY

April 1983 marked the 40th Anniversary of the formation of ETPS at Boscombe Down. So by late 1982 plans were already afoot to celebrate this milestone in a suitable fashion. As I was now the PTFW, the Boss passed the baton to me to get things going. I recruited Sqn Ldr Mike Grange, our Aerosystems Tutor, to give me a hand. One of the early suggestions was to see whether we could win some sponsorship to help with the inevitable costs of such a 'do'. I remember making trips to London with Mike and visiting Shell House, among others, to talk over the possibilities with the appropriate PR folks. We also travelled to Newport Pagnell to talk to the people at the Aston Martin car company. We were shown around and allowed to sit in their latest luxury and futuristic driving machines.

Many of our targeted sponsors came up with the goods, so we now had a budget. Various meetings narrowed down the format for the day as well as actually choosing the date on which we would hold the celebration, whom we would invite and how we would allocate responsibilities around the staff and student body. The programme evolved into an afternoon static display and open house in the school premises with a 'home-grown' flying display. The evening would be a dinner in the Mess followed by dancing and socialising over drinks. During the afternoon many 'Old Boys' turned up and I was privileged to help a US graduate of No. 2 course to climb into and spend time in reverie in the cockpit of one of the Harvards. Some members of my old course turned up along with many distinguished test pilots from around the world. It was a fitting and enjoyable day with much fun enjoyed by our visitors and families.

Earlier in the year an approach had been made by the BBC Children's TV programme *Blue Peter* to do a piece about the school in its 40th year. After discussions it was agreed that the presenter Simon Groom would fly in a Hunter to do an inverted spin and in a Scout helicopter to experience an engine-off landing. I was tasked with completing the fixed-wing bit and Sqn Ldr Dave Reid with the rotary-wing adventure. I suggested to the producer that Simon should come and fly with me in a Hawk first, to see how he got on with high performance aeroplanes and all that goes with them: this was agreed. So on 4 May I met up with the tall, rather willowy young presenter and proceeded to get him ready. While I was flying during the morning Simon was checked over by our doctor, Charles Macallister, kitted out by Tony Gee and shown how an ejection seat works by John Eatwell. All this was filmed for the eventual broadcast. Simon and I met up again after a light lunch and

I briefed him for our flight. It would be a general handling sortie on which we would try a few aerobatics and a spin or two to see how he got on. In the event it went very well until about five minutes before I had planned to land. We were just descending to join the circuit at Boscombe when Simon alerted me to the fact that he was feeling unwell. I told him to get his sick bag out, take off his mask and turn his microphone off. I then told him to use his bag if necessary, that I would fly as gently as I could and land straight away. He came back 'on air' as we rolled down the runway saying that he felt a lot better and asked me what he should do with his bag. 'Just give it to the man that comes to help you unstrap,' I said. 'There will probably have been a few bets riding on that!' Simon was due to come back for the Hunter trip a few days later. However, during his next show he had done some sort of unarmed combat and got injured. So we were put on hold. He was eventually fit to fly with me in the Hunter on Tuesday 14 June. I had asked the ground crew to leave the drop tanks empty as I planned to go up to 40,000ft and carry out the inverted spin directly, so giving Simon's tummy the minimum disturbance while still getting the job done. The camera crew were stationed around the aeroplane and cockpit as we strapped in and I was asked to point out the spin panel and say a few words about what we were going to do. I hadn't been briefed on this bit so I made something up. I ended with words that would come back to haunt me via all the old buddies who saw the eventual broadcast: 'You may or may not enjoy this, but don't worry, Simon, I'll have it all under control.' The folks from the photographic section had fixed a couple of cameras in the cockpit; one facing Simon, so that he could prove that it was really him doing this crazy thing and one looking across the cockpit at me. I had the switch that would run them both when the time came. We took off and climbed to 40,000ft. This was much higher than we had flown in the Hawk and Simon was impressed by the view. I cleared everything with the radar controller and the ground pilot for the spin and made sure that Simon was ready. Then we went into an inverted spin via a rolling entry and I held it until the JPT was reaching its limit. 'Isn't it incredible?' I said for posterity. Simon replied with a higher pitched 'Amazing!'

We recovered and went home. He was feeling OK and we didn't have a repeat of the previous sortie. By the time that we landed we had been airborne for all of forty minutes. Simon was pleased and relieved. The ground crew presented him with a polished and engraved Hunter starter cartridge, which he proudly displayed in the studio on the day of the transmission. My kids were impressed only a little that their daddy had been on *Blue Peter*, and a tiny bit more that he had met Simon Groom, but they were very disappointed that he hadn't met the *Blue Peter* dog-of-the-day, Goldie! It later transpired that the internal camera facing Simon had failed just after we had entered the spin.

Fortunately we did have a recording of his face before he lowered his tinted visor so the kids could see that it was really him. What the producers wanted was shots of someone with a helmet, showing its *Blue Peter* badge, and the tinted visor down during the spin. One of our engineers, Brian Hemming, volunteered to be Simon's stand-in and we just went up and filmed a couple of inverted spins with the camera on top of the instrument panel viewing Brian's head. On the programme they used some of that and edited it in over the original soundtrack – it all looked very genuine. They also asked if we could get some external shots while the Hunter was spinning. Fortunately we had already done that during some filming in 1982 for a Central Office of Information film. On that occasion John Thorpe had volunteered to fly a Hawk with one of our photographers in the back and I had another on board the Hunter with me. I knew already that John was an exceptional pilot but I had thought that chasing an inverted spin would be nigh on impossible. In the event we had a couple of goes at it and on the second I was aware of a red, white and blue shape flashing by the cockpit – not that far away! As I recovered JT's voice came loud and clear over the radio: 'DON'T TURN LEFT!' So I didn't. Then he appeared as if by magic on our left wingtip to follow us home. The resulting video was amazing and showed the world just what a masterful pilot JT was. I was glad that I had no idea at the time just how close he had got!

Another spin-off (excuse the pun!) from the anniversary year was a proposal from Wg Cdr Chris Greaves, via Allan 'Woody' Wood of the Boscombe Down Workshops, that an ETPS First Day Cover be designed and flown. In negotiations it was agreed that 1,000 covers would be prepared and that we would fly all 1,000 at 1,000mph in the Lightning. Accordingly on 25 April 'Woody', having been medically cleared to fly and fully kitted out, met me by the Lightning. He was carrying a cardboard box. I hadn't realised just how much room 1,000 envelopes occupied. The Lightning is a very dense aeroplane and has little or no space for cardboard boxes. So I told Woody that he would have to sit with the box on his knees! If we had to eject he would have to take it with him! To reach 1,000mph I had to calculate the indicated Mach number, which meant translating mph to knots and then, using the forecast temperature at 36,000ft, applying the numbers to my little-used Dalton Aviators' Computer to get the answer. When I'd got that I decided that we would go for 1.5 Mach to make sure that we had travelled for a minute or two at 1,000mph. We took off and climbed at 20,000ft per minute on the familiar south-west track over the English Channel. I levelled off and when the London Military controller told me I turned left into the supersonic corridor. Once on heading I selected full afterburner and we accelerated smoothly through the 'sound barrier'. Allan was wide-eyed, sitting there quietly taking it all in. 'We're going faster than our sound now, Woody,' I said. 'So it's no good shouting!'

Soon the speed arrived at 1.5 Mach and I cancelled the afterburners but held full, dry power to hold the speed for at least a minute; it seemed the right thing to do! Then I slowed down gently and once we were subsonic I got clearance to turn left back towards Boscombe Down. During the recovery I talked through everything that I was doing and showed Woody the autopilot approach. I kept my hands clear of the controls right down to a couple of hundred feet then disconnected 'George' and landed. Job done! Well, actually not quite job done. I then had to take the box home and sign every single envelope in exactly the right place and, having been given my share of the stamps, stick them on, very carefully, absolutely upright with just the right amount of envelope showing around their top and right edges! But it was all well worth the effort and I got another Lightning flight out of it!

37 CHOOSING A NEW PATH

The year 1982 was as busy as ever but, while I was running to keep up, my wife, Mo, had very little to do. She had worked while we were living in Bedfordshire, but now she was finding herself with a lot of time on her hands. In the middle of the year she came across information on a government subsidised Training Opportunities or TOPS Course in Systems Analysis. She followed this up, went to take the 'entrance exam' and passed! Eventually she was notified that the course would be a six-weekly residential one, based in Swindon. So she was looking forward to that, with all the possibilities of a satisfying second career ahead.

That year's 22 April meant something significant for me: my 38th birthday; significant because it was a potential exit point from the RAF, with a sizeable gratuity and a deferred pension. As I was on a Permanent Commission it was my call. During late 1981 I had been telephoned by a personnel officer, known as my Desk Officer, to ask whether I was going or staying. I told him that I probably had some prospects of getting a test pilot's job in industry. He advised me that if I decided to stay then I could be selected to go to the RAF Staff College at the end of my time at ETPS. However, he warned, that was by no means a given, competition for places was stiff and, in his words, 'You're not getting any younger.' I could take a hint. I contacted some of the 'mates' in BAe and by April I had decided that I would stay with the RAF; prospects outside were in decline and none of the locations were that attractive.

Mo went off to Swindon in early August and started her course. After she had finished all her training things became quite different at home, but I put that down to the stress that Mo was finding and the uncertainty she had about her next steps back into full-time employment. Of course that uncertainty was not helped by my own over my future.

On Friday 5 November I arrived back from Honington, where I had spent the week supervising the Buccaneer Preview Team. When I got home we got the family ready for that annual British Beano – Bonfire Night. There was to be a fireworks display outside the gates of Boscombe and then mulled wine and nibbles in the Officers' Mess. We went along, but all the time I could sense that things were far from warm between us. When we got home and were alone I asked what was wrong.

Mo told me that she had fallen in love with one of the guys on the course and that he had asked her to marry him. Well that explained a lot – but I didn't see it coming! We talked long into the night. But in the end it was to be divorce. At the beginning of 1983 I had taken over the reins of the horse called Principle Tutor Fixed Wing and one of the traditional duties of the PTFW was to host a party at home for all the fixed-wing course students and staff. By now I was friendly enough, in a fairly platonic way, with a lady who lived in Oxford and her name was Linda Cooper. Eventually I was emboldened enough to ask her if she would like to come and help me host the party, which was to be on a Friday night in late March. Linda was a fabulous hostess and no doubt some of the staff wondered whether this was my new 'partner'. I didn't commit myself one way or the other! However, over the coming months we realised that our friendship had blossomed into love. I couldn't see that coming either! By Christmas 1983 I was sure. I hid her engagement ring in a chocolate wrapper and gave her the box on Christmas Eve. The last nine months had been a tale of growth and recovery; it now felt right. During the year Linda had told me that she had decided to start going to church again, something she hadn't done regularly for quite a long time. That struck a chord with me too. I had been brought up to go to church and Sunday School and had a yearning to start again. We went, when I was in Oxford at the weekends, to the nearest church to Linda's home – St Ebbe's. My private life was slowly recovering from the shock and awe of the divorce. I was now a single parent, trying to manage a very busy working life and keeping house and home together. However, there were some odd things about this new way of living. Such as going down into Amesbury, in uniform, on Thursday mornings and queuing in the Post Office for the Family Allowance (as Child Benefit was called then) among all the ladies and OAPs. After a few weeks the lady behind the counter took pity and gave me a form so that I could get the money paid into my bank account.

Many of my colleagues had no idea how difficult it could be at times, well all except John Thorpe. Earlier, before Mo and I had actually separated, he came into my office.

'What's up, mate, you don't seem to be yourself these days?' I told him, confidentially, that we were going to get divorced. Before he could stop himself he blurted out,

'Oh, thank goodness for that – I thought your gastric ulcer had come back!' Then he realised what he'd said and turned on the sympathy. I forgave him – after all he was my best buddy.

By the middle of 1983 I had decided what I would do if I didn't get into Staff College: I would change my terms of service to Specialist Aircrew and keep flying as long as I could. I thought about applying to return to the front line in Germany, now twenty years since I was there for the first time. Now there were Buccaneers, Phantoms, Jaguars and Harriers and the Tornado was coming into squadron service. Back to low-level operations – but also back to QRA! When I thought more about it two things came to mind. One was walking out to the same aircraft type every day. By now I had served for eight years on flying units where I had flown an average of six very different types every month. That would take some getting used to. The other was that I was a long time away from that strike/attack world and approaching 40; I decided that I would, if necessary, do something completely different. So I rang my Desk Officer to answer the question that had started this train of thought.

'About those options for the non-Staff College route,' I said. 'I'd like to transfer to Specialist Aircrew and go either to Search and Rescue helicopters or VC10s.' My rationale was that I already knew how to fly helicopters and SAR bases were usually near the seaside in nice parts of the UK. On the other hand I would like to learn to fly big aeroplanes properly and the VC10 Squadron was based near Oxford, where Linda and I were planning to buy a house.

'OK, old boy, I'll put that into the mixing pot. I'll call you when the Staff College selections are out, then we'll action Plan A or B as required. Cheers.' In the autumn of 1983 the call came. 'Mike, you're off to No. 76 Course at the RAF Staff College starting at the end of next February. Best of luck!'

So that was it. I was going to take another step up the career ladder, a bit belatedly at my age, but I never had aspired, or had the talent, to go to the top floors. I just hoped, fervently that I would get to fly again. I shouldn't have worried. I would do another fifteen years in the test flying world. But that, as they say, is another story.

APPENDICES

Appendix A: A Brief Lesson in Aerodynamics

Here I will try to set out, in the simplest of terms, the way that an aircraft flies and the forces that act on it while doing so, as well as explaining some of the more esoteric terms that might have crept into my story from time to time. Those who wish to know more should seek further reading in books by the likes of world-renowned aerodynamicists Babbister, Maughame, Hill or the very readable, late and much-missed Darrol Stinton.

So here we go! When a powered aeroplane[1] is in steady flight there are four forces acting upon it. The force that holds it in the air is *lift*, generated primarily by the wings. In level flight this force is equal and opposite the aeroplane's *weight*, which pulls it towards the centre of the Earth. If the aeroplane is flying at a steady speed then there are two forces acting in equal and opposite fashion to each other in the horizontal plane; one is the *thrust* from the engine(s) pulling or pushing forwards and the other is *drag* from air-resistance pulling backwards. An important factor in the way that these forces are balanced is related to the point through which the weight always acts, known as the aeroplane's *centre of gravity* (CG). This can vary with the way that the variable bits of the aeroplane's load are distributed; these bits are such things as cargo, passengers, the crew, fuel and, in some cases, weapons. The CG should always remain within defined limits or loss of control may occur. Some variation of the CG may occur in flight as the weight of some of these items reduce, such as fuel, or the dropping of bombs or cargo by parachute. Passengers moving about also will have a transient effect on the position of the CG, especially when they transfer some of their bodily contents to the WC tanks at the rear of the aircraft!

An important factor is that the three forces of lift, thrust and drag do not all act, as the weight does, through the CG. Where they act in relation to the CG will vary with the design of the aeroplane. But because they do not act through the CG they each can cause a *moment* around the CG tending to push the nose up or down in a variable way. To help control this moment and to allow for the

---

1   The term aeroplane does not cover helicopters or autogyros, whereas the term aircraft can include these or any other form of craft that flies.

variations that come from a whole range of changeable factors another surface is usually added to the tailplane.[2] This is called the *elevator*, or, in American, the 'stabilator' and is connected to the pilot's *control column* (often called the *stick*), which allows the pilot to move the aircraft's nose up or down as necessary for any given condition of flight. That movement is called *pitch* and it acts around an axis that passes from side to side through the CG; this axis can be easiest to envisage as a line from wingtip to wingtip in a straight-winged aeroplane. The way that the aircraft behaves around this axis is described as its *longitudinal stability*.

But flying in straight lines is not sufficient to guarantee a safe arrival; although many an airline pilot may feel that the only time the aircraft is turned through any significant amount is when it has landed at its destination and has to make its way to the terminal building! In the very early days of aviation the pioneers soon discovered that they needed to control their direction as well as their elevation. So they copied boats and put a *rudder* on the back end. This was controlled by the pilot's feet with a centrally pivoted bar near the floor; it was, unsurprisingly, called the *rudder bar*. So we ended up with aeroplanes having another moving surface at the back end, much like a tailplane and elevator, but mounted vertically. A fixed part, the *fin*, that gives stability and a moving part, the rudder, that allows control. Movement initiated by the rudder acts around an axis that runs vertically through the CG and is referred to as *yaw*; the way that the aircraft behaves around this axis is described by its *directional stability*. An important element in this respect is something called *sideslip*, which is when the air no longer comes directly at the aircraft's nose but comes slightly from one side. Sideslip can have an effect on many things: lateral control and stability, drag and structural stress among them.

But this arrangement alone was insufficient for total control because when the rudder was used one wing or the other would usually go up or down. This also happened in even the lightest of gusts of wind or thermally induced turbulence. Somehow those magnificent men had to find some way of varying the lift of each wing of their flying machines in a controllable manner. The first attempts at doing this was by stretching wires from the end of the wings to the pilot's control column or wheel. These wires would then be moved by the pilot to twist the wing and so increase the lift on the wing that had gone down, reduce the lift on the other wing and so regain equilibrium with the wings once more level. This method was called wing-warping.

2   For simplicity I have put the stabilising element in its usual position at the rear of the aeroplane. However, there are aircraft that have it at the front end; in this case it is called a Canard. Now seen often on modern fighters, such as the Typhoon and Rafale, it was the original arrangement on the Wright Flyer and other early flying machines.

However, as flying machines became less like gossamer butterflies and stronger and sturdier the effort required by the pilots to warp the wings became too much. So some bright spark put small flaps at the back of the wing, near the end, where they would have the most effect. Perhaps the first such bright spark was French because these things became known as *ailerons* (*aile* being French for wing). The ailerons allow movement around the third axis, which effectively runs from nose to tail, and that is called *roll*; the way that the aircraft behaves around this axis is described by its *lateral stability*. Invariably the lateral and directional stabilities of aeroplanes interact in such a way that it is nigh impossible to isolate one from the other.

In order to allow some shorthand in the description of stability and control and the manipulation of the associated mathematical equations, terms called stability derivatives were invented. They come from alphabetical labelling of axes, motions and quantities; some in Arabic and some in Greek. Many of these terms become a natural part of the test pilot's vocabulary!

All the above are the major elements of something called *stability and control characteristics* and are fundamental as to how any particular aircraft handles. This is the prime concern of designers and test pilots. Questions as to how easy or hard the aircraft is to fly become paramount during design, development and testing and is the province of the test pilot. Whereas stability and control parameters are described mathematically, thus objectively, the way that the aircraft responds and feels to its pilot is subjective. In order to try to give some measure of objectivity to the variable of pilot opinion a numerical scale was first introduced by the USA's National Advisory Committee for Aeronautics (NACA) at their Ames Laboratory, outside San Francisco in California; NACA became NASA (the National Aeronautics and Space Administration) in 1958. The man who drove the development of the scale was George Cooper and the Cooper Pilot Opinion Rating Scale was initially published in 1957. After several years of experience gained in its application to many flight and simulator experiments, and through its use by the military services and aircraft industry, the scale was modified in collaboration with Robert (Bob) Harper of the Cornell Aeronautical Laboratory and became the Cooper–Harper Flying Qualities Rating Scale in 1969, a scale which remains the standard for measuring flying qualities.

The flow chart for the use of the scale is illustrated below. The CHFQRS is used constantly to help test pilots determine whether some sort of change is required to improve or ameliorate difficulties they find in an aircraft's handling that may affect its safety or its ability to fulfil its in-service role.

Apart from stabilty, control and handling qualities another important aspect of development that a test pilot may be employed in is wrapped up in the term 'Performance'. This can be anything from fuel consumption, so defining

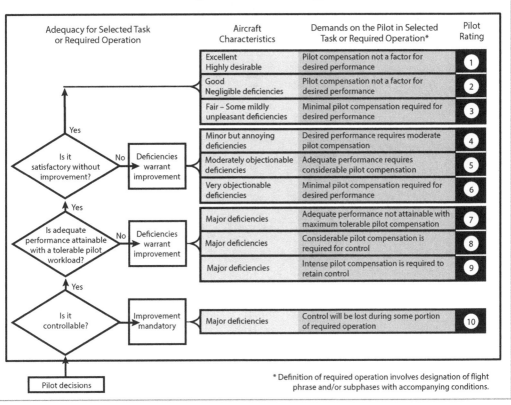

Handling Qualities Rating Scale

how far the aircraft can fly or remain in the air, to its maximum speed or rate of turn. The latter elements form part of what is known as the 'Flight Envelope', as in the rather gung-ho sounding test pilot talk of 'pushing the envelope'!

In reality all test flights, regardless of their primary objective, allow test pilots to evaluate many things and form opinions as to the utility of the machine or system under test. Although some subjectivity is inevitable the overall aim is to report the results as objectively as possible and supported by scientifically acceptable data. It's not a case of a test pilot just whizzing round the sky for an hour, landing and declaring, 'I'll give it a five. Refuel it and let's get it into production!'

Appendix B: Cockpit Illustrations

Illustrations from the aircrafts' Aircrew Manuals and Pilot's Notes, all courtesy of Mach One Manuals (www.mach-one-manuals.net)

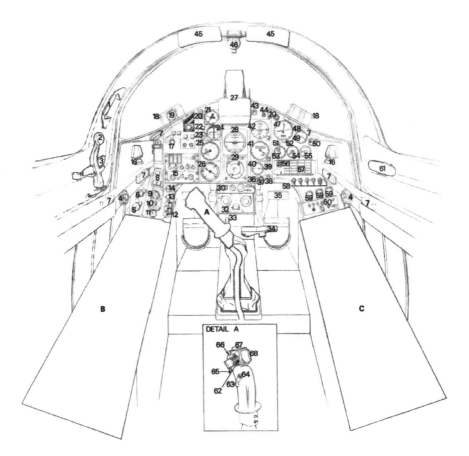

Hawk T1

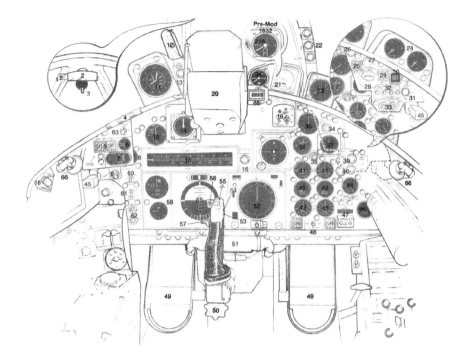

Buccaneer S2B

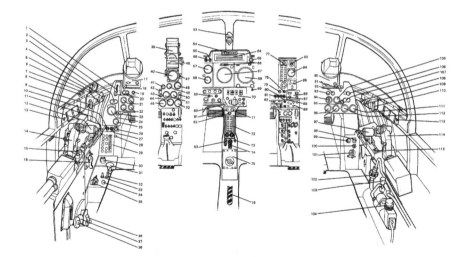

Lightning T5

Arrangement of Panels in Cockpit

Andover CC2

Devon C1

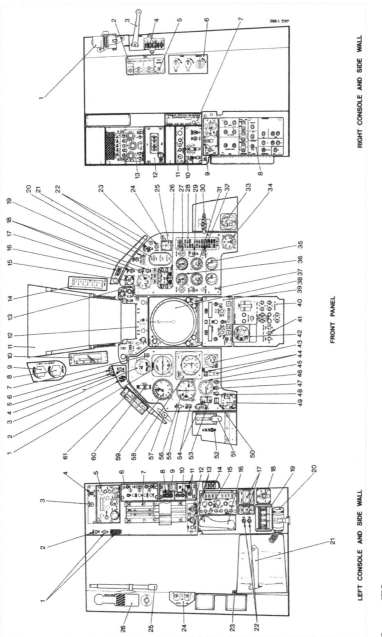

RIGHT CONSOLE AND SIDE WALL

FRONT PANEL

LEFT CONSOLE AND SIDE WALL

Jaguar T2

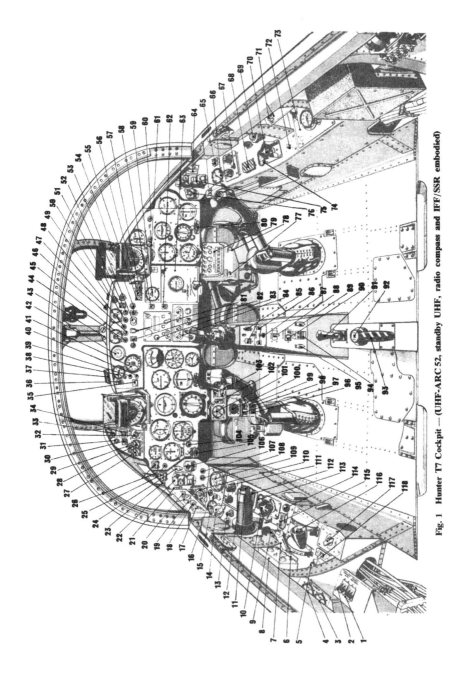

Fig. 1 Hunter T7 Cockpit — (UHF-ARC 52, standby UHF, radio compass and IFF/SSR embodied)

Hunter T7

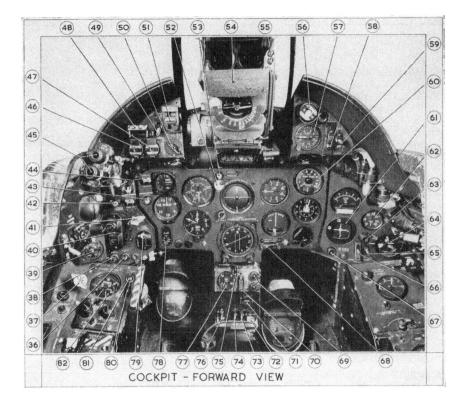

COCKPIT - FORWARD VIEW

Hunter F6A

INDEX

Lightning Source UK Ltd.
Milton Keynes UK
UKOW07f0654100115

244286UK00002B/29/P